Microsoft® Visual Basic .NET™ Programming Fundamentals

Souleiman Valiev

Frontenac

Microsoft® Visual Basic .NET™ Programming Fundamentals

Copyright © 2008 by Souleiman Valiev

Printed and bound in the United States of America.

ISBN   978-0-9802029-0-8

LCCN   2008922419

1. Programming. 2. Microsoft. 3. .NET. I. Valiev, Souleiman. II. Title

Attention libraries, colleges and universities: Quantity discounts are available on bulk purchases of this book for educational purposes. The publisher offers discounts on this book when ordered in quantity for special sales. Please use the order form located at the end of the book. For more information, contact: Marketing Department, Frontenac, P.O. Box 322 Huntington, New York 11743-0322 USA or email: FrontenacBooks@gmail.com

About the Book

If you decided to begin an exciting career in computer programming, then this is the book for you. This book will help you acquire solid knowledge and many practical hands-on programming skills. The book is intended for beginners. The selection of topics is designed to help you learn the fundamentals of Visual Basic .NET programming and Visual Studio .NET development tools. The book is based on Visual Studio .NET 2005 and .NET Framework 2.0.

You will learn how to design graphical user interface; understand Visual Basic .NET data types and variables; how to use ADO .NET components to program application data access; analyze application error types and ways to prevent them; and how to use Visual Studio to debug applications.

Visual Basic .NET is an object-oriented language, thus it is important to understand its concepts. This book provides simple descriptions and explanations of the main object-oriented concepts and their practical uses. Once you have designed and tested a project, you need to know how to install and deploy it on the end user machines. This book shows you how to create setup projects and publish the application using the ClickOnce technology. Each chapter in this book is accompanied by a relevant lab project that will allow you to consolidate your knowledge and practice your new skills. If you are looking for a self-paced Visual Basic .NET fundamentals training course, this is it.

Acknowledgments

I want to take this opportunity to express my gratitude to Alisher Valiev for constructive discussion of the book, reviewing the manuscript and providing a lot of valuable suggestions. Thanks to Microsoft Corporation for technical information on Visual Studio .NET and various betas and upgrades.

Contents at a Glance

Table of Contents

Part I   Introduction to Programming

Introduction
to
Programming

Chapter 1: Introduction to Programming

Introduction to Programming

In this Chapter:

You will learn how to create Visual Basic .NET application, how to design the program's graphical user interface and write programming statements. You will complete Lab 1 and create your first Visual Basic .NET project.

Chapter 1 at a Glance

➢ Introduction

➢ Creating User Interface

➢ User Interface Functions

➢ Using Forms and Controls

➢ Form Control

➢ Writing Code

➢ Programming Semantics

➢ Programming Syntax

➢ Programming Statement Basics

➢ Summary

Introduction

To create programs in Visual Basic .NET, you will use the Microsoft Visual Studio .NET development program. It is a suite of programs that provides developmental functionality and can be used to create various types of applications. In this book, we will consider desktop applications and will discuss the basic concepts of .NET programming.

Developing Windows applications has two main aspects: designing a program's graphical user interface (GUI) and writing code. Designing a user interface is aimed at creating a series of program screen images that are displayed to a user when a program runs. Writing code allows the implementation of the program's functionality. When you write a program's code, you create something known as the application source code, which is used to generate the program's executable file. In the rest of this chapter, we will discuss these two aspects of application development in more detail.

Creating a User Interface

You may know from your experience of using various programs that when a program runs, it generates one or more images on computer screen referred to as windows or user interface. As the term implies, the user interface facilitates user interaction with the program or interfaces the user with the program.

User Interface Functions

When you create a desktop application, you would normally start by creating a user interface. What does a program user interface do? Think about a user interface as a program's control panel. The users will rely on it as the only tool to communicate with the program. When you design a user interface, you employ various visual elements such as buttons, textboxes and labels to function as virtual operation tools.

These visual elements may generally perform three main functions:

- ➢ Transport user input to the program.
- ➢ Present the program's output.
- ➢ Invoke a certain program action.

In Lab 1, we will show you how to create a program's user interface. Note that the hardest part of this work is done for you by Visual Basic .NET behind the scenes. Therefore, your part in the design work is relatively easy. Initially, it will mainly consist of adding controls to a form and setting their properties.

Using Forms and Controls

Form Control

If you take a look at an empty form shown in Figure 1.0, you will see that a form is a kind of visual template that is used to generate a window-like image. As for controls, they are used to paint visual elements on the form. Thus, the form and controls are programmable user interface building blocks.

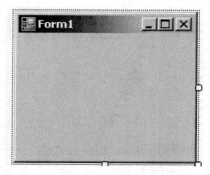

Figure 1.0 A Windows form control.

<u>**Note:**</u>

A form is a pre-defined class that is used to generate a window-like image. You can use it as a foundation to build your program's screen. Controls are smaller classes with less functionality then the form and are used to present programmable visual elements.

It is essential to note that the form is a special control that fulfils two important missions: it paints the program's window and serves as a container for other controls. Thus, if we were to separate the roles in this scenario, we should say that the form is a parent control and all other controls are child controls.

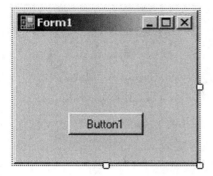

Figure 1.1 A form with a button control.

For example, in Figure 1.1 you can see a form that contains one button control. We will discuss the form and controls in more detail in Chapter 6.

Writing Code

Writing code is not exactly similar to writing a freshman English composition. On the one hand, a programming language is not as rich and expressive, which should make it simpler. On the other hand, it deals with a lot of abstractions that make it complicated. Therefore, the creators of programming languages try to make everything possible to narrow the gap between the two. The results of this noble work can be seen in Visual Basic .NET and other programming languages where the programming semantics and syntax closely resemble their human language counterparts. However, you should realize that a programming statement is not equal to a sentence in a natural language and a human language syntax has very little to do with a computer language syntax. Thus, the use of these terms in programming is relative but it allows us to create a very useful analogy.

Having said that, let's look at what you need to know to be able to write code. Of course, there are quite a lot of things but it would make sense to begin with understanding what programming syntax and semantics are.

Programming Semantics

When you write code, you would use a lot programming keywords that essentially constitute a programming language vocabulary. For example, according to MSDN's Visual Basic Language Reference, Visual Basic .NET is built on approximately 190 reserved and 39 unreserved keywords. That's probably not a gigantic lexical arsenal. For your information and comparison, C# is even more laconic as it counts only 77 keywords. If you, by any chance, wonder how these less than a couple hundred words languages can produce powerful programs, don't kill yourself, just remember what the ancients said: "One line of code is worth a thousand words."

And as for writing an English composition, according to some estimates a college graduate's vocabulary may include 15, 25 or even 60 thousand active words. That's the headword count only and does not include different senses, inflicted forms and compound words.

When you begin writing your own code, remember that you cannot use the reserved keywords words as names for your procedures or variables simply because your code will not compile. You may use unreserved keywords in your code but it is not recommended as it can lead to subtle errors and make your programming composition hard to read. Note that in a programming language, keywords can play different roles. They can be procedure names, class names, data type names, constants, attributes and so on. Therefore, when we talk about programming semantics, we refer to the meaning of these programming language keywords.

Let's take a look at some examples. For example, *Integer, String, Char, Date, Single, Double, Boolean* keywords are used to represent primitive data type names. The programming semantics of most of these keywords is very close to what they mean in your native language. For example, *Integer* represents whole numbers, *String* signifies text and *Char* denotes single characters. So the idea is that we want the meaning of programming keywords to be as transparent as possible. By transparency we mean being close to your native language semantics.

This becomes even more important when you dig deeper into programming grammar and start differentiating between programming nouns and verbs. There is a general programming convention to assign nouns to class properties and use verbs to name class methods. For example, the form class that we talked about earlier has such properties as *Text*, which represents the text that appears on the form's title bar, *Size, Location, Cursor* and many others that contribute to the form appearance and most of them are nouns. The form's methods *Show, Close* and *Hide* are verbs and their semantics truly reflect the nature of actions that these methods can perform. This means that they can show, close or hide the form accordingly.

Let's take one more example: the *Console* class. It can be used in a console application; for example, to write to the screen or to read the command line text typed by a user. For example, the *Console.WriteLine* method can write a line of text on the screen and the *Console.ReadLine* can read a line from the screen. Therefore, the semantics of these two Console class methods names exactly coincide with the nature of actions performed by them.

The above examples illustrate transparent programming semantics, which we can enjoy in Visual Basic .NET thanks to a tremendous work accomplished by its developers. That's the good news. The bad news is that when you have to read, maintain or modify your fellow programmer's code, you may not be so lucky. As a matter of fact, in many cases you may have to deal with a lot of totally non-transparent programming semantics. If a programmer does not follow recommended naming conventions, which we will talk about in Chapter 5, things may get even worse than just non-transparent semantics. For example, what object variable names such as *data* or *tree* can tell you about themselves? First of all, we have no idea if *data* is an object or a simple variable. It would be hard to guess that *data* is a *DataTable* object variable and *tree* is a *TreeView* object variable. Note that abiding to naming conventions help to reduce the guesswork in reading and understanding code. Now let's talk about programming syntax.

Programming Syntax

Programming syntax is a set of rules of building a programming statement. It explains how to put together procedure names, variables and keywords to create a valid programming statement. To learn coding, you need to know how programming statements are formed, what the syntax rules are, how to use the keywords, how to call a function, how to pass parameters and much more. For example, to invoke a procedure all you need to do is type the procedure name and pass all required parameters. Thus, your code to call the *CreateReport* procedure may look like this:

```
CreateReport(strReportName, strRegion)
```

Here's the first syntax rule, which you can learn from the above example: You should always pass parameters to a procedure by enclosing them in parentheses. Even if you do not pass any parameters, you should still type the empty parenthesis. The simplest programming statement is, probably, a variable declaration. Its syntax includes four elements in the following order:

Dim + VariableName + As + DataType

For example:

```
Dim strModelDesc As String
```

The next simple example is an assignment statement where you assign a value to a variable or property using an assignment operator (=). For example:

```
strModelDesc = "Sony VX203"
```

In an assignment statement, you actually write to a variable or property. Note we will discuss variables in Chapter 5.

The core element of any code is a procedure, which we will discuss in more detail in Chapter 12. When you create your own function or subroutine procedures, you should follow a number of syntax rules. A procedure code must be enclosed in the opening and closing wrapper lines. The opening line should contain the procedure type keyword *Sub* or *Function* followed by the procedure name and the argument list in parentheses. Function procedures must also define a return data type.
For example:

```
Sub ProcedureName(Parameters)
      'Procedure code
End Sub
Function FunctionName(Parameters) As ReturnType
      'Procedure code
End Function
```

The third type of procedures are called event procedures. Because they are wired to events and are automatically executed when events occur. This fact is reflected in their opening line syntax. Besides what is defined in a regular sub, they also contain the keyword *Handles* followed by the event name. For example:

```
Sub ProcedureName(Parameters) Handles Object.EventName
      'Procedure code
End Sub
```

When you take a closer look at code written in procedures, you will find other syntax rules. For example, to control how your code executes and to make decisions, you need to use the so-called execution control structures. The simplest of them is the *If* block. A single selection if block looks like this:

```
If intQuantity > 0 then
        'The If block code
End If
```

The *if* block opens with the test condition statement and is closed by the *End If* statement. If the test condition evaluates to true, the *if* block code is executed otherwise it is skipped. The syntax for a double selection if block adds the *Else* keyword to the structure:

```
If intQuantity > 0 then
        'The first selection
Else
        'The second selection
End If
```

The *if* block allows testing multiple conditions. In this case, the *ElseIf* keyword is used and the syntax looks like the following:

```
If intQuantity > 100 then
        'The first condition code
ElseIf intQuantity > 50
        'The second condition code
ElseIf intQuantity > 10
        'The third condition code
End If
```

We will consider the *if* blocks in more depth in chapter 8. Obviously, in this discussion we only scratched the surface of this topic but this should be enough to give you a general idea of what programming semantics and syntax are.

A Programming Statement

Writing code requires knowledge of programming language concepts, syntax, semantics and much more. Structurally, programming code is made up of modules, procedures and statements. Modules are made up of a certain number of procedures, and procedures in their own turn consist of a set of programming statements. A programming statement is the smallest integral unit of code.

Note:

A programming statement is the smallest integral unit of code. It can be as small as one word or contain multiple words and expressions. It is an uninterrupted line of code that can perform a certain programming task.

In Visual Basic .NET, code written on one line is considered one statement. If you want to continue a statement on the next line, you should use the underscore (_) character to indicate that the statement is continued on the next line. The end of the line is automatically considered to be the end of the statement.

In each programming language, there are rules as to what is considered to be the end of the statement and how the spaces are dealt with. For example, C# code editor ignores any extra spaces and it looks for a semi column as the indicator of the end of the statement. The Visual Basic code editor automatically eliminates unnecessary spaces at the time when you type code or press Enter. Writing code is an essential part of creating a program. A program without some code cannot provide any functionality. For each task or action performed by an application, you have to write code that will implement it.

Summary

In this chapter, we have introduced you to fundamental aspects of graphical user interface design, writing programming statements, programming semantics and syntax. Programming code is a human readable set of programming statements that are grouped into procedures, and procedures in their own turn are assembled into modules that make up a program. If you were able to get so far, then you are ready to create and test your first Visual Basic .NET application. We strongly recommend that you proceed to complete Lab 1. Good luck!

Lab 1: The ShowTime Project

ShowTime

In this Project:

You will build a very simple program called ShowTime. The functionality of the program is obvious from its name. The program will show the current time when the user clicks on the "Show Time" button. The lab has four main sections: Create Project Folder, Design the User Interface, Write Code and Test the Program.

Create the Project Folder

Creating a project folder should always be the first step in your project creation routine. You can create a new folder from DOS command prompt or by using the Windows Explorer. We recommend learning both methods. Remember, it is important to keep up your DOS skills. Furthermore, you may need them when you start working in a real enterprise environment.

Using the DOS Command Prompt

To create a project folder, you need to know the following DOS commands:

md – stands for "make directory."

cd – is for "change directory."

To create a new folder on your local drive, do the following:

- On the Start menu, choose Run.
- In Vista, choose Start/All Programs/Accessories/Run.
- In the Open dropdown, type *cmd* and click OK.
- To move to the root directory, type *cd * and press Enter.
- To create a new folder, type *md Labs* and press Enter.
- To get into the *Labs* directory, type *cd Labs* and press Enter.
- To create the project folder, type *md Lab1* and press Enter.
- To check if the *Lab1* folder has been created, type *cd Lab1* and press Enter. Your command prompt should show: *C:\Labs\Lab1>*.

If you successfully completed the above steps, you should have created two folders. Remember to create project folders for each lab.

Using the Windows Explorer

- On the Start menu, choose All Programs/Accessories/Windows Explorer.
- In the Windows Explorer, choose drive *C* or other local drive.
- In the right-hand pane, right-click any blank area.
- On the popup menu, choose New/Folder and type *Labs*.
- To open the *Labs* folder, double-click it and create *Lab1* folder.

Create User Interface

Create a New Project

If you have successfully created your project folder for this lab, you are ready to create your first project. Please complete the following steps:

- On the Start menu, choose *All Programs/Microsoft Visual Studio .NET*.
- On the Start Page, click on the *Create Project*...link.
- In the Project Types pane, choose *Visual Basic*.
- In Templates, choose *Windows Application*.
- In the Name textbox, type the name of the project: *ShowTime*.
- In the Location textbox, type the path to the project folder: *C:\Labs\Lab1* or navigate to it and click OK.

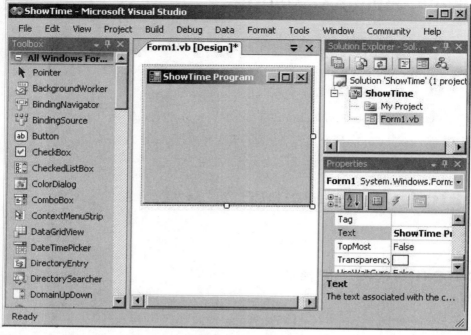

Figure 1. The ShowTime project in Visual Studio .NET.

If you successfully completed the above procedures, you should see your new project in Visual Studio .NET Integrated Development Environment (IDE). By default, Visual Studio will show the Form Designer and the Solution Explorer in its main window.

At this stage of your lab work, you have accomplished two important things: you have created a project folder as well as a skeleton of a new project. Visual Basic .NET has done a considerable amount of work to create a bare bones project for you. Now you are going to use it as a foundation to build your project.

Your newly created project should look like the one shown in Figure 1. Make sure that you open and position all Visual Studio components as they appear in the picture. You will need them to continue your work. Note that there should be at least four components open in the main window: the Form Designer, the Solution

Explorer, the Properties window and the Toolbox. Here's what you need to do to open any of them.

- To open the Solution Explorer, click on this ⬚ button in the main window toolbar.
- To open the Toolbox, click on this ⬚ button in the main window toolbar.
- To open the Properties window, click on this ⬚ button in the main window toolbar.
- To open the Form Designer, double-click the Form1 file in the Solution Explorer.

Set the Form Properties

When Visual Studio created the skeleton of your project, it used the default values to set its properties. For example, the form's Name property is set to Form1 and the Text property, which you may see in the form's title bar, is set to Form1 as well. Typically, in your project you will change some of these properties while others may be left to use the defaults. To change the Text property of the form:

- Right-click the form and choose Properties.
- In the Properties window, scroll to the Text property and type: *ShowTime Program*.

Add Controls

In this project, you will add two controls to the form: a Button and a Label.

Before you begin, make sure that both the Form Designer and the Toolbox are open and displayed in the Visual Studio main window.

To place controls on the form, complete the following two steps.

- In the Toolbox, double-click the Button control. It should appear on the form. Alternatively, click on the Button control and drag and drop it onto the form.

- Add the Label control using one of these methods.

Set Control Properties

In this part of the lab, you will set the properties of the Button and Label controls. To make this process quicker and easier, you should keep the Form Designer and the Properties window open and visible. Pay attention that when you click on any control on the form it will be automatically selected in the Properties window. This may help you save time because you won't have to select the control as it will be selected automatically. All you need to do is type or choose a desired property value.

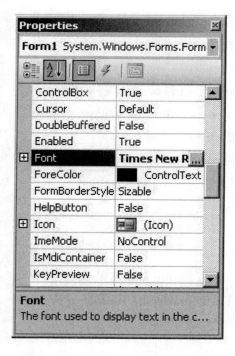

Figure 2. The Font property.

Set the Button Properties

In the Properties window, select the Name property and type *btnShowTime*. Then select the Text property and type *Show Time*.

Set the Label Properties

In Figure 2, you can see a snapshot of the Properties window that displays the properties of the Label control. To find a certain property, use the scroll bar and when you find it, just click on it. If the property has a dropdown or a dialog box to select values from then you will see a small downward arrow or an ellipsis button. Clicking on it will bring up a dialog box to choose values from. Set the following Label properties:

- Set the Name property to *lblTime*.
- Set the Text property to *Current Time*.
- Set the TextAlign property. Click on the downward arrow and click in the middle of the white rectangle. This will center align text in the label.
- Locate the Font property and click on it. Click on the Ellipsis button. In the Font dialog box select: Times New Roman, Bold, Size 14 and click OK.
- Set the AutoSize property to False.

Note that it is not absolutely required to set all of the above properties of the Label control. Your project will still work if you do not change these properties. You can limit your efforts to the first item in the list: the Name property. It must be set because we will reference it in code. When you are done with the form and controls, your newly designed form should look like the one shown in Figure 3.

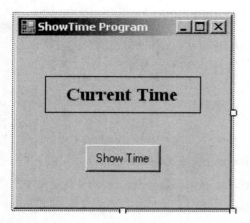

Figure 3. The ShowTime form design view.

In this form, you set control properties at design time. There is another way to do exactly the same. You can set properties programmatically by writing code that will set them when the program runs. You will have a chance to practice the second method when setting the label control's Text property.

Save your Work

It is important to frequently save your work. You may lose your work at any time. To save your project, click on the Save button or press Ctrl + S.

Write Code

In this part of your project, you will write the program's code. In terms of functionality, this program is expected to perform one simple task: show current time. When the user clicks on the "Show Time" button, it will read the current time from the system and display it in the label control. To write code, double-click the "Show Time" button. You should see an empty click event procedure like this:

```
Private Sub btnShowTime_Click(ByVal sender As Object, ByVal e
```

```
As EventArgs) Handles btnShowTime.Click
             'Procedure code
End Sub
```

Type this code:

```
lblTime.Text = Format(DateTime.Now, "hh:mm:ss")
```

When you are done, your button click event procedure should look like the following:

```
Private Sub btnShowTime_Click(ByVal sender As Object, ByVal e
As EventArgs) Handles btnShowTime.Click
             lblTime.Text = Format(DateTime.Now, "hh:mm:ss tt")
End Sub
```

The code that you wrote does two things. It obtains the current time from your computer system and formats the time value to show hours, minutes and seconds and then assigns it to the label's Text property. Please save your work.

Test the Application

To run and test the application, click on the Start button or press F5.

Figure 4. The ShowTime application at runtime.

Click on the Show Time button. Does the program display the current time correctly?
You should see a window like the one shown in Figure 4.

Congratulations! You have successfully completed Lab 1.

Part II   Visual Studio .NET Development Tools

Visual Studio .NET Development Tools

Chapter 2: Visual Studio .NET Components

Visual Studio .NET Components

In this Chapter:

You'll learn how to use the Visual Studio .NET Integrated Development Environment components to develop your own applications using Visual Basic .NET as a programming language.

Chapter 2 at a Glance

- ➢ Visual Studio .NET Development Tools
- ➢ Using the Start Page
- ➢ New Project Dialog Box
- ➢ Creating a New Project
- ➢ Project Types
- ➢ Application Templates
- ➢ Opening a Project
- ➢ The Solution Explorer
- ➢ The Toolbox
- ➢ The Form Designer
- ➢ The Properties Window
- ➢ The Code Editor
- ➢ Understanding IntelliSense

Visual Studio Development Tools

In Chapter 1, we have briefly introduced you to Visual Studio .NET IDE. Now we will take a closer look at each Visual Studio component. Let's first recap a few important points. Visual Studio .NET is a program that you can use to create your own applications in any .NET language. Normally, you should select your programming language before you select the project type. Visual Studio can be used to create a new project from scratch or to continue working on an existing one. The last but not least, you can customize your Visual Studio in accordance with your preferences such as what language you would like to use and how the development components should appear and behave.

As mentioned earlier, when developing a program you will accomplish two major types of work: designing graphical user interface and writing code. Creating a graphical user interface helps to build a visual presentation of the program while writing code is important to implement its functionality. It is essential that both types of development work can be accomplished using Visual Studio. That's why it is called an integrated development environment.

Learning how to use Visual Studio components is something that you need to do at the very beginning of your .NET training. This chapter's primary goal is to help you to do just that. In the following sections, we will consider each Visual Studio component in more detail.

The Start Page

The Start Page is the first screen that you'll see when you open Visual Studio. It is essential to learn how to use it from the very beginning. To open Visual Studio, on the Start/All Programs menu, select Microsoft Visual Studio .NET. You should see a Start Page similar to the one shown in Figure 2.0 or Figure 2.1 depending on the Visual Studio version.

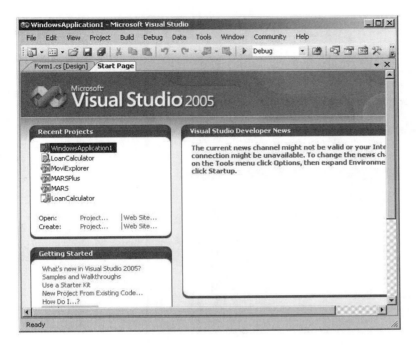

Figure 2.0 Visual Studio .NET 2005 Start Page.

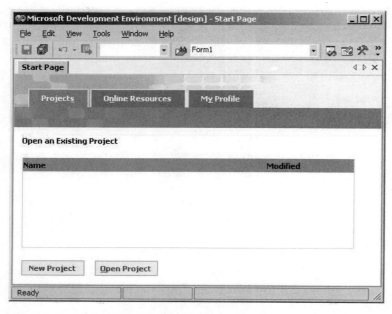

Figure 2.1 Visual Studio .NET 2003 Start Page.

The Start Page Features

The structure of the Start Page is simple. In Visual Studio 2005, there are four panes: Recent Projects, MSDN, Getting Started and Visual Studio Headlines, which are mostly self-explanatory. The Recent Projects pane is the place where you can see links to your recently opened projects or create a new project. The Getting Started pane provides help in various development areas. It lists recently posted web articles and Visual Studio events.

Tip:

Notice that the Recent Projects section has a very cool feature. When you hover the mouse cursor over the project name link, you can see the full path to the project folder in the status bar. This feature may prove useful when you need to quickly check the location of the project folder and files.

In Visual Studio 2003, the Start Page structure is noticeably different. In the left-hand pane you can see links to various sub-sections of the page, such as Get Started, My Profile, What's New, Online Community, Headlines, Downloads and others. When you click on the section link, its content are shown in the right-hand pane. Each sub-section provides its own set of useful features. For example, the Get Started section has the Projects and Find Samples tabs and two buttons: New Project and Open Project.

The Projects tab, which is selected by default, is designed to list the names of projects that you recently worked on and the dates they were opened. By clicking on a project name link, you can open a corresponding project. If you need to create a new project, you should click on the New Project button. If you do not see a link to a project that you would like to open, just click on the Open Project button, navigate to the project or solution file and click Open.

Note:

The Start Page offers a lot of features that will help you make your development work easier and faster. It gives you quick access to recently opened projects, helps to open existing projects not shown in the recent projects list or create new projects from scratch and provides links to Visual Studio web resources.

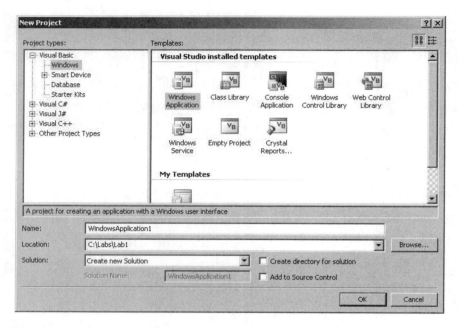

Figure 2.2 Visual Studio .NET 2005 New Project dialog box.

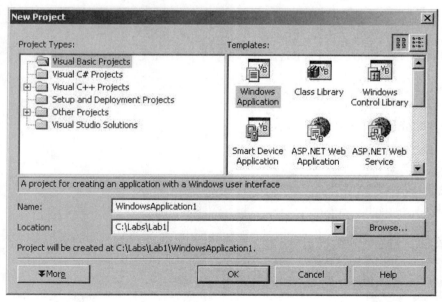

Figure 2.3 Visual Studio 2003 New Project dialog box.

New Project Dialog Box

The New Project dialog box comes into play when you need to create a new project. Open Visual Studio and click on Create Project link. You should see the New Project dialog box similar to the one shown in Figure 2.2 or Figure 2.3 depending on your Visual Studio version.

Your work in the New Project dialog box may be divided into four steps. You should complete each step before you proceed to the next stage of your new project development. Here's what you need to do:

- ➢ Select the Project Type
- ➢ Select the application Template
- ➢ Enter the project Name
- ➢ Enter the project Location

Creating a New Project

Take a closer look at the New Project dialog box. In the upper left-hand side, you can see the Project Types pane. In the upper right-hand side there is the Templates pane, which shows application templates such as Windows Application, Class Library, Console Application, Windows Service and others. In the lower part of the dialog box, you can find the project Name textbox and the project Location dropdown list box.

Normally, to create a new project you need to do the following: Choose a project type and application template; Make up a name for your project; Enter a path to the project folder or use the Browse button to navigate to it. We recommend that you always create a project folder before completing the above steps. Of course, you can create the project folder on the fly or have Visual Studio .NET create one for you. In this case, you may not always be sure where the project folder was created. We will walk you through each step and show you what you have to do to successfully complete the process.

Note:

In Visual Studio 2005, the New Project dialog box has a "Create directory for solution" checkbox, which is checked by default. This will make sense if you plan to have multiple projects in one solution. If you leave it checked, it will always create two nested project folders with the same name. This may become annoying if you don't like deeply nested folders. Uncheck it once and Visual Studio will remember it thereafter.

Project Types

Selections made in the Project Types pane are used to determine the language you are going to create this project in. It is important to remember that in most cases it is here that you will make a decision as to what programming language to use in the project. Also note that this action is not only limited to selecting a programming language. Other choices are not always language related and may include more specialized project types such as Setup and Deployment Projects, Database Projects, Blank Visual Studio Solutions and others.

Selecting a project type allows you to choose a programming language and then determine the nature of your new project by selecting the application template. Remember, when you create a new project from scratch you may want to follow this routine: Select project type, select application template and then enter project name and project folder path.

Application Templates

Visual Studio .NET offers a variety of application templates to choose from; for example, Windows Application, Class Library, ASP.NET Web Application and others.

The main reason why you need to use templates is because it helps you to build a skeleton of your new project. In fact, if you use a template, you will not build the project from scratch. It will be pre-built for you. That's the way Visual Studio .NET works. It always does a lot work for you behind the scenes. In this case, it will actually build the foundation of the application in accordance with the selected application template. Thus, when you select a template, you actually request Visual Studio .NET to build the basis for a certain application type.

However, it does not mean that you cannot build a project from scratch. As a matter of fact, you can and we strongly recommend you to do it at least sometimes. This will give you a chance to better understand what kind of work is done for you when you use an application template.

Paradoxically enough, to build a project from scratch, i.e., without using templates, you need to use an Empty Project template. In the Project Types pane, expand Visual Basic node and highlight the Windows node. In the Templates pane, select Empty Project and click OK. When the new project is created, it will be completely empty. There will be no references or modules added, except the My Project folder, which will be used to store project settings files if you create such and other project information files; for example, Application.myapp, AssemblyInfo.vb and others.

Project Name

Names do matter in any times, epochs and environments. Deciding what name to give to your new project is no exception. Naming a project is simpler then selecting a project type or template, but there are certain things that you need to know and follow.

First, in Visual Basic .NET, as in any other programming language, there are naming rules and conventions. For example, the project name cannot be one of the reserved Visual Basic .NET keywords. The following are some of the keywords, which you may easily recognize, used in Visual Basic .NET: *New, Option Explicit, As, Dim, File, Integer, String, System.*

Second, you may need to take precautions to avoid project naming conflicts. Note that name clashes can occur when you accidentally use the same name for two different projects or when your fellow developer, without knowing it, uses your project name. Naming conflicts can be avoided by creating elaborate and well-thought namespaces. Note that Visual Basic will always assign a default namespace that is the same as the project name. You can change this name whenever you need to.

Third, always try to make your project name meaningful and reasonably short.

Project Location

By location, we mean a path to a physical folder where all project files will be stored. Thus, in the location dropdown list box, you need to enter a full path to the project folder. This step has a few very important things to remember, especially if you have little or no experience in creating file folders and handling project files in general. We do not recommend using the default folders created for you by Visual Studio. Pay attention that if you do not create a specific project folder for your new project, Visual Studio will create one for you and place all project files in it. As we already mentioned, it will be a good idea to develop a habit of creating a project folder before you start creating a new project. This way you will have good control over where the project files are stored.

In the New Project dialog box, type your project folder path or navigate to it using the Browse button. Remember, you can create your new project folder by using the Windows Explorer or the DOS command prompt methods described in Lab 1. If you use DOS, all you need are two simple commands: *cd,* which stands for "change directory" and *md* - for "make directory."

When you are done with the project folder, you can either type a full path to that directory in the location dropdown or navigate to it. Visual Basic will start working to create your new project. It won't take more then a few seconds before your project comes to light. In the next section, we will show you how to work with Visual Basic .NET project in the Visual Studio IDE.

Opening a Project

In Figure 2.4, a snapshot of a test project opened in Visual Studio .NET 2005 is displayed. Your screen may look different for a number of reasons. For example, because we have adjusted the default size to make it more compact, it shows only those components that we need in this discussion.

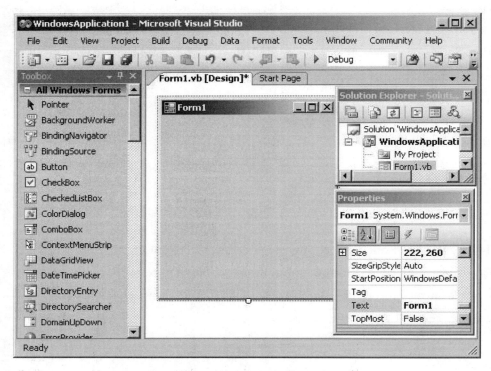

Figure 2.4 Visual Basic .NET project in Visual Studio IDE.

Visual Studio successfully integrates a suite of programs. It consists of the main window, which allows you to open a number of child windows or tabbed documents. In Visual Studio 2003, it is a combination of multiple document interface (MDI) and tabbed document interface (TDI) where some components such as the Solution Explorer, the Toolbox and the Properties window are implemented as windows while others, such as the Code Editor or the Form Designer, are designed as tabbed documents. In Visual Studio 2005, the Solution Explorer, the Toolbox and the Properties window can be either a tabbed document or a window. More about this can be found in the Solution Explorer section. In this design, each tabbed document or window is a separate program, which provides its own functionality. When you open any program, it comes up pre-loaded with data related to the project opened in the main window. Thus, child windows and documents are always aware of the project opened in the parent window.

Take a closer look at Figure 2.4, which displays a newly created VB .NET project in Visual Studio's main window. When we started the project, we selected the Windows Application template, so Visual Studio created a typical Windows desktop application. Notice that the snapshot displays four development components: the Toolbox, the Form Designer, the Solution Explorer and the Properties window.

The Solution Explorer

The Solution Explorer is a component that you are going to use very often to manage your project classes, modules, files and much more.

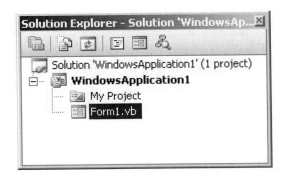

Figure 2.5 The Solution Explorer.

A snapshot of the Solution Explorer window is shown in Figure 2.5. This tool, as most other Visual Studio components, has the following functional elements: the title bar, the toolbar and the tree view. Each item comes with its own handy context menu. Note that the toolbar is built dynamically for each tree view node to reflect the node functionality.

If you take a closer look at Figure 2.5, you will notice that the form's toolbar displays six tiny buttons: Properties, Show All Files, Refresh, View Code, View

Designer and View Class Diagram. When you highlight the solution node, only two buttons will be displayed: Properties and Add New Solution Folder. By the way, if you need to find out the name of any of these buttons, hover the mouse pointer over it for a few seconds and the button name will show up in the tooltip. Most of these buttons are self-explanatory so we won't spend time describing them. However, it will be very useful if you learn how to toggle docking, hiding and tabbing. We will discuss this in the next section.

Using Context Menus

We will use the Solution Explorer context menu, which is shown in Figures 2.6 and 2.7, as an example of how to toggle component location. Each Visual Studio component can be set to one of the following options: *Docked, Floating, Hide* and *Auto Hide.* In Visual Studio 2005, they can also be tabbed. You can set or reset component's behavior using its context menu, which pops up when you right-click its title bar.

Figure 2.6 Visual Studio 2005 Solution Explorer context menu.

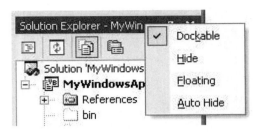

Figure 2.7 Visual Studio 2003 Solution Explorer context menu.

Using this functionality, you can "glue" a component to one side of the main window. This feature is called docking. By default, most component windows are docked, which, of course, can be changed at any time. If you don't like docking, you can let the component "float" by checking float. This will allow components to migrate and be anywhere, even outside the main window.

Note that Hide will simply hide a component until you bring it up using the View menu or otherwise. If Auto Hide is on, the component window is displayed automatically when you hover the mouse over its icon. Auto hide can be set only when the component is docked. We'll talk more about the auto hide feature in the Toolbox section.

It won't be an exaggeration to say that the Solution Explorer is a central navigation point to almost anything you may have in your project. Technically, it is just another window that shows a tree-like view of all files associated with your project. But from the functionality perspective, not only does it allow you to view all the project files but you can also invoke the functionality related to each item. For example, you can navigate to the Form Designer or to the Code Editor or the Properties window.

To start playing with any of the above-mentioned components, you need to highlight an item and click on one of the buttons at the top of the window or right-click the item and use its context menu. For example, to view the form in design mode, you need to highlight it and click on the View Designer button. To view the form's code, click on the View Code button or press F7. Now let's walk through each item that can be displayed in the Solution Explorer tree view.

Note:

When you work with any item in the Solution Explorer, remember the following: First, any item except the solution name and references represents a corresponding project file; Second, each item has its own context menu, which is a very convenient shortcut to its functionality. For example, if you right-click the References node and select Add, you will be taken to a dialog box that allows adding references to code libraries.

Solution Name

The first item listed in the Solution Explorer is the solution name. Note that Visual Studio will normally set the solution name to the first project name. If you have multiple projects in one solution, you may want to change the solution name to something appropriate for the entire solution. If you right click the solution name, a context menu will popup like those shown in Figures 2.8 or Figure 2.9, depending on the Visual Studio version.

Figure 2.8 Visual Studio 2005 Solution Name context menu.

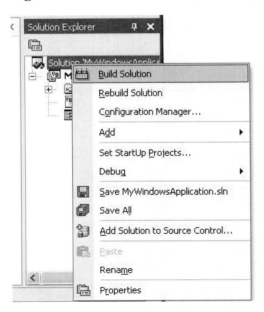

Figure 2.9 Visual Studio 2003 Solution Name context menu.

You can use the solution name context menu to access solution level functionality such as Build or Rebuild solution, Open configuration manager dialog box, Add folder, Add new project, Add new or existing item and so on.

Adding References

The next item in the Solution Explorer is References. When you use other libraries and projects in your project, you need to reference them. You can view existing references and add new ones by using the context menu. Remember, adding references provides the compiler with information about the external library file location, classes and types, the library name and much more. The compiler uses this information to load the library file and also verify its validity when the project is built.

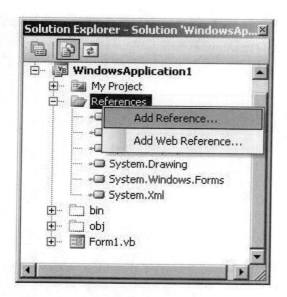

Figure 2.10 The References context menu.

One of the ways to add references to your project is to use the References node context menu. Right-click References and choose Add References. This will bring up the Add References dialog box shown in Figure 2.11. By default, the .NET tab should be displayed, which you can use to select the .NET framework libraries. The COM tab provides access to legacy components so you can reference COM DLLs created using a non-.NET version of Visual Studio. Using the Projects tab, you will be able to reference other projects. If the library that you need to reference is not listed in the .NET or COM tabs, you have to navigate to it. Click on the Browse tab and navigate to the desired DLL file. The Recent tab will display your recently referenced libraries.

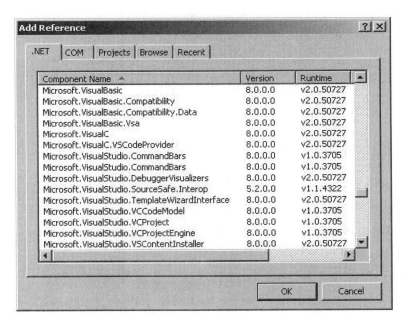

Figure 2.11 Add References dialog box.

Remember that references to most often used .NET Framework classes are added to your project by default when you create a new project. If you expand the references item in the Solution Explorer, you will see references to five major FCL libraries: *System, System.Data, System.Drawing, System.Windows.Forms* and *System.*

XML. Adding these powerful classes to your project is enough to create some simple projects, but when things get complicated you have to add more and more classes.

Assembly Info

An assembly in the .NET world is a unit of executable code. Whenever you create a project, you will ultimately compile it into an assembly, which could be an EXE or a DLL. AssemblyInfo.vb file in your project is a place where you may enter information that describes the project assembly. This may include such things as assembly title, assembly description, assembly company name and a lot of other characteristics. You can enter this information directly into the AssemblyInfo.vb file or just enter it in the project properties windows and Visual Studio will enter it into the AssemblyInfo.vb file for you. The good news is that in most cases, especially at the initial stages, you won't have to enter any data into the AssemblyInfo.vb file.

Form File

In your Visual Basic .NET project, you may have one or more forms. Each form will actually represent a corresponding graphical user interface or window. Initially, the form class file will be the main place where you will write code. Of course, in a more complex project you may have multiple forms and classes.

When you select the form file node, you have two choices: Open the form designer to do user interface design or open the code editor to code the form class. Therefore, from the form node you can choose View Designer or View Code. The following actions can be performed with the form node in the Solution Explorer:

Click on the Form node:

When the form node is highlighted, you can do the following:

➢ Open the Form Designer by clicking on the View Designer button.

➢ Open the Code Editor by clicking on the View Code button.

➢ Open the Properties window by clicking on the Properties button.

Double-click the Form node:

➢ Double-clicking the form node will open the Form Designer.

Right-click the Form node

➢ Right-clicking the Form node will open its context menu.

The form node context menu brings together all available commands and actions that you can perform on the form.

Form Context Menu Items:

➢ Open - Opens the form in the Form Designer.

➢ Open with - Allows you to open the form file with a program of your choice.

➢ View Code - Opens the form in the Code Editor.

➢ View Designer - Opens the form in the Form Designer.

➢ Exclude from project - Removes the form file from the project.

➢ Properties - Opens the Properties window.

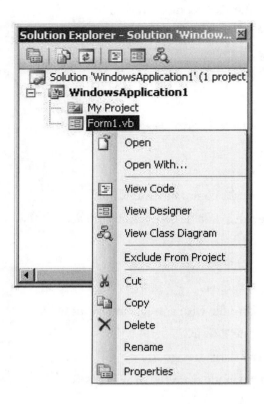

Figure 2.12 The form node context menu.

All other items on the context menu such as Delete, Rename, Cut and Copy are self-explanatory. To wrap up our discussion of the Solution Explorer functionality, let's recap. The Solutions Explorer is a very important tool to manage your project inventory. It allows you to view all files that belong to your project in a tree-view style, select any item and open it either to write code or to do graphical design work. Also, you can add, rename or delete files, add or rename projects, open the Properties window and so on.

The Toolbox

The Toolbox is a graphical design component that stores a collection of controls that can be used to create a user interface. It is a developer's virtual toolbox.

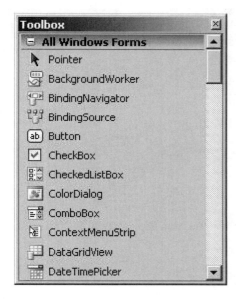

Figure 2.13   The Toolbox.

The arsenal of all toolbox controls is divided into several categories such as All Windows Forms, General, Data, Components and others. Each category of controls is stored in its own tab. In Figure 2.13, the All Windows Forms tab is displayed.

Note:

We mentioned the term control many times. What is a control? In a very simplified and brief definition, a control is a class that paints a certain visual element on the form and implements functionality related to it. Thus, a control is a virtual device that has dual nature. On the one hand, it paints an image that can be a part of a graphical user interface. On the other hand, it is a unit of code that implements functionality associated with this visual element.

Now let's take a look at how to place controls on the form.

Opening the Toolbox

To start playing with controls, you need to open the toolbox. There are at least three ways to do this:

- ➤ Click on the Toolbox button in the main window toolbar.
- ➤ On the View menu, choose the Toolbox menu.
- ➤ Press Ctrl + Alt +X.

Tip:

Remember, before opening the Toolbox you should have the Form Designer open. This really makes sense because you need the form to be visible before you try to place controls on it. If you try to open the Toolbox while the form is not displayed, the latter will come up empty.

The toolbox is truly a very important asset in a developer's programming arsenal. Earlier in this chapter we mentioned that your development work would, in most cases, comprise two major types of creativity: graphical design work and coding. The Toolbox is your main tool to accomplish the former.

The AutoHide Feature

In Visual Studio, all window-based components implement external behavior features such as Dockable, Hide and AutoHide. Here we will use the toolbox as an example of how the AutoHide feature works.

Figure 2.14   The toolbox AutoHide feature.

If you take a closer look at Figure 2.14, you may notice a tiny pin on the title bar. By clicking on this pin you can toggle the AutoHide feature on and off. When it is on, you can open the toolbox by hovering the mouse cursor over its icon. Moving the mouse cursor out of the toolbox area will automatically close it.

How to Place Controls

Now it's time to learn how to place controls on the form. We counted three main methods:

> ➢ Double-click a control in the toolbox.
> ➢ Click on a control and then draw it on the form.
> ➢ Drag and drop a control onto the form.

The Double-Click Method

Using the double-click method is very easy. When you use this method, the control will be randomly placed on the form. If you double-click the same control again, the next control will be placed on top of the previous one. Don't be surprised if you don't see the previous control, just drag the last control and you'll see the previous one underneath. You may safely pile up as many controls as you want and then drag them to any desired location on the form.

The main drawback of this method is that you cannot control where on the form the control will land. This may be an issue if you already have some controls on the form. You may accidentally drag the wrong control and as a result will have to reposition controls, which you have already placed on the form. Of course, this inconvenience may be easily avoided if you handle your controls carefully. Also, when you use this method, .NET will draw the control in a default size, which you can change later.

The Mouse Draw Method

This method is simple enough and we think it may become one of your favorites. First click on a desired control in the toolbox then move the mouse cursor to a location on the form where you want to draw the control. You will notice that the mouse cursor turns into a plus sign with a tiny icon that symbolizes the selected control. Now press the left mouse button and holding it down start drawing the control. Remember, when you release the mouse button, your drawing session will end and you won't be able to continue drawing.

The place where you start drawing will be the control's location. Of course, you can change both the size and the location after you finished the initial drawing. Just click on the control and drag it to a new location or resize it by moving the mouse cursor. The main advantage of this method is in the freedom to choose where to draw the control and setting its initial size. Pay attention that when you click on a control on the form, it gets highlighted and the mouse cursor changes to an Arrow Cross.

To move a control from one location on the form to another, you need to do the following: Click on it and while holding the left mouse button down, drag it to a new location.

The Drag and Drop Method

The essence of this method, as you may guess, is in dragging and dropping a control from the toolbox to the form. Click on a control and then while holding the left mouse button drag the control to a desired location on the form. When you reach the target location, drop the control by releasing the mouse button. With this method you can choose where on the form you want to place the control but you cannot control its initial size. We recommend that you practice using each of the methods described above and make sure that you complete this chapter's lab where you will find more details on how to use each method.

Adding Code Components

Besides controls, the toolbox contains code components. The difference between a control and a component is that a control is a visual programmable device that has a certain visual image associated with it. Components have no visual representation - they provide valuable functionality but remain invisible like phantoms of the form. Essentially, they are units of code that you may be interested to add to your project to use their functionality. The simplest example of a component is the *Timer*. Other commonly used components are *ErrorProvider, ImageList, EventLog, MessageQueue* and *BackgroundWorker*.

You should place components on the form the same way as controls. The only difference is that they will not show up on the form but will be displayed in a special place right under the form called the component tray.

Note:

The main difference between controls and components is that components do not have visual representation and they won't appear on the form. They provide valuable functionality and work as plug-in code units.

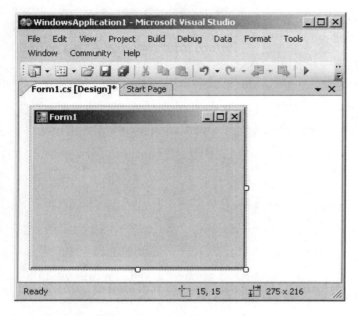

Figure 2.15   The Form Designer tab.

The Form Designer

The primary mission of the Form Designer is to provide capability to design the form. The main part of this work is focused on visual modeling of the form, which should result in building a corresponding graphical user interface. This makes the form designer a very important tool in accomplishing multiple user interface design tasks. In Visual Studio .NET, the Form Designer component is built as a tabbed document and cannot be converted into a window as other components; for example, the Toolbox or the Solution Explorer. A tabbed document normally bears the form name and the word "design" [Design], which is meant to make it easy to differentiate between the Form Designer and, for example, the Code Editor tabbed document. The form name on the tab should help to easily identify a form file from among other project files opened in VS .NET.

The tabbed document design will allow you to have multiple form and code files open in your Visual Studio environment at the same time. Note that every time you open a form in the form designer, Visual Studio opens a new tabbed document. If you have multiple documents open, the tab labels will shrink to provide space for others. A great thing about this tabbed document layout is that it puts all opened files at your fingertips and you can easily access them by just clicking on the corresponding tab.

The Properties Window

The Properties window is a Visual Studio component that is designed to provide a direct access to form and other controls properties.

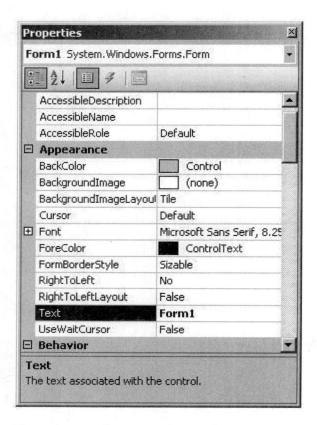

Figure 2.16 The Properties window.

The Properties window shown in Figure 2.16 has a relatively simple structure. It has a title bar, a dropdown list box that displays the name and type of selected object, a toolbar, a large list box that shows property names and values and a property description pane at the bottom. The composition of the toolbar and the properties list box may vary for each control type because they are built dynamically for each object. For example, the form toolbar will show the following buttons: Categorized, Alphabetical, Properties and Property Pages. The first two buttons are used to determine how the properties will be displayed—in alphabetic order or grouped into categories. If you click on Categorized, all properties will be displayed by categories such as Accessibility, Appearance and Behavior. In Figure 2.16, the properties are categorized.

Note that clicking on the Events button will display all events associated with the object. You can use this if you need to lookup the control events or create an event handler procedure. To set a certain property, you need to select that property and either type in the property value or select it from a dropdown box.

The Code Editor

Since programming code is a text, it can be written using any text editor such as Notepad or WordPad. Some programmers prefer to use Notepad to write all their code. However, specialized code editors offer a lot of additional features that may help to increase productivity and reduce errors. The Visual Basic .NET code editor is one of them. It comes with a number of built-in features designed specifically for code editing. To get the first impression of the Visual Basic .NET code editor, look at Figure 2.17 that shows an excerpt of Form1 form code.

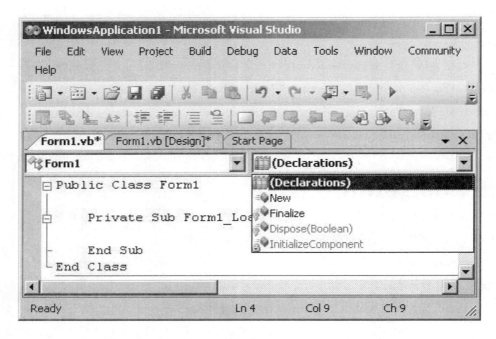

Figure 2.17 The Visual Basic .NET code editor.

Note:

The Visual Basic .NET code editor component is a text editor with a long list of useful features such as Auto Syntax Check, Auto List Members, Auto Quick Info and many others that help to make code writing much easier.

The Code Editor Layout

The first thing that we want to draw your attention to is the code editor layout. If you look at Figure 2.17, you will notice that the code editor tab has two dropdown boxes and a large textbox. The left-hand side dropdown is called Class Name. It displays all controls placed on the form. Note that once a control or component is added to the form, it becomes an object.

The right-hand side dropdown box is called Method Name. It displays a list of method and event procedure names associated with the object selected in the left-hand dropdown. When you select an object in the Class Name dropdown, the Method Name dropdown will be refreshed with all methods and event procedures that are available for that object. If you are ready to write code, all you need to do is select an object, then select a procedure associated with it and start coding.

The Code Editor Features

The code editor comes with a lot of built-in features. In the following sections, we will consider them in more detail.

Text Color

You may have already noticed that the code text is displayed in different colors. If you did not change the default configuration, your code editor will use the following text colors: black, blue, red and green. Code is displayed in blue and black where blue is used for keywords, and black for variables and operators. Green is used for comments and red for literal values. For example:

```
strRegionName = "East Coast"
```

In the above assignment statement, the *strRegionName* variable name and the assignment operator are black and the value assigned to it is red. To comment a code line you need to place an apostrophe at the beginning of the line. Remember, comments are ignored by the compiler and are used to describe or interpret the code logic or to write memos. Code text coloring is helpful in many ways. It helps to read code faster, to easily recognize certain parts of code and identify errors.

Syntax Check

The Visual Basic .NET code editor does automatic syntax check at the time when you type your code. This is a really valuable feature because it allows you to see errors even before you finished typing your statement. To see the syntax check feature in action, try this: On a new line type () and press Enter. What you typed will be underlined with a wavy blue line. This blue line normally indicates a syntax error or other problem. To find out what's wrong, just hover the mouse pointer over that line and the error message will be displayed in a tooltip below the line. In our test case, the message should say "Syntax error." Try another test: Type the keyword *Call* followed by *()* and press Enter. This time the blue line should appear under the parentheses and the error message should say "Expression expected."

The code editor will not prevent you from typing wrong statements but it will always give you a hint if something is wrong. If you choose to ignore these quiet signs of errors, your code will not compile and you will get these errors reported in the Output window when you try to build the project.

Cool Tip:

To play with the code editor, try this: On a new line type any word and press Enter. Did your code editor add empty parentheses after the word? Then on the same line after the parentheses type any word again and press Enter. Did the code editor put that word inside the parentheses? Isn't the Visual Basic code editor cool!

The IntelliSense

The IntelliSense provides valuable lookup and code completion functionality. It includes the following main functions: List Members, Parameter Info, Quick Info and Complete Word. We cannot stress more how handy IntelliSense is. Keep in mind that by default, Visual Basic .NET code editor is set to automatically run the first three above-mentioned functions. You can reset this feature in the Tools/Options/Text Editor menu. Additionally, you can explicitly invoke any IntelliSense method by using the corresponding menu or a hotkey combination, which we will show you later.

List Members

As we mentioned earlier, the Auto List Members and Parameter Info are enabled by default. It means that these two features will work automatically whenever you type code in your code editor. The List Members function is called as soon as you type a keyword or an object variable name followed by (.). This function displays all members of the object variable class in a popup list box like the one shown in Figure 2.18.

Figure 2.18 The IntelliSense List Members.

In the above example, Auto List Members display all members of the Console class. Note that the term members in this context means all public properties, methods, events and constants defined in the class. To use the Auto Complete feature, you need to select a member and press the Space key or double-click and the selected member name will be typed for you. If for some reason the List Members feature does not work or you need to see the list of members again, you can manually call this function by selecting Edit/IntelliSense/List Members menu or just pressing Ctrl + J. Remember, the IntelliSense will work only if you referenced the corresponding code library and included the *Imports* directive in your class code.

Parameter Info

The Parameter Info function displays method parameters information. This feature relieves you from necessity to remember what parameters, data types and return value types a function or a subroutine requires. This information will always be at your fingertips thanks to the IntelliSense Parameter Info feature. The function works similar to List Members discussed earlier.

When you type the opening parentheses after the method name, the Parameter Info will immediately show a list of all parameters defined in that method. If the method is overloaded, the number of overloads will be displayed and you can see each overloaded method parameter list by pressing on the down or up arrow. Let's, for example, look at the *WriteLine* method of the Console class.

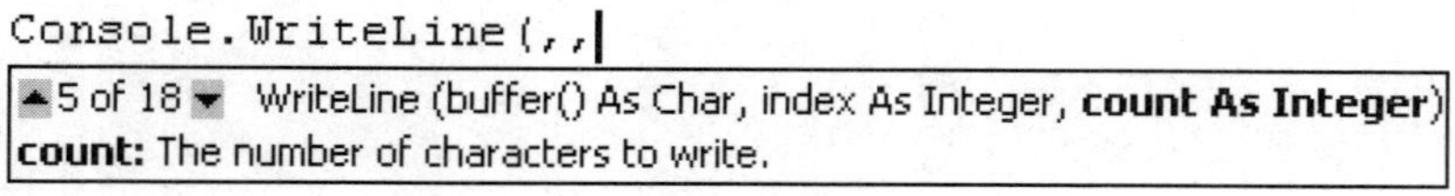

```
Console.WriteLine(,,|
```
▲5 of 18 ▼ WriteLine (buffer() As Char, index As Integer, **count As Integer**)
count: The number of characters to write.

Figure 2.19 The IntelliSense Parameter Info function.

Type *Console.WriteLine* followed by open parenthesis. You should see something similar to Figure 2.19. If you type a comma, the next expected parameter will be displayed in bold, and if you press the down arrow the next overloaded function parameter list will be displayed. To manually call the Parameter Info function, choose

Edit/IntelliSense/Parameter Info menu or press Ctrl + Shift + Space. Remember, this will work only if you already typed the opening parenthesis.

Quick Info

You may have already noticed that when you hover the mouse over an object variable, the IntelliSense displays a tooltip message. This message is used to show information related to that object variable class or class members. In fact, the message content may vary depending on a number of factors. For example, if you type:

```
String.Format(...)
```

When you hover the mouse cursor over *String*, the Quick Info will show a message *String*, which signifies the shared class name. Now do the same with the method name *Format*. You should see a message saying: *Public Shared Function Format(argument list) as String*. That's the design time information. But if you do it when the application runs in the debug mode, the Quick Info will show the current value of the variable.

The Auto Data Tips

The Auto Data Tips is another form of statement completion help implemented by the IntelliSense. In your project, you will have to declare variables of various data types. Visual Basic .NET offers a great variety of built-in standard data types. Thanks to the Auto Data Tip function, you don't need to remember all these data types when you want to write a variable declaration statement. Let's assume you want to declare a string variable as follows:

```
Dim strReturnValue As String
```

When you type the keyword *As* and press Space, the Auto Data Tip will show a list of all available Visual Basic .NET data types. This works similar to the List Members function discussed earlier. If you want the code editor to complete your statement, just select a data type and press the Space key or double-click the selection.

Summary

In this chapter, you have learned how to use the Visual Studio .NET development tools. We recommend you to review it whenever you have questions related to the use of the Start Page, the New Project dialog box, the Toolbox, the Form Designer, the Solution Explorer, the Properties window and the Code Editor.

Lab 2: The Desktop Calendar Project

Desktop Calendar

In this Project:

You will create a Windows application that will look like a desktop calendar. Functionality wise, it will simply display the day, month, year and current time. This project will allow you to consolidate your knowledge of form controls and practice using the Properties window and other Visual Studio development components.

Create the Project Folder

Using the DOS Command Prompt

To create a project folder, you need to know the following DOS commands:

md – stands for "make directory."

cd – is for "change directory."

To create a new folder on your local drive, do the following:

- On the Start menu, choose Run.
- In Vista, choose Start/All Programs/Accessories/Run.
- In the Open dropdown, type *cmd* and click OK.
- To move to the Labs folder, type *cd Labs* and press Enter.
- To create a new folder, type *md Lab2* and press Enter.
- To check if the *Lab2* folder has been created, type *cd Lab2* and press Enter. Your command prompt should show: *C:\Labs\Lab2>*.

Using the Windows Explorer

- On the Start menu, choose *All Programs/Accessories/Windows Explorer*.
- In the Windows Explorer, choose *C:\Labs*.
- In the right-hand pane, right-click any blank area.
- Choose *New/Folder* and type *Lab2*.

Create a New Project

To create a new Windows Application project, complete the following steps:

- On the Start menu, choose *All Programs/Microsoft Visual Studio .NET*.
- On the Start Page, click on the *Create Project...*link.

- In the Project Types pane, choose *Visual Basic.*
- In the Templates pane, choose *Windows Application.*
- In the Name textbox, type the name of the project: *DesktopCalendar.*
- In the Location textbox, type the path to the project folder: *C:\Labs\Lab2* or navigate to it and click OK.

If you successfully completed the above steps, you should see your new project in Visual Studio .NET IDE. By default, Visual Studio will show the Form Designer and the Solution Explorer in its main window. Now you can enhance the project by adding controls and writing code.

Add Controls

Right-click any free space on the form and choose Properties. Find the form Text property and type: *Desktop Calendar.* Add label controls according to Table 1.

Table 1. Label controls properties.

Label Name	Font Size	TextAlign	Text
lblMonth	18	MiddleCenter	February
lblDay	48	MiddleCenter	7
lblYear	24	MiddleCenter	2009
lblTime	16	MiddleCenter	12:23:12 PM
lblCurrentTime	10	MiddleCenter	Current Time:
lblEnabled	14	Left	Disabled

Table 1 presents property settings of all label controls used in this application. Note that each label has a specific programmatic name that actually signifies its role in the program. For example, lblMonth will be used to display month and lblDay to show the day and so on. To set the Font properties, first click on the Font property in the Properties window and then click on the ellipsis button. Set all labels Font Style to Bold and Font Name to Times New Roman. Add one button control and set its properties as follows:

Name = btnEnable;

Text = &Enable.

Add the *Timer* component. Set its *Interval* property to 1000. Note the interval property is measured in milliseconds (*ms*) and is used to determine the frequency at which the timer fires its *Tick* event. By setting the interval property this way, we will make our timer tick every second. Note that when you add the timer component, it will not appear on the form but will be placed on the component tray below the form.

Figure 1. The Desktop Calendar form design view.

When you complete the user interface design, your form should look like the one in Figure 1.

Write Code

Before you start writing code, check if you properly completed the form design work. First, check if all your label controls are positioned and named in accordance with their role in this program. For example, make sure that lblMonth is used to display months and lblDay - days and so on. Your coding work in this project will be limited to creating two small procedures. Both procedures are wired to control events, one to the button click event and the other to the timer tick event.

Write code in the btnEnable button click event procedure. On the form, double-click the btnEnable button. Visual Basic will open the code editor in the empty button click event procedure that may look like this:

```
Private Sub btnEnable_Click(ByVal sender As Object, _
        ByVal e As EventArgs) Handles btnEnable.Click
End Sub
```

Type the following two lines of code:

```
Timer1.Enabled = True
lblEnabled.Text = "Enabled"
```

When you are done, your entire procedure should look like this:

```
Private Sub btnEnable_Click(ByVal sender As Object, _
        ByVal e As EventArgs) Handles btnEnable.Click
        Timer1.Enabled = True
        lblEnabled.Text = "Enabled"
```

End Sub

The first line of code enables the timer so it will start ticking. The second line changes the Text property of the lblEnabled label to "Enabled" to signal that the timer is running. Write code in the *Timer1_Tick* event procedure. On the components tray, double-click *Timer1*. The code editor should open *Timer1_Tick* event procedure. Type six lines of code. After you are done coding, your procedure should look like this:

```
Private Sub Timer1_Tick(ByVal sender As Object, ByVal _
                        e As EventArgs) Handles Timer1.Tick

    Dim dtCurrentDateTime As DateTime
    dtCurrentDateTime = DateTime.Now
    lblMonth.Text = Format(dtCurrentDateTime, "MMMM")
    lblDay.Text = dtCurrentDateTime.Day
    lblYear.Text = dtCurrentDateTime.Year
    lblTime.Text = dtCurrentDateTime.ToLongTimeString
```

End Sub

We will now walk you through the code in the timer tick event procedure. In the first line, we declare a DateTime variable called *dtCurrentDateTime* that will be used to store the current date and time value. The second line of code assigns a current date and time value retrieved from your computer system to it.

In the rest of the code, we manipulate the *dtCurrentDateTime* variable to extract and if necessary format parts of date and time values such as month, day, year and time. For example, the third line extracts the month value and converts it from numeric format to month name and then assigns it to the *lblMonth* label. The fourth and the fifth lines do the same with the day and year values. Finally, the sixth line extracts the time value, formats it to show hours, minutes, seconds, AM/PM and then assigns that value to the Text property of the lblTime label control.

Note that code in the btnEnable click event procedure will be executed when you click on the Enable button. Since by default, the timer Enabled property is set to false, it would not run when we start the program and as a result, the timer will not fire its tick events. But as soon as the user clicks on the Enabled button, the timer will start ticking and all labels will be refreshed.

Save your Work

To save your work, click on the Save button on the toolbar or press Ctrl + S. We remind you to save your work every once and a while. You may lose your valuable work at any time if something unexpected happens.

Test the Application

Press F5 to start the application. Visual Basic will run the program and show the form. Verify if the program works. Check the following:

- Does the form show correctly all hard-coded values in month, day, year and current time labels?
- Click on the "Enable" button and check if all labels are refreshed with the current date and time values.
- Check if the value of the lblTime label is refreshed every second.

Congratulations! You successfully completed this project.

Extra Credit Task

For those of you who were not challenged by this simple project, we have an extra credit task. As you know, this program has a button that enables the timer. It would be nice if there was a button that would disable the timer or even better, if the same button could do both. Therefore, you have to add code to the btnEnable button click event procedure that will always check the status of the *Timer1* component and if it is enabled disable it and visa versa. Good Luck!

Chapter 3: Visual Studio .NET Navigation Tools

Visual Studio .NET Navigation Tools

In this Chapter:

You will learn how to use Visual Studio .NET navigation tools. You will be introduced to the Tabbed Document Interface and learn how to find and open Visual Studio .NET components using three main navigation tools: the Solution Explorer, the Toolbar and the Menu bar.

Chapter 3 at a Glance

- ➤ The Visual Studio .NET Main Window
- ➤ Understanding Tabbed Document Interface
- ➤ The Menu Bar Functionality
- ➤ Exploring Menus
- ➤ File Menu
- ➤ Edit Menu
- ➤ View Menu
- ➤ Project Menu
- ➤ Build Menu
- ➤ Debug Menu
- ➤ Format Menu
- ➤ Tools Menu
- ➤ Window Menu
- ➤ Help Menu
- ➤ The Toolbar Functionality
- ➤ Customizing Toolbars
- ➤ Using Additional Toolbars

The Visual Studio .NET Main Window

The primary mission of the Visual Studio .NET main window is to organize and streamline your development work by providing quick access to multiple components and tools. In other words, the main window is a navigation point from which you can start and manage all of your creative activities. To do this efficiently, you should know how to quickly access components and tools you need. In this chapter, we will show you the ways to access major development tools from the Visual Studio .NET main window.

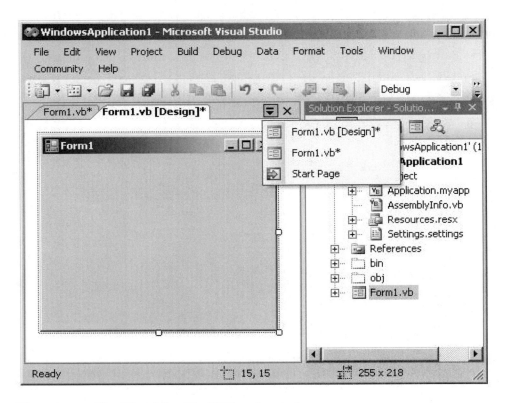

Figure 3.0 The Visual Studio .NET main window.

Tabbed Document Interface

By default, the Visual Studio .NET main window layout is set to the Tabbed Documents Interface (TDI) mode. The alternative is the Multiple Documents Interface (MDI) mode. To set or reset this, go to Tools/Options/Environment/ General and select a desired window layout option. If you are not sure what an MDI mode is, let us remind you that; for example, MS Word is built as an MDI program and previously, before .NET versions of Visual Studio, used it too. In MDI there is one parent window that can open multiple documents in child windows, which will always be displayed inside the parent window.

In the TDI design, each document is opened as a tabbed document, not a window. For example, in Figure 3.0 there are three open tabbed documents: the Start Page, the Form1.vb (Design) and Form1.vb. When you have multiple documents open, you have two quick ways to access them: you can click on the tab or if it is not visible click on the Active Files box, which is next to the Close box and choose the document from the dropdown menu.

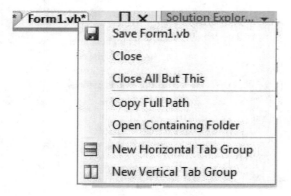

Figure 3.1 The tabbed document context menu.

Additionally, each tabbed document provides a context menu of its own. A snapshot of Form1.vb tabbed document context menu is shown in Figure 3.1. This context menu allows you to deal with this and other open documents in a number of ways. You can save changes to the file, close the tab, close all but this tab and perform other actions.

The Menu Bar

If you take a closer look at the upper part of the Visual Studio main window shown in Figure 3.0, you may notice two navigation panels: the Menu Bar and the Toolbar. The Menu Bar displays a row of menus right under the title bar. This is probably the most powerful navigation tool as it provides access to almost any functionality available in Visual Studio.

When you study the menus, pay attention to icons and hotkeys displayed before and after each menu. In most cases, if the sub-menu shows an icon before its name, then this item can be also placed on the toolbar and the same icon will be displayed on the corresponding toolbar button. The same rule applies to hotkeys. If a hotkey is available for a menu item then you should see it after the menu name.

File Menu

The first item on the menu bar is the File menu. This menu functionality is centered on manipulating solutions and project files and performing such actions as: Open, Save, Save As, Add and many others.

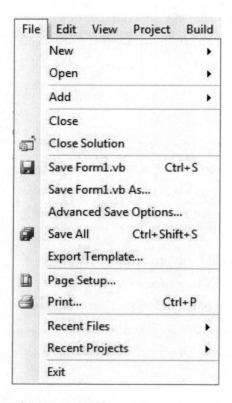

Figure 3.2 File menu.

The File menu snapshot is shown in Figure 3.2. Below is a brief description of each sub-menu:

New – allows creating a new project, website, file or project from existing code.

Open – allows opening a project, a file or converting a project.

Add – new project, new website, existing project, existing website.

Close – will close the selected document.

Close Solution – will close the selected solution.

Save Form1 – will save changes to Form1 file.

Save Form1 As – allows saving Form1 file with a different name.

Save All – saves changes to all files in this solution.

Recent Files - shows links to recently opened files.

Recent Projects – shows links to recently opened solutions and projects.

Exit – will close Visual Studio .NET.

Note *Save* and *Save As* menus will show a module name only if it is highlighted in the Solution Explorer.

Edit Menu

The Edit menu is mostly related to the code editor functionality. Thus, if the latter is not open it will be empty. That's why it will make sense to have the code editor open before you use this menu.

Undo and Redo – are used to cancel or move to previous or the next state of changes made to an open document. Remember, you may click on this menu or the corresponding toolbar button multiple times to return to a certain state of changes made to a document. Undo takes you back to the previous state and Redo moves to the next. The icons used for these actions are the forward and backward bound arrows. If you look at the Toolbar in Figure 3.0, you should see these two buttons. Chances are that you will use Undo and Redo as often as Backspace in Word. Both are included in the standard toolbar by default.

Cut, Copy, Delete, Paste and *Select All* are self-explanatory.

Find and Replace – allows performing text search and replacing actions. You may search for any character, word or combination of words. This function may be useful when in real-world projects you have dozens of pages of code and need to quickly find a certain literal expression or a variable.

Remember these shortcuts:

Quick Find: Ctrl + F.

Quick Replace: Ctrl + H.

Go To – sends the cursor to a specified line of code. Just enter the code line number in the dialog box and press Enter. If your code lines are not numbered, you can set this feature in Tools/Options/Text Editor/Basic by checking the Line Numbers checkbox. Having code lines numbered is really helpful in large projects.

Advanced – has a lot of sub-menus. We will mention two, which we consider very useful. *Comment Selection* - comments out the selected code. *Uncomment Selection* - does just the opposite. Notice that the corresponding buttons are included in the standard toolbar by default.

IntelliSense – we covered it in the code editor section in Chapter 2. Remember, all IntelliSense features are turned on by default and they should work when you type code. However, if you want to run a certain IntelliSense feature manually then you can do so by using a corresponding menu item or the hotkey. For example, say you typed File – and IntelliSense showed you a list of all members that belong to the File class and then somehow you lost the member list view and want to see it again. You can do this by choosing Edit/IntelliSense/List Members or by pressing Ctrl + J and the members list will appear again.

View Menu

The View menu allows you to open almost any Visual Studio component. When you learn its functionality, remember that for each direct access sub-menu there is an icon, a menu name and a hotkey combination. For example, as you can see in Figure 3.3, the Code Editor can be opened using the Code menu or F7 hotkey. The Form Designer can be launched using the Designer menu or with the Shift + F7 hotkey combination. Below is a brief description of each sub-menu:

Code or F7 – opens the Code Editor.
Designer or Shift + F7 – opens the Form Designer.
Server Explorer – opens a window that shows servers.

Solution Explorer – opens the Solution Explorer.

Class View – shows the Class View window.

Object Browser – opens the Object Browser window.

Error List – shows project compilation errors.

Output – shows project build results.

Properties Window or F4 – opens the Properties window.

Task List – shows current project tasks.

Toolbox – opens the Toolbox.

Other Windows – shows sub-menus such as Command window, Start Page and others.

Toolbars – shows a list of toolbars that can be added to the main Toolbar.

Full Screen – toggles the main window full screen mode.

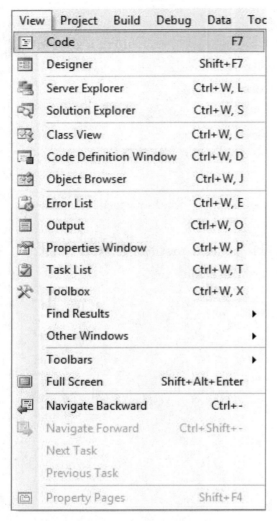

Figure 3.3 View menu.

Project Menu

The Project menu is designed to help you deal with various project level development tasks such as add new or existing items, modules or files, modify project properties and others. For example, you can add a new form or a class to your project. Of course, many of these functions can be invoked from the Solution Explorer and the corresponding context menus.

Build Menu

Using the Build menu or F6, you can build or rebuild the whole solution or certain projects in the solution. If you have multiple projects in a solution and need to build only a certain project, you should first highlight it in the Solution Explorer and then invoke this menu or press Shift + F6.

Debug Menu

This menu opens the door to a lot of debugging actions. Essentially, debugging is a process of finding and correcting programming errors. It will be covered in more detail in Chapter 10. Here we will give you an overview of the Debug menu functionality.

Windows – allows opening the Breakpoints and the Immediate windows.

Start Debugging or F5 – is used to start a project debugging session.

Start Without Debugging or Ctrl + F5 – runs a project without debugging.

Step Into or F11 – allows stepping into a procedure and executing code line by line.

Step Over or F10 – executes without stepping into code.

New Breakpoint – creates a breakpoint on the line where the cursor is placed.

Clear All Breakpoints – deletes all breakpoints in the project.

Disable All Breakpoints – disables all breakpoints without deleting them.

Format Menu

The Format menu will assist you in positioning controls on the form. Note that you won't see it on the main window menu bar unless the form designer is open. That's because the Format menu is used to arrange controls on the form. Also, you won't be able to run any of its sub-menus unless you first select one or more controls on the form. This menu functionality is useful to properly position multiple controls on the form especially when the form is densely populated with controls.

Align – aligns selected controls to the left, right, center, bottom or top.
Make Same Size – resizes all selected controls to the size of the first selected control.
Horizontal Spacing – equalizes horizontal spaces between selected controls.
Vertical Spacing – equalizes the vertical spaces between selected controls.
Center in Form – centers selected controls on the form horizontally or vertically.
Lock Controls – locks selected controls to disallow property changes.

Let's consider one example of how formatting can be applied to positioning controls on the form. Let's assume that you have five button controls positioned one below the other in the right-hand side of the form. To improve the appearance of the form, you may want to make sure that horizontal positioning and vertical spacing between each button is exactly the same. Select all five buttons by clicking on the first one then while holding the Ctrl key down click on each button to add it to the selected group. Open the Format menu and choose Vertical Spacing/Make Equal and then Horizontal Spacing/Make Equal.

Cool Trick:

The above-described operation has one drawback—manual selection of each control in a group of controls. We can recommend a trick that does just the same. Press the left mouse button and move the cursor to lasso all desired controls into a rectangle. When you release the mouse button, all controls inside the rectangle will be selected.

Tools Menu

The Tools menu exposes a number of advanced functions that are not covered in this book. However, there is one menu that we will touch upon briefly. It's the Options menu, which can be used to customize your Visual Studio .NET IDE. For example, you can customize your Text Editor settings. Note that the Text Editor and the Code Editor that we discussed earlier are different names for the same component. The Text Editor settings could be set to apply to all Visual Studio languages or to each language separately. We recommend keeping it separate for each language. The default settings may initially satisfy all your needs and you may not need to change them. However, it will be useful to know what Text Editor features are set by default and how you can change them if you need to. Go to Tools/Options and select Text Editor. You should see All Languages node and individual nodes for each programming or database language. Select Basic for Visual Basic.NET. In the right-hand pane you should see three sections: Statement Completion, Settings and Display. Note that all Statement Completion settings are related to the IntelliSense features such as Auto List Members and Parameter Information, which you can set here.

Window Menu

Some of the Window menu features are similar to those in Word or other well-known programs. As you may know, a typical Window menu in an MDI program allows you to view a list of all open documents. This functionality is also present in the Visual Studio Window menu. But we would like to tell you about a few cool features such as Split, New Horizontal Tab Group and New Vertical Tab Group. These sub-menus will allow you to split your tabbed document page horizontally or vertically. In other words, you can divide one document into two sections. The split border is adjustable.

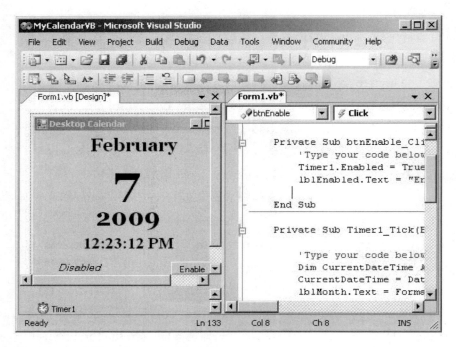

Figure 3.4 The Vertical Tab Group.

The *New Vertical Tab Group* divides the main window vertically into two sections.
For example, Figure 3.4 shows a vertical tab group in which the left tab shows the
form in design view and the right one displays the code. This feature may prove very
useful if you like to do design work and coding at the same time. This may allow you
to have the same form module displayed in design and view code modes at the same
time. The main difference of tab groups from splits is that the former can display two
different documents as a group of tabs, which are already open in Visual Studio. You
cannot pre-define what a tab's combination should be but you can toggle the tabs
by clicking on the Move to Next Tab Group. The Move to Next tab Group menu will
be displayed only after you have selected one of the tab groups. For example, if you
selected New Vertical Tab Group and then open the Window menu, again you will

see two menus: New Horizontal Tab Group and Move to Next Tab Group. The trick is that by moving to the next tab group you actually ask to create a new combination of pages in the tab. The splits, on the contrary, just divide one document into two halves.

New Horizontal Tab Group – the same as the vertical tab group but works horizontally.

Note:

The Tab Groups menu works well when there are multiple documents open in Visual Studio. If you have only one file open, the Tabs Group menus won't be displayed. Therefore, before you start playing with this functionality, have several documents open. Then create one tab group and try to swap pages in the tab group by using the Move to the Next Tab Group menu. When you need to return to a normal display mode, just close one of the tabs.

Help Menu

Learning how to most effectively use all help resources is extremely important. It will help you resolve a lot of issues and problems not only while you are learning but, most importantly, when you start working on your own. The Help menu is a gateway to a number of help documents, knowledge base articles and other resources.

Help is available in two modes: online and offline. To use help offline you need to install MSDN, which comes with Visual Studio .NET. To work online, you should be connected to the Internet. The methodology built into help functionality is based on providing a search engine that allows exploring the above-mentioned resources by index, a keyword or a word combination.

The Toolbar

The Toolbar has one significant advantage over the menu bar—each toolbar button provides a direct access to functionality it is associated with. However, the toolbar offers just a fraction of functionality available in Visual Studio because its capability is dependent on the real estate it can use. Although Visual Studio offers dozens of various toolbars, only a few can be placed on the main window. By default, only the Standard and the Text Editor toolbars are displayed.

Figure 3.5 The Toolbar.

The Standard toolbar is set to display a certain number of buttons by default. The selection of buttons is, probably, based on the assumption that they are the ones most often used. Of course, you can change it and we will show how. If you examine the toolbar shown in Figure 3.5, you will see that it displays the following buttons: Create New Project, Add New Item, Cut, Paste, Copy, Undo, Redo, Navigate Forward, Navigate Backward, Start, Solution Configurations, Solution Explorer, Properties, Toolbox, Object Browser, Command Window and Start Page. You can customize it by removing or adding more buttons. To add or remove buttons, click on a little downward arrow called Toolbar Options and choose Add or Remove Buttons/ Standard. You should see a long list of available buttons that can be added or removed from the toolbar. If a button is already added, you should see a checkmark before its name.

Additional Toolbars

To add more toolbars or customize your development environment, right-click any place under the title bar but before the tabbed documents. You should see a list of additional toolbars. When you click on any toolbar, it will be immediately added to the main window. Note that sometimes a newly added toolbar may be floating anywhere in the main window. Just drag it to an empty place in the toolbar area.

Summary

In this chapter, you have learned how to use Visual Studio .NET to access its main components and tools. Visual Studio offers multiple ways to open and manage documents from its main window. Each navigation method discussed here has its own strengths and weaknesses and it's up to you to decide which ones to use in your development work. To consolidate your knowledge of Visual Studio navigation tools, we recommend you complete Lab 3.

Lab 3: The Temperature Converter Project

Temperature Converter

In this Project:

You will create a Temperature Converter program. It will be designed to convert Fahrenheit values to Celsius. This lab will give you a good chance to practice skills learned in chapters 1, 2 and 3. If you have any questions or don't know how to deal with a certain error, review a related topic in one of the previous chapters and try to fix the problem. Note that most of your potential errors may be related to such trivial things as typos, spelling and wrong naming of variables.

Create a New Project

- ➤ Create the *Lab3* project folder.
- ➤ Open Visual Studio .NET
- ➤ Create a new Windows Application project.
- ➤ Set the project Location to C:\Labs\Lab3.
- ➤ Set the project Name to *FCConverter*.

Design User Interface

Begin with changing the form class and file name. In real-world projects, you may want to give your forms some meaningful names. Changing the form name may require corresponding changes in a number of places in the project. Fortunately, in Visual Studio 2005 most of this work is done for you. However, in Visual Studio 2003 things may get tricky; we'll tell you why later. In the Solution Explorer select Form1 file, right-click it and choose Rename. Type frmConverter.vb. In Visual Studio 2005, you should get a message asking if you would like this change be applied to all references of Form1. Click Yes.

In Visual Studio 2003, there will be no such notification and your form file name change will pass unnoticed. Continue your work. Open the code editor and change the form class name to frmConverter. This should also be accepted without any noise. Try to build the application. You should get an error like this: "Sub Main was not found in FCConverter.Form1." To fix the problem, do the following: Bring up the Solution Explorer, right-click *FCConverter* project name and choose Properties. If you see a message saying "There are no property pages for the selection," click OK to close and then repeat the operation. Now you should see the project Property Pages window. Find the Startup Object dropdown and select frmConverter, click Apply and then OK. Now try to compile the application again. You should get no errors.

Normally, any project must have a startup object, which could be a form or a shared subroutine procedure called *Main*. By default, Form1 is set as your project startup object. However, when you change the form name, it is gone. When compiler fails to find Form1, it checks if there is the *Main* subroutine, which it can't find as well. Then it generates a misleading error saying that Form1 does not have a Sub Main procedure. A simple solution is to set the startup object to a new form name, which you did. Of course, if you are using Visual Studio 2005, you are spoiled because all this work is done for you.

Add Controls

Add controls to the form. Note that the GroupBox control in this project should be placed before other controls since it is a container control. You don't need to name the labels because they will be used to display static data. Note that the use of ampersand (&) character in the Text property of buttons is intended to create a hotkey combination. Add all controls and set their properties according to Table 1.

Table 1. The frmConverter form controls.

Control Type	Property Name	Value
Form	Name	frmConverter
-/-	Text	Temperature Converter
-/-	StartPosition	CenterScreen
GroupBox	Text	Temperature Conversion:
Label	Text	Fahrenheit
Textbox	Name	txtFahrenheit
Label	Text	Celsius
Textbox	Name	txtCelsius
Button	Name	btnConvert

-/-	Text	&Convert
Button	Name	btnClear
-/-	Text	Cl&ear
Button	Name	btnClose
-/-	Text	Cl&ose

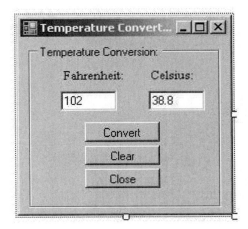

Figure 1. The FCConverter form.

When you complete your design work, your form should look like the one shown in Figure 1.

Write Code

You will have three buttons in this application so you need to write code in their click event procedures. Then you will write code that does the conversion work using a formula to convert a temperature given in Fahrenheit into Celsius. Note that in this lab you will also write code to validate user input.

Write code in the Convert button click event procedure. Double-click the btnConvert button. This should open an empty *btnConvert_click* event procedure. Your complete procedure should look like this:

```
Private Sub btnConvert_Click(ByVal sender As Object,
   ByVal e As EventArgs) Handles btnConvert.Click
   'Write code below this line:
   Dim intFahrenheit As Int32 = 0
   If txtFahrenheit.Text.Length = 0 Then
      MessageBox.Show("Enter temperature in Fahrenheit.")
      Exit Sub
   End If
      intFahrenheit = Convert.ToInt32(txtFahrenheit.Text)
      txtCelsius.Text = (intFahrenheit - 32) * 0.5555
End Sub
```

Here's a brief interpretation of the above code. In the first line we declare *Int32* variable to store the Fahrenheit value. In the second line we check the length of the text entered in the txtFahrenheit textbox to validate the user input. In this case we want to make sure that the user entered some value. If this test returns true, which means nothing is entered, we show a message box asking the user to enter a value. The fourth line calls the Exit Sub method to leave this subroutine procedure because if the user did not enter anything it does not make sense to continue. The sixth line reads the value entered in the textbox, converts it from string to integer and then assigns it to the *intFahrenheit* variable. We need to convert a string to an integer because we cannot do math operations with a string. In the seventh line we apply the conversion formula and assign the result to the txtCelsius textbox. Write code in the btnClose button click event procedure to close the form. Your code should look like this:

```
Private Sub btnClose_Click(ByVal sender As Object, _
     ByVal e As EventArgs) Handles btnClose.Click
     Me.Close()
End Sub
```

Write code in the btnClear button click event procedure. This code will delete text in both textboxes.

```
Private Sub btnClear_Click(ByVal sender As Object, _
     ByVal e As EventArgs) Handles btnClear.Click
     txtFahrenheit.Text = ""
     txtCelsius.Text = ""
End Sub
```

Save your Work

To save your work, click on the Save button or press Ctrl + S.

Test the Application

Test the application. Note when you use Debug/Start menu or press F5, Visual Studio will try to build the application and then run it. If there are errors, build will fail. Correct errors and try again. When you can run the application, check the following:

- Check if all labels, textboxes and buttons are displayed correctly. Check if the buttons display correct captions.

- Without entering any value in the Fahrenheit textbox, click on the Convert button. You should get an error message prompting you to enter a value.
- In the Fahrenheit textbox, enter 68 and click Convert. You should get the result of 19.998 displayed in the Celsius textbox.
- Test the Clear button functionality. When you click on this button, the text in the Fahrenheit and Celsius textboxes must be erased.
- Test the Close button. Clicking on it should shut down the program.

Congratulations! You successfully completed Lab 3.

Extra Credit Tasks

For those of you who are not challenged by this simple project, we have two extra credit tasks. Your temperature converter program has a lot of vulnerabilities. Think about it in terms of how smart the program is and how error-proof it is. Consider a few "What if" cases and how your program would behave in these situations. For example:

1. What if the user enters a non-numeric value? Will the program be able to continue or fail?
2. What if the user wants to convert from Celsius to Fahrenheit?

We will help you to answer these questions. In case 1, the program will fail because it does not check if the entered value is numeric. Trying to convert a non-numeric value into an integer or doing a mathematical operation with a string value will cause an error. In this case, you may get a very confusing .NET error message saying: "Input string is not in correct format." Case 2 requires modification and enhancement of project code to allow conversion from Celsius to Fahrenheit.

Extra Credit Task 1

Modify the program and make it smart enough to identify if the temperature value entered by a user is numeric. There are many ways to do it. Here's a hint for a simple solution. Use the *IsNumeric()* VB .NET built-in function to test the value entered by the user before you apply the formula. If you combine the absence of value check, which is already in place, with the data type validation then your code may look like this:

```
If txtFahrenheit.Text.Length = 0 Then
     MessageBox.Show("Enter temperature in Fahrenheit.")
```

```
      Exit Sub
ElseIf Not IsNumeric(txtFahrenheit.Text) Then
      MessageBox.Show("Please enter a numeric value.")
      Exit Sub
End If
```

Extra Credit Task 2

Conversion from Celsius to Fahrenheit. First, you may need to add two radio buttons to the application. Name one of them *radioFahrenheit* and the other *radioCelsius*. To convert from Celsius to Fahrenheit, the user should check radioFahrenheit and to do the opposite use radioCelsius. In your code you need to check which radio button was checked and decide which formula to apply accordingly. Below is the code that does it. Your code may look different but you got the idea:

```
If radioFahrenheit.Checked = True Then
      txtFahrenheit.Text = (intCelsius - 32) * 1.8
Else
      txtCelsius.Text = (intFahrenheit - 32) * 0.5555
End If
```

Good Luck!

Part III   Data Types

Data Types

Chapter 4: Visual Basic .NET Data Types

Visual Basic .NET
Data Types

In this chapter:

You will learn Visual Basic .NET data types and the concepts of Value Types and Reference Types. You will consider the main characteristics of data types. A profound knowledge of these concepts is key to your successful learning of Visual Basic .NET programming.

Chapter 4 at a Glance

- ➢ The Role of Data Types
- ➢ The Heap and the Stack
- ➢ Value Types
- ➢ Numeric Data Types
- ➢ Non-Numeric Data Types
- ➢ Reference Types
- ➢ Classes, Types and Objects
- ➢ Principles of Type Casting
- ➢ Object Type
- ➢ Comparing Value and Reference Types
- ➢ Boxing and Unboxing

The Role of Data Types

Data processing is one of the most important operations in any program. To deal with data in an application you will use programming data types that can represent the real-world data types. You should declare in advance what type of data you will be dealing with. To do so you first need to find out what programming data type is the best match for your data. This way you can make sure that the selected data type will best represent the actual data used in a program. Then you will need to declare a variable of that data type, which will store the data.

In the .NET world, data types are classified into two main categories: *Value Types* and *Reference Types*. In the following sections we will discuss them in more detail. But before that, we will briefly introduce two memory utilization concepts: the *Heap* and the *Stack*.

The Heap and the Stack

Before we delve into details of this topic we would like to draw two useful analogies. In human memory, information is stored easily without data type classification, formatting and measuring how much space and what type of memory is needed to hold it. Of course, this is not the case with the machine memory. Machines save information, humans memorize it. There are many theories that explain how that happens. A common understanding is that information is first exposed to a short-term memory and then gradually moved to a long-term memory.

Obviously enough, handling data in a program excludes the memorizing aspect but it does require an efficient combination of short-term and long-term memory mechanisms. This is where the concepts of the *Stack* and the *Heap* come into play. The stack can be considered a highly dynamic short-term memory to pile up small and simple data and the heap is a pro-type of a long-term memory that is used to store large and complex data. Now that we have introduced you to the heap and the stack, we need to tell you what makes them so different. There are three major factors: memory size, means of data retrieval and methods of memory release.

Memory Size

Memory allocated to the stack is relatively small and so are items stored in it. It can be any primitive data type variable with a size that can range from 1 byte to 16 bytes. For example, the *Char* data type that represents single characters uses 1 byte of memory. *Int16* integer – 2 bytes, *Int32* - 4 bytes, *Date* – 8 bytes and *Decimal* - 16 bytes. References to objects that can also be stored on the stack take 8 bytes.

The heap memory is significantly larger and is used to store objects. We won't go into details of classes and objects here since we will discuss this topic in Chapter 11. But we will give some examples of object sizes. First of all, objects are instances of classes. Typically, the size of an object is a sum of class implementation code plus class instance data. For example, if your class code is 1000 bytes and you have defined 10 *Integer* properties in it, your object size can be about 1000 + (20 * 4) bytes. How big can an object get? Small and medium size objects should not exceed 85,000 bytes. If they do, they will become large objects. Does it matter? Yes, it does. Small and medium size objects are stored on a regular managed object heap while large objects are stored on a large object heap (LOH). This topic is out of scope of this book but it is worth mentioning that garbage collection on LOH is different and is not as fast and frequent as on the normal heap.

Data Retrieval

In terms of data retrieval, the stack is a simple memory utilization mechanism. The commonly used analogy is a pipe. When the stack stores data, it gives each item an incremental index and pushes it into a virtual memory pipe. When it's necessary to retrieve an item, it reverses the process and pops up one item at a time until it gets the one with the right index. This principle of data retrieval is known as First in Last out (FILO). The stack defines and uses two simple methods: *Push* and *Pop*. The push method stores data and the pop method retrieves data. Thus, in the stack, no search and find procedure is necessary to retrieve data.

Now that you are familiar with the stack it will be easy to understand what makes it so different from the heap. With the heap things are principally different. When an object is stored on the heap, a pointer is created to reference that object. This object reference is then used to identify the object on the heap. When you need to access the object to invoke its methods or retrieve data you first need to do a reference search to find the object on the heap and then use it.

Memory Release Method

On the stack, memory used by a variable is released immediately after the variable goes out of scope. This mechanism provides high performance and efficiency of memory use. On the contrary, any memory used by an object on the heap is not released immediately after it is no longer needed. This work is delegated to the .NET Common Language Runtime (CLR) memory housekeeping service called Garbage Collection (GC). Therefore, the memory release is delayed until the next garbage collection occurs.

This memory management mechanism relieves a programmer from a critically important memory management task. On the other hand a programmer loses the ability to control the memory release process. This brings us to another .NET concept known as a non-deterministic destruction. What this concept means is that in your program you do not have the power to determine when an object can be destroyed and the memory it uses released. Object destruction or memory release in .NET is totally a prerogative of the CLR and its garbage collection "department". If all the above-mentioned abstractions do make sense to you, then you are ready to learn two cardinal .NET data type concepts: Value Types and Reference Types.

Value Types

In order to understand what Value Types are you need to make a distinction between primitive data, such as numbers or characters, and complex data, such as types and objects. This distinction is important because in .NET the former belongs to the value types category and the latter to the reference types. Note by primitive data we mean data that carries a simple, single value. This could be an integer, a decimal, a character, a text or a date. In the following sections, we will discuss Visual Basic .NET value types.

Numeric Data Types

Visual Basic.NET implements a set of numeric data types, which are presented in Table 1. Please devote some time to study the characteristics of each type. When you do so, notice that the most important point in this classification is how the value range represented by a type relates to the amount of memory necessary to store it. In most cases, the relation is quite simple: the greater is the range, the more memory is required. You may also notice that some types in Table 1 have exactly the same characteristics. For example, *Short* and *Int16*, *Integer* and *Int32* represent the same data types. That's because they are a legacy of VB 6. The VB 6 *Integer* is represented as *Short* in VB .NET and the VB 6 *Long* is *Integer* in VB .NET.

Table 1. Visual Basic .NET numeric data types.

Type	Description	Memory Size	Value Range
Byte	8-bit unsigned integer	1	0 to 255
Short	16-bit signed integer	2	-32,7682 to 32,767
Int16	16-bit signed integer	2	-32,7682 to 32,767
Int32	32-bit signed integer	4	-2,147,483,648 to 2,147,483,647
Integer	32-bit signed integer	4	-2,147,483,648 to 2,147,483,647
Long	64-bit signed integer	8	-9,223,372,036,854,775,808 to 9,223,372,036,854,775,807
Int64	64-bit signed integer		
Single	32-bit number	4	-1.5_10E45 to 3.4_10E38
Double	64-bit number	8	-5.0_10E324 to 1.7_10E308
Decimal	Decimal number	16	-1.0_10E28 to 7.9_10E28

Note: In Table 1 (E) is used to denote exponent.

Interpretation of Numeric Types

If you examine Table 1, you may wonder why there are so many data types that represent numbers. Well, this has to do with a number of reasons. The first important classification criterion is the value range represented by a type. For example, compare the maximum value of *Byte* and *Long*. The second factor is the separation of types that can represent decimals from those that denote whole numbers. And the last, but not least, is the signing factor and the level of precision of decimals. Thus, we can classify all numeric data types by the following criteria: value range, precision and signing.

Memory Size and Value Range

Each data type requires a specific amount of memory to store. In case of positive whole numbers the relationship is simple—the greater the number the more memory is required. In case of signed numbers we need twice the memory to represent the same range because the value can stretch in both directions—positive and negative.

The range of values represented by data types varies. Each numeric type is designed to store only a certain range and has a defined minimum and maximum, which should not be exceeded. Trying to assign values that exceed the value range will cause an Overflow exception.

Note:

To prevent overflow errors, you should verify the maximum or minimum values by referencing the type's Maximum and Minimum properties of the data type.

Precision Factor

Visual Basic .NET has three floating point data types that may be used to represent decimal numbers. These are *Single, Double* and *Decimal*. Decimal types should be used to provide a required level of numeric precision. We will discuss this topic in more detail in the Decimals section.

Signing Factor

As you already know, numeric data types can be signed or unsigned. Signed numbers allow both positive and negative numeric values. The unsigned numeric data types can only be used to represent positive numbers. Pay attention that all Visual Basic .NET numeric data types are signed except one: the *Byte*. The byte in Visual Basic is unsigned and it can represent numbers from 0 to 255. For your information, unsigned numeric data types are implemented in other .NET languages; for example, C#. To give you an idea of the difference that the signing can produce let's remind you that a singed byte can store numbers from -128 to 127. Thus, the main advantage of unsigned numeric data types is that they allow storing larger positive numbers with smaller amount of memory used. This feature can be useful for better memory utilization when you have to deal with many large numbers.

When you examine value range column in Table 1, pay attention that all signed types minimum value is a negative number and the maximum value is a positive number. Finally, we would like to stress that the main advantage of having this wide variety of numeric data types is that it allows you to choose the type that will best represent your numeric value and at the same time provide optimal memory utilization.

Decimals

Numeric data types designed to represent decimals are shown in Table 2.

Table 2. Decimals.

Type	Minimum	Maximum	Precision	Memory
Single	-1.5_10E-45	3.4_10E38	7	4
Double	-5.0_10E-324	3.4_10E308	15/16	8
Decimal	-1.0 10E-28	7.9 10E28	28	16

In Table 2, the value range is represented by the Minimum and Maximum values. The Precision column denotes the number of decimal places and the Memory indicates the memory used. To understand how this works, let's look at how the *Single* and *Double* differ from each other. The maximum value of a non-decimal part of a double is significantly larger than that of a single and it also provides a twice higher level of precision because it can carry a maximum of 16 decimal places, while the single can provide only 7. Note that decimals are designed to provide a higher level of precision, obviously, at the expense of the value range of their non-decimal part. Therefore, decimals should be used with smaller numbers that require a significantly higher level of precision.

Precision in Action

You may be wondering when precision is essential and if it really matters in real-world situations. Let's look at an example where the level of precision may cause a significant difference. If you know how decimal number precision mechanism works you may skip this section. Let's say your program needs to calculate a currency exchange transaction where 120 million Euros were bought at the exchange rate of 1.1945897879989989. In your calculation procedure you decided that using five decimal places would be good enough to calculate the dollar amount of this trade.

120,000,000 * 1.19456 = $143,347,**200**

When you found out that your results did not tie up with the audit numbers you decided to calculate using all 16 decimal places.

120,000,000 * 1.1945699879989989 = $143,34**8,398**

If you compare the numbers you'll see that the second calculation has a difference of $1,198. This example shows how precision works when you deal with a financial transaction that requires both large numeric values and high precision.

Using Numeric Data Types

Visual Basic .NET has a number of data types that are designed to represent numeric values. When you make a decision of what data type to choose you need to know how big the maximum value you want to store will be and if it's going to be an integer or a decimal. If precision is important, you may further need to know how many decimal places will ensure the required level of accuracy. Once you have made these decisions you are ready to choose your numeric data type. Of course, there is always the memory usage that will come into play when the application stores a lot of data.

Non-Numeric Data Types

There are not too many non-numeric data types: *String, Char, Date* and *Boolean*. Note that the string is a special type and we will cover it later in this chapter. Non-numeric data types are listed in Table 3.

Table 3. Non-numeric data types.

Type	Description	Size
Char	Represents characters	2
Date	Represents date and time	8
Boolean	Represents True/False	4
String	Represents text	8 + (2 * string length)

Interpretation of Non-Numeric Data Types

In the non-numeric data types category we will consider *Char, String, Boolean* and *Date*.

Char

Char is used to represent single characters. Note you should not assign more than one character to a char variable. If you attempt to do so, only the first character will be stored and the rest will be truncated and no error will occur. If you need to convert a string to a char, you may use the *Parse* method defined in the char class as follows:

```
Dim chrVariable As Char
chrVariable = Char.Parse(StringValue)
```

String

The String is not a value type but we consider it here because it represents primitive data. The string is designed to represent a sequence of characters. The capacity of a string is dependent on your computer resources and may range from 1 to billions of characters. The *String* class is defined as an immutable class, which makes it different from other reference types in .NET in general. The string immutability is used specifically to make it behave as a primitive data type. Therefore you cannot edit the content of a string object variable. Let's say you created a string variable and assigned a value to it. Then you decide to replace a few characters in it. In this case the following will happen. A copy of data stored by the sting variable will be made with your changes applied and then assigned to a new string object and the variable made to reference this new string object. The old string object will be dereferenced. Let's consider two examples.

Case 1.

```
Dim strA As String
Dim strB As String
strA = "test"
strB = ""
strB = strA
```

Case 2.

```
Dim objClassA1 As New ClassA
Dim objClassA2 As New ClassA
```

```
objClassA1 = objClassA2
```

When in Case 1, we assign *strA* variable to *strB* variable a copy of *strA* data is made and assigned to a new string instance referenced by *strB*. The variable data is copied and a new string instance for *strB* is created. As a result both will have their own copy of data and will point to different string objects. Case 2 illustrates a normal object reference behavior. In this assignment statement only the object reference is copied. Thus, after the assignment statement is executed object variables *objClassA1* and *objClassA2* will point to the same object in memory and as a result will reference the same ClassA class instance.

Date

The *Date* and *DateTime* types are used to represent date and time. The date values stored may range from midnight 01/01/0001 to midnight 12/31/9999. So you can create a programmable time machine to travel from midnight of January 1 of year 1 to midnight of December 31, 9999. The date class has something that could be called a satellite type—the *TimeSpan* type that can be very useful to measure time difference between two date instances. For example:

```
Dim tspDiff As TimeSpan
Dim dtStartDate As Date
Dim dtEndDate As Date
Dim intDiffDays As Integer
Dim intDiffHours As Integer
tspDiff = dtEndDate - dtStartDate
intDiffDays = tspDiff.Days
intDiffHours = tspDiff.Hours
```

The *TimeSpan* object relieves you from tedious work of calculating the difference between the two dates. Just assign the date difference to the *TimeSpan* object and then extract the difference in any desired units: days, minutes or seconds.

Boolean

Boolean is used to represent one of two logical values: *True* or *False*. Both values are keywords in Visual Basic .NET. Note under the hood, Boolean values are stored as 16-bit numbers. Although you can assign numbers to Boolean variables, it's not recommended to mix logical and numeric values because numeric conversions of Boolean values may produce different results.

Reference Types

In the following sections we are going to talk about the reference types. We will also discuss the main characteristics of a generic object type and look at methods of type casting.

Classes, Types and Objects

We will now look at types from a perspective of a logical triangle of classes, types and objects. This will, hopefully, help us to briefly describe the relationship between these three abstract entities. Please find a more detailed discussion of classes and objects in Chapter 11. Classes represent pieces of reusable code that can provide useful functionality. A type is a collection of exposable class characteristics. Objects are instances of classes.

Classes and Types

What's the difference between classes and types? Types contain only exposable class features such as public methods, properties and events and do not include implementation or private members. Thus, only the exposable features of a class will make up the class type.

Types and Objects

Why is typing important? Typing methodology is used in programming as a powerful program safety tool. One of the biggest problems that may occur at runtime is when your program is trying to read or write to a wrong memory address. In fact, it would be more correct to say not wrong memory address but wrong memory structure or cliché. For example, if you try to save object X data into memory laid out for object Y, it may cause serious problems, such as data corruption, program crash and so on.

Type is an abstraction. However, in .NET there is a place where you can find a full type description. It is called metadata. In a .NET assembly each class is placed into a module. Each module has metadata, which describes its type. Therefore, when the runtime builds an object it reads the metadata. Thus, types are supposed to be unique and attempts to store object data that belongs to one type in a memory built for another type should be considered illegal. But you may ask, what if I really need to store data created for one object in the memory created for another object? Well, programming types are not cast in stone so they can be forged. Even though you would be violating the principles of strong typing, it's totally legal to convert types. Moreover, this need is understood and addressed ever since the object-oriented programming came into being. This brings us to a more practical programming topic: Type Casting.

Type Casting

You can convert objects from one type to another by *Type Casting*. In Visual Basic .NET, type casting can be performed *implicitly* or *explicitly*. Implicit casting is a built-in Visual basic .NET feature. This means you can assign an object of one type to another object and let Visual Basic figure out if a conversion is possible and do it. Thus, the actual type conversion is done for you behind the scenes. Explicit conversion is managed by you. You have to select and call a method that you think can do the job. More about casting in Chapter 11.

Object Type

In .NET there is a special type called *object* that is the root of all objects, which means each and every class in the .NET world must derive from it. The *object* can be used as a universal type conversion media. You can convert any type to an object and when necessary do the reverse, convert back to a specific type. This feature is widely used in various .NET collection classes where many class members are defined as objects. Finally, thanks to object and the liberalism of Visual Basic .NET compiler, late object binding is possible in Visual Basic. We will talk more about object binding in Chapter 11.

Value Types and Reference Types

Now let's now sum up what you have learned about value and reference types.

Major Characteristics of Value Types

- Value Types represent primitive data.
- Value Types are allocated memory on the stack.
- Value Types are fast and use less memory.
- Value Types are destroyed as soon as they go out of scope.

Major Characteristics of Reference Types

- Reference Types represent object data.

- Reference Types are stored on the heap.
- Reference Types are removed by Garbage Collection.

Boxing and Unboxing

This is a final knockout topic, although it has nothing to do with rings and rounds. To better understand the subject matter, in the terms *Boxing* and *Unboxing* the root element *Box* should be associated with the word *Object*. Hence, boxing should be understood as an action in which we put a value type variable data into an object wrapper. We kind of lock the value type data into an object shell. As a result, a value type variable data is converted into a reference type. Therefore, by boxing we formally transform a value type into a reference type. Unboxing is just the opposite. Boxing and unboxing are two special procedures that are used to reconcile the differences between value and reference types.

```
Dim objA As New Object
Dim intValue As Integer = 777
objA = intValue      'Boxing
intValue = objA      'Unboxing
```

In the above code, we declared and instantiated a generic object variable *objA* and an integer variable *intValue*. Then we assigned an integer variable to an object variable, in which case boxing is performed. In the next statement, we *unbox* the integer value by assigning the object variable to the integer variable.

Summary

In .NET, data types are classified into two major categories Value Types and Reference Types. Value types are designed to represent primitive data such as numbers, dates and characters and are stored on the stack. The stack is allocated a relatively small memory and is designed as a dynamic memory utilization mechanism. Value types consume less memory and provide better performance. Reference types are used to represent objects and are stored on the heap. The generic object is a root class for all .NET classes and can be used as a universal type conversion media. Boxing and unboxing techniques are used to remedy type conversion constraints and help to cross the boundaries between the value and reference types.

Lab 4: The Loan Calculator Project

Loan Calculator

In this Project:

You will create a loan calculator program. The name of the program speaks for itself. It is supposed to calculate monthly payments, interest paid and total payments on principal plus interest types of loans. In this project you will consolidate your knowledge of data types, type conversion and practice using numeric data types.

Create a New Project

> ➤ Create *Lab4* project folder.
>
> ➤ Open Visual Studio .NET.
>
> ➤ Create a new Windows Application project.
>
> ➤ Set the project Location to *C:\Labs\Lab4*.
>
> ➤ Set the project Name to *LoanCalculator*.

Design User Interface

Add Controls

Add controls and set their properties according to Table 1.

Table 1. The LoanCalculator form controls.

Control Type	Property Name	Value
GroupBox	Text	Loan Information:
GroupBox	Text	Payment Information:
Label	Text	Loan Amount:
Label	Text	Down Payment:
Label	Text	Interest Rate:
Label	Text	Loan Fees:
Label	Text	Loan Term:
Label	Name	lblResults
Label	Font	(size 10)
TextBox	Name	txtLoan
TextBox	Name	txtDown
TextBox	Name	txtInterest
TextBox	Name	txtFees
TextBox	Name	txtTerm
Button	Name	btnCalculate
Button	Name	btnClose

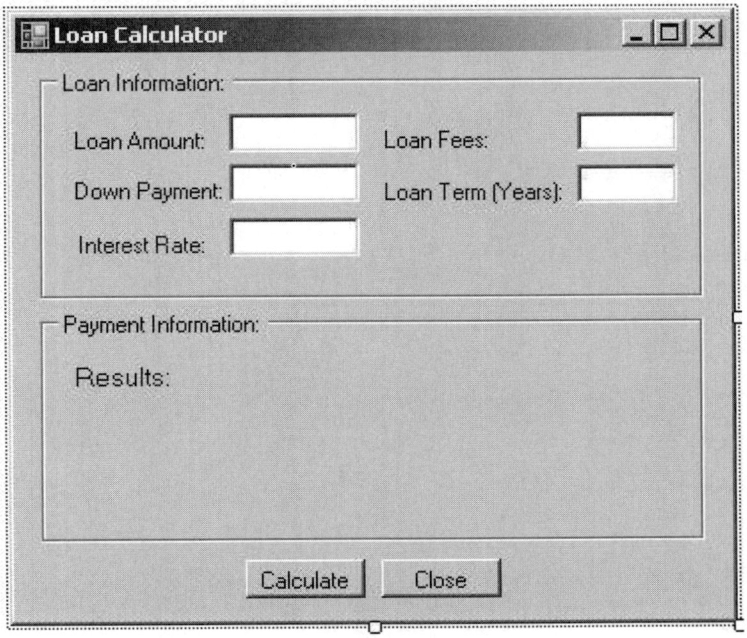

Figure 1. The LoanCalculator form.

When you complete the design work, your form should look like the one shown in Figure 1.

Write Code

Write the Calculate and CheckInput procedures. These procedures are presented in Listing 1.

Listing 1. Private procedures.

```
Private Sub Calculate()
      Dim str As String
      Dim intLoanAmt As Integer
```

```
Dim intDown As Integer
Dim intFees As Integer
Dim intBalance As Integer
Dim dblIntsRate As Single
Dim intLoanTerm As Integer
Dim sngInterestPaid As Single
Dim intTermMonths As Integer
Dim dblMonthlyPmt As Integer
Dim intTotalPaid As Integer
Dim dblYon As Double
Dim dblXon As Double
Dim dblZon As Double


If Not CheckInput() Then
      Return
End If


intLoanAmt = Convert.ToInt32(txtLoan.Text)
intFees = Convert.ToInt32(txtFees.Text)
intDown = Convert.ToInt32(txtDown.Text)
intBalance = Convert.ToInt32(intLoanAmt - intDown +
intFees)
intLoanTerm = Convert.ToInt32(txtTerm.Text)
dblIntsRate = Convert.ToDouble(txtInterest.Text)
intTermMonths = intLoanTerm * 12
dblYon = dblIntsRate / 1200
dblXon = dblYon + 1
dblZon = Math.Pow(dblXon, intTermMonths) - 1
```

```
        dblMonthlyPmt = (dblYon + (dblYon / dblZon)) * intBalance
        intTotalPaid = dblMonthlyPmt * intTermMonths
        sngInterestPaid = intTotalPaid - intBalance
        str = "Loan balance =" & Space(11) &
        intBalance.ToString & vbCrLf
        str = str & "Loan Term =" & Space(16) &
        intLoanTerm.ToString & " years" & vbCrLf
        str = str & "Interest paid =" & Space(13) &
        sngInterestPaid.ToString & vbCrLf
        str = str & "Total paid =" & Space(17) &
        intTotalPaid.ToString & vbCrLf
        str = str & "Monthly payment =" & Space(5) &
        dblMonthlyPmt.ToString
        lblResults.Text = str


End Sub


Private Function CheckInput() As Boolean


Dim strErr As String = ""
If txtLoan.Text.Length = 0 Then
        strErr = "Enter loan amount" & vbCrLf
End If


If txtDown.Text.Length = 0 Then
        strErr = strErr & "Enter down payment" & vbCrLf
End If
If txtInterest.Text.Length = 0 Then
```

```
        strErr = strErr & "Enter interest rate" & vbCrLf
End If


If txtFees.Text.Length = 0 Then
        strErr = strErr & "Enter fees" & vbCrLf
End If


If txtTerm.Text.Length = 0 Then
        strErr = strErr & "Enter loan term" & vbCrLf
End If


If strErr.Length > 0 Then
            MessageBox.Show(strErr)
        Return False
Else
        Return True
End If
```

The *Calculate* procedure implements the loan calculation formula. First, it calls the *CheckInput* function to verify if any values were entered into the textboxes. The absence of value is considered an error and a corresponding error message is assigned to the *strErr* string variable. At the end of the procedure you check this variable and if it contains errors, you display them in the message box and set the *CheckInput* function return value to false. This return value is checked by the *Calculate* procedure. If it is false the procedure stops processing by calling the *Return* command. Then the *Calculate* method extracts the values entered in the textboxes and converts them into corresponding numeric data types. Note that some parameters such as loan amount, down payment and fees will use whole numbers so they are declared as integers. For other variables such as interest rate and for some intermediate rate calculation parameters, precision is important so they are declared as doubles.

Note that we divided the monthly loan payment calculation formula into multiple parts to simplify the syntax and also help you follow the computation logic. Once the monthly payment amount is calculated, you will use it to generate the total amount paid. In this case it is equal to monthly payment times the loan term.

Listing 2. The Event Handlers.

```
Private Sub btnCalculate_Click(ByVal sender As System.Object,
ByVal e As System.EventArgs) Handles btnCalculate.Click
      Calculate()
End Sub


Private Sub btnClose_Click(ByVal sender As System.Object, ByVal
e As System.EventArgs) Handles btnClose.Click
      Me.Close()
End Sub
```

Listing 2 contains two event handler procedures. From the btnCalculate button click event procedure, you will invoke the Calculate procedure. The btnClose button click event procedure is used to close the application. Please find these procedures in Listing 2 and type them into your project.

Test the Application

Now it's time to test, and if necessary, debug the application. First try to build the project. Check the Output window for any errors or warnings. To open the Output window, on the View menu, choose Output. Read error messages, and try to correct them and then re-build the project.

Functionality Testing

Press F5 to start debugging. If there are no errors, Visual Studio will run the application and show the form. Perform program functionality testing. The program accepts loan information and calculates monthly payments, total payments and the interest payment. Note that the formula is based on accrued interest and better suits mortgage calculations but can be used for other loan types as well. Enter the following test case information:

Loan amount = 350000

Down payment = 30000

Interest rate = 5.75

Loan fees = 2000

Loan term = 30

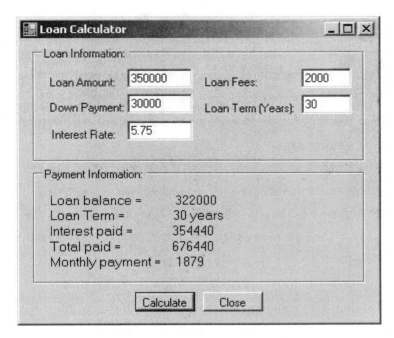

Figure 2. The LoanCalculator at runtime.

Click Calculate. The calculation results should be formatted and displayed in the lblResults label control as shown in Figure 2. For the above test case you should get monthly payment equal to $1879. If you get a different number, check your code for errors, fix them and try again. Congratulations! You successfully completed Lab 4.

Extra Credit Task

For those of you who were not challenged by this simple project, we have one extra credit task. This application is not protected from invalid data entry. This becomes even more important since we are using input data in mathematical operations. We have a general data input check but, of course, it is not enough. User input should check if it is of a valid data type. Since in all cases we deal with numbers, we just need to verify if the value entered is a number.

Here's a hint. Before you allow the application to use data entered by a user, you need to check if it is of an expected data type. To implement this task you may use the Visual Basic .NET built-in function *IsNumeric* that takes one parameter, the input value, and returns true if the expression can be converted into a number. Here's a sample code that uses this function.

```
If Not IsNumeric(txtLoan.Text) Then
     MessageBox.Show("Please enter a number")
     Return
Else
     intLoanAmt = Convert.ToInt32(txtLoan.Text)
End If
```

While you are working on this task try to think about why you would need to call *Return* or *Exit Sub* command in this code. Of course, you may create your own solution—after all, it's your extra credit. But if you can't invent anything new don't give up, just use the hint. Good Luck!

Chapter 5: Data Types and Variables

Data Types and Variables

In this Chapter:

You will learn how to handle data types and variables. In a typical application you may have to deal with data of different type, size and origin. Your program may need to process static and dynamically changing data. To program such data manipulation tasks you need to know how to create temporary data storage devices called variables, how to declare and name them, understand variable access modifiers and variable scope concepts. This is the chapter where you will consider all that and much more.

Chapter 5 at a Glance

- ➤ A Variable Mission
- ➤ Variables and Memory
- ➤ Variable Declaration
- ➤ Variable Naming Rules
- ➤ Variable Naming Conventions
- ➤ Data Type Selection
- ➤ Using Value Types
- ➤ Using Reference Types
- ➤ Variable Scope

Introduction

In your program you may need to store and use data that can be either created internally or obtained from external sources. A program's internal data bank may be created by using information hard-coded into variables and constants at design time. For instance, a database name, a connection string, a file name and other information may be stored in variables. The data used in an application can also be obtained from external sources such as databases, files or entered by a user. To handle data in a program you need to use variables. Variables are temporary storage devices that provide fast access and allow changing values held by them as many times as necessary.

It may sound paradoxical but variables are divided into two major categories: variables and constants. Constants are a special type of variable used to store values that cannot be changed at runtime. Thus, if you need to use some static values such as coefficients or rates you may assign them to constants.

A Variable Mission

Apparently, the term variable indicates the fact that this is something that may change. In fact, this meaning is "glued" to the term in many branches of science. For example, in mathematics a variable means an expression that may vary or fluctuate. As we mentioned earlier, a variable in programming means a data storage name that is associated with the memory that holds that data.

A variable fulfils the following tasks:

 - ➢ Associates a human readable and meaningful name with a computer memory address.
 - ➢ Serves as a reference to dynamically changing data.
 - ➢ Helps to enforce data typing restrictions.

It is essential to realize that variables are a significant part of any application code. More importantly, variables provide a number of services, which are briefly stated at the beginning of this section. From a functionality perspective, a variable is a convenient mechanism of storing data at runtime, which provides fast access and dynamic value changes.

The terms design and runtime were briefly mentioned in this chapter. Now, let us consider how they relate to the variable concept. All your development work prior to application compilation falls into the design time category. A declaration of a variable is a request to reserve a suitable memory for it. Note that a variable declaration statement is not an executable code. You may verify this statement and we strongly recommend you to do so. Select a procedure that has at least one variable declaration and place a breakpoint on its first line. Run the application in the debug mode and notice if the declaration statement is executed or skipped. It should be skipped. The only time it may be executed is when a variable declaration is combined with the variable initialization or instantiation. From a practical standpoint, using variables requires knowledge of how to declare, initialize and read or write to them. In the following sections, we will discuss these questions in more detail.

A Variable Declaration

Creating variables begins with writing a variable declaration statement. To write a proper declaration statement, you need to learn naming rules, naming conventions and data types, which we discussed in the previous chapter. The declaration syntax and rules vary in different programming languages. We will now look at how variables are declared in Visual Basic .NET.

First, you should decide what data type your variable is going to represent. Next, you need to make up a variable name. Finally, you should determine what visibility level or scope the variable needs. These three aspects of variable declaration are the most important factors that must be considered every time you create a variable. The syntax of a variable declaration statement is simple enough and would normally consist of three main parts. Procedure variables should start with the keyword *Dim* followed by the variable name and then the keyword *As* followed by the data type keyword. Class level variables should begin with the access modifier keyword; for example, *Public*, and the rest is the same as in procedure variables. For example:

Procedure Variable Declaration:

```
Dim dblTotalAmount As Double
```

Class Variable Declaration:

```
Public m_decAmount As Decimal
```

Variable Naming Rules

Of course, you can name your variable whatever you deem necessary or appropriate but your creativity in this area may be limited by a number of must-follow Visual Basic .NET rules and some optional naming conventions commonly used not only in Visual Basic but in many other programming languages.

Visual Basic .NET Variable Naming Rules:

> ➤ A variable name cannot be a Visual Basic reserved keyword.
> ➤ A variable name cannot contain special characters.
> ➤ A variable name cannot be a number.
> ➤ A variable name should be a single word.

Using Keywords

The first rule is straightforward and clear enough. You may not use any of Visual Basic .NET reserved keywords because they are reserved for Visual Basic use. For example, you may not use such words as *Dir, DirectoryInfo, End, Stop, Start, Exit, Sub, Procedure, Handles* and many others. You may find a full list of Visual Basic .NET keywords in MSDN documentation.

Special Characters

Using special characters in your variable names is not a good idea. The compiler will reject such variable names. Note that the error message will be posted by the compiler as a friendly reminder and in most cases will not give you any clue that the error is caused by the use of special characters. You may see these error messages in the IntelliSense. Again, do not expect the error message to tell you that using special characters in variable names is not allowed. We will show you some examples of such error messages later in this section. Let's first identify what should be considered special characters. The following are examples of special characters that cannot be used in variable names:

{ } , . : ; " ' [ ] \ | * % # @ < >

Thus, if you write a declaration like the one below, it will be rejected:
Wrong: Dim intNB> As Integer

The error message that you may see in the IntelliSense should look like this: "End of statement expected." It's not an easy task to interpret the compiler's logic used to generate such error messages. However, we may guess that the compiler is, most probably, driven by the following logic. Since everything before the illegal character is correct, the statement must end here. In fact, "Dim intNB" is a legal variable declaration even though the "As" part of the declaration is omitted. In such cases VB .NET will default the variable data type to object. Here's another example, which will not compile:

Wrong: `Dim *intNB As Integer`

In this case, the compiler may produce this error message: "Identifier expected." Again, its logic is similar to the following: your declaration statement ended right before the "*" sign but you did not enter the variable name (identifier) yet. That's why the error message states that the identifier is expected. Thus, all you have in your declaration statement is the keyword *Dim*; the rest is not accepted by the compiler.

Using Numbers

A variable name cannot be a number or start with a number. This rule is obviously very simple. Therefore, trying to use numbers as variable names will definitely fail and generate an error. For example, if you try a variable declaration like the one below, you will get an error.

Wrong: `Dim 777 As Short`

In this case, your error message should say: "Identifier expected." It means that the compiler does not accept the number as a variable name and concludes that the variable name is missing. It is equally wrong to start a variable name with a number. Thus, the following declaration will also cause "Identifier expected" error:

Wrong: `Dim 777Lucky As Int16`

However, it is legal to use the number at the end or in the middle of the variable name. For example, *intLucky777* or *intLucky777Num* are valid variable names.

Data Types Shorthand

Although you may not use special characters in variable names, you can use some of them as part of shorthand variable declaration syntax. For example, $ can be used as shorthand for the String data type, @ - for Decimal, # - for Double and so on. Therefore, the following declarations are completely legal and valid.

```
Dim MyString$
Dim MyDecimal@
Dim MyDouble#
```

And are equal to the following:
```
Dim MyString As String
Dim MyDecimal As Decimal
Dim MyDouble As Double
```

Variable Naming Conventions

As it always happens, there are rules and there are exceptions. That's absolutely true about variable naming as well. We have already covered the main restrictive rules and some exceptions, and now it is time for recommendations. Naming conventions belong to this category. They are not mandatory rules but we strongly advise you to follow them.

Most naming standards are rules that were developed and accumulated in programming as recommendations to follow. Having said that, it is equally important to stress that naming conventions are meant to make code more readable, maintainable and understandable. Most of these rules exist in the form of several well-known naming conventions, such as Pascal, Camel, Hungarian, Prefix and Underscore notations or cases. Let's briefly look at some of them.

Pascal Case

When more than one root word is used in the variable name, you may need to find a way to make them distinct and easily recognizable within the variable name. To achieve this goal, in Pascal Case each root word element in the variable name is capitalized. For example:

```
ProductName
OrderNumber
TypeInstanceName
```

Camel Case

According to Microsoft MSDN documentation, Camel Case is characterized by the first letter of a variable being a lower case and all subsequent root words being capitalized. For example:

```
productName
orderNumber
typeInstanceName
```

Underscore Notation

There are different variations of underscore notations. In the most well-known one, all root word elements are lower case and separated by an underscore. For example:

```
product_name
order_number
```

```
type_instance_name
```

Underscore Notation in combination with all words in the upper case is typically used to define constants. For example:

```
TAX_RATE
LOG_FILE_NAME
STUDENT_COEFFICIENT
```

Of course, using a certain naming style may be a matter of personal and esthetical preference. But adhering to a certain naming convention helps to make code much more readable and understandable. You may find more recommendations on naming conventions in Microsoft's MSDN help documentation under the Naming Guidelines category.

We will conclude this section by giving a few examples of how these naming guidelines can be applied to create various types of identifiers. According to MSDN all variables, class names, class methods and namespaces should be Pascal Case. Parameter names and protected class field names should be Camel case and constants—a combination of underscore case with words in upper case.

Selecting Data Types

It is recommended that before writing a variable declaration statement you should decide what data type would best represent the variable data. Review all available data types and choose the one that best fits the data requirements. For example, if you need to store a relatively large amount of text, the String data type is your best choice. If you want to store whole numbers, then one of the integer data types should be used. With numbers it is essential to know what value range the variable may be expected to hold and then select an appropriate type. For example, if you know that the number stored will be between 0 and 255, you may use the Byte. If your variable data will consist of single characters, then the Char data type should be good enough.

What we have discussed so far is more or less common to both value types and reference types variables. However, there are some considerable differences in how you would use these two variable categories, which we will discuss in the following sections.

Using Value Types

To sum up the above discussion, we want to point out that using variables may require the following actions:

> Data type selection.

> Making up variable names.

> Writing variable declaration statements.

> Variable initialization.

> Reading or writing to variables.

We have discussed most of the above except variable initialization and reading/writing to variables, thus we will remedy that shortcoming in this section.Let's say you declared a variable *dtStartDate* as the *Date* type. Before you can reference it in code, it must be initialized. Variables must be initialized before they are referenced in code. Initializing a variable is equal to simply assigning some valid value to it. In Visual Basic .NET you don't have to initialize variables because VB does it for you behind the scenes. In our case the Date variable will be initialized to a default date and time of 1/1/1900 12:00:00. You can verify that by using the IntelliSense. Hover the mouse pointer over the variable name and the value held by it will be displayed. Alternatively, you may execute the following code:

```
Dim dtStartDate As Date
Dim strDate As String
strDate = dtStartDate.ToString()
```

As previously mentioned, you can initialize a variable in the declaration statement; for example:

```
Dim dtStartDate As Date = Date.Now()
Dim dtNextDate As Date = "12/31/2009 10:12:21"
```

After the declaration and initialization you may use the variable either to read the value it holds or to write to it.

Reading and Writing to Variables

To read or write to a variable you need to write an assignment statement. The syntax of an assignment statement is as follows: The variable to which you want to write should be placed on the left side of the assignment operator. For example:

```
strProductName = "Camcorder"
```

To read from a variable you should place it on the right side of the assignment operator. For example:

```
strProductName = txtProduct.Text
txtBirthday.Text  = dtBirthday
lblBirthMonth.Text = dtBirthday.Month
```

When you write to a variable you may either read the value from another variable or use a literal value. Keep in mind that when you assign a value to a variable, you need to verify if it is of the right data type, and if not convert it. The good news is that to a certain extent you do not need to worry about conversions because Visual Basic will do implicit conversion for you. For instance, in the last two examples we read the variable *dtBirthday* and assign its values to the *txtBirthday* textbox and the *lblBirthMonth* label. In both cases, conversion is necessary, which is implicitly done by Visual Basic. Of course, you should not be totally spoiled by Visual Basic and be aware of conversion issues that we will talk about in Chapter 8.

Using Reference Types

Using reference types is significantly different from value types. The difference becomes obvious when you simply compare the list of actions for value types presented earlier with a similar list for reference types.

Actions Related to Reference Types:

> Referencing class libraries.

> Writing the Imports directives.

> Writing object variable declarations.

> Instantiating object variables.

> Reading or writing to object properties.

> Calling object methods.

> Handling object events.

In the rest of this chapter, we are going to cover each of these items in more detail. We will begin with references to class libraries.

Adding References

Normally you should begin working with any object variable by adding a reference to a corresponding class library in your project. When you create an object variable you deal with a certain class code, which should be available for the compiler to load it. Therefore, by adding a reference to a class library, you simply show the compiler where the class assembly file is located and also request that a reference to that library be added to your project description.

Using Class Libraries

From a practical perspective, it is useful to classify all class libraries into at least three major categories: .NET Framework Class Library (FCL); classes created by vendors or the so-called third parties; and classes created by you or your colleagues. The reason why you should be aware of this is simple enough. The FCL classes are created by Microsoft and are shipped with the .NET Framework and Visual Studio .NET. This relieves you of the necessity to copy files to your machine and know where a particular class assembly file is located.

With the third-party classes and classes developed by your company or yourself, you first need to make sure that the corresponding files are copied to your machine. You do not need to register anything. However, if the assembly where a class resides is strongly named then you need to GAC it using the GACUTIL utility. Then when you add reference to a class you need to navigate .NET's Add Reference manager to the DLL assembly file. These are the main things that you need to remember when dealing with different categories of classes. It is also common to break down class libraries into standard and custom classes, in which case FCL should belong to the first and the third party and company classes - to the second.

Types of Class Libraries:

- ➤ .NET Framework Class Library (FCL)
- ➤ Vendor Class Libraries
- ➤ Company Class Libraries

Referencing .NET Framework Classes

As we have already mentioned, when you use FCL classes you do not have to bother with copying assembly files to you developer machine. In case of commonly used classes, you even need not add references because they may be already added for you by Visual Basic .NET. Although, in case of the FCL classes the compiler knows where the corresponding files are located, you still need to add references. Because FCL is a huge depository of classes and you need to specify which classes should be referenced in your project. Remember our talk about a skeleton of a new project created for you by Visual Basic? When this is done Visual Basic, typically, adds references to some major libraries, such as *System, System.Data, System.Xml* and some others depending on selected project template.

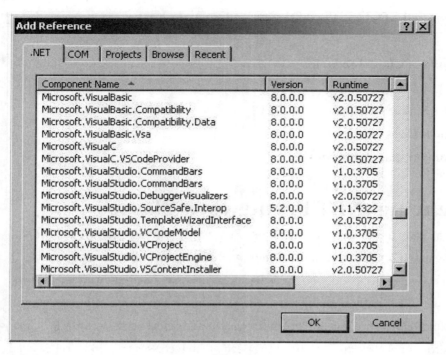

Figure 5.0 Visual Studio 2005 Add Reference dialog box.

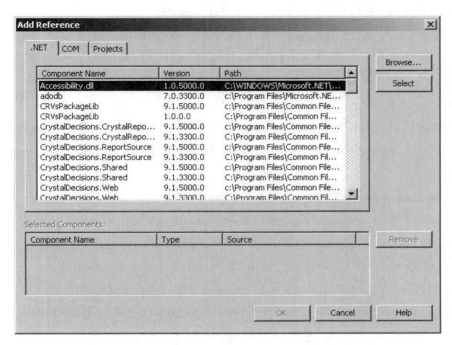

Figure 5.1 Visual Studio .NET 2003 Add Reference dialog box.

The procedure of adding a reference to any FCL class or namespace is simple. In the Solution Explorer, right-click the References node and choose Add Reference. You should see a dialog box like the one shown in Figure 5.0 or Figure 5.1 depending your Visual Studio version. FCL classes are listed in the .NET tab, which should be open by default. In Visual Studio 2005, select one or more items and click OK. In Visual Studio 2003, highlight a desired library and click Select. The selected library will appear in the Selected Components pane. Repeat the procedure to add more items and then click OK to finish. When the Add Reference dialog box closes, verify if the reference was actually added to your project. In the Solution Explorer, expand the References node and the reference should be there. If you need to remove any previously added reference, just highlight it and press Delete.

Referencing Third-Party Classes

The first thing to worry about when you deal with the third-party or company-developed classes is that you need to make sure that all the necessary assembly files and dependencies are copied to your developer machine. Please note that an assembly may contain one or more classes and should have the DLL filename extension. When you want to use a certain class you need to copy its assembly file to your machine. Do not expect to see these classes in the .NET tab of the Add Reference dialog box.

To add a reference to a custom class, use the Browse button and navigate to the folder where the assembly file is located. Remember, you should select a file with the DLL filename extension. The rest of the procedure is the same. Once you have added all necessary references you may want to add the corresponding *Imports* directives to make all added class libraries visible in your code editor and the IntelliSense. Remember, the imports directives must be added in each class code module where you expect to use the referenced libraries.

Adding the Imports Directives

Adding the *Imports* directives is a matter of convenience and is not something that is required. However, this action saves a lot of extra typing and in some cases may help you to prevent namespace and class name ambiguity or conflicts. Remember, the imports directive must be typed at the very beginning of your class code before the class declaration. For example:

```
Imports System.IO
Public Class Form1
```

In the above code, the imports directive for *System.IO* namespace precedes the form class declaration. Adding the imports directive enables the IntelliSense to provide coding help features, which we discussed in Chapter 2. Furthermore, you won't need to type the so-called fully qualified class names to create an object variable. You can enter the name of the class itself or select it from the Auto Data Tip. Let's say you decided to create a *FileInfo* class object variable. Your declaration statement may look like the following:

```
Dim objFileInfo As FileInfo
```

If you do not have a corresponding imports directive then your declaration should use the fully qualified class name and will look like the following:

```
Dim objFileInfo As System.IO.FileInfo
```

Remember, if you use a class name without a corresponding namespace imports directive you will get a compilation error such as: "Type 'FileInfo' is not defined."

Note:

When using the *Imports* directive, you need to know which namespace your class is defined in and use that namespace, not the class name. Use the Object Browser to look up what namespace your class belongs to. Once you are able to locate the class just copy and paste its full namespace into your imports directive.

Variable Declaration Summary

Before you declare an object variable, you need to add a reference to a corresponding class library. For the third-party and company classes you also need to copy assembly files to your machine. Then you have to make up your object variable name. Note that for object variables the same naming rules that we discussed earlier apply. When you type the *As* keyword, the IntelliSense will show a dropdown to select a namespace or class name from. If you added corresponding imports directives, then you should be able to find the class name in the dropdown. If you did not you should type a fully qualified class name. You may use the IntelliSense to search and find namespaces and classes. Once you found a namespace or class, press Space to have it typed for you.

Instantiating Object Variables

Instantiation is an important part of the object variable creation process. Once you are done with object variable declaration you have to instantiate it before you can use it. Why do you need to instantiate an object variable? When you declare an object variable you just announce that you need to reserve memory laid out for a particular type. When you instantiate an object variable, an instance of a corresponding class is created and a reference to it is assigned to your object variable.

Remember, when you instantiate an object variable a new instance of a class is created. You may have several object variables of the same class in your project and in each case the runtime will create a new instance of that class. To create a new class instance the *New* operator is used. For example, to instantiate the *DirectoryInfo* object variable your code may look like this:

```
Dim objDirInfo As DirectoryInfo
objDirInfo = New DirectoryInfo(strDirPath)
```

If a class constructor requires parameters, you should pass them at the time you instantiate the object variable. Note when you type the opening parenthesis after the class name the IntelliSense will show you all parameters expected by the class constructor.

What happens if you try to use the object variable before you instantiate it? You will get a notorious error, "Object reference not set to an instance of an object."

Figure 5.2   Object variable instantiation error.

A message box or an error like the one shown in Figure 5.2 may popup in any program. Remember that your code will compile correctly even if you do not properly instantiate your object variables. The truth is, if you do not instantiate your object variables, Visual Basic will do it for you. However, Visual Basic does the minimum part of the job. It will simply set an object variable to *Nothing* (null), which is good enough to compile the application but not good enough to run it because the object variable reference must be set to a corresponding class instance. To experiment with object variable instantiation, try this code:

```
Dim objStreamRdr As StreamReader
If objStreamRdr Is Nothing Then
      MessageBox.Show("Object reference is set to Nothing")
End If
```

The worst part of the "Object reference not set to an instance of an object" error is that it will popup at runtime and if not handled properly may cause the application to fail. In most cases, object reference errors may be caused by improper sequencing of declaration and instantiation statements or simply because of the instantiation failure. We mention this fact to emphasize how important it is to write properly sequenced object variable instantiation statements. The problem can be solved by properly writing the object variable instantiation code and by checking the variable status. In fact, you can easily intercept such errors by checking if the object variable is instantiated. A simple check if the object variable is equal to null will do the job. For example:

```
If Not objStreamRdr Is Nothing Then
      'Use the object variable
Else
      'Handle the error.
End If
```

In the above code, we first test if the object variable is not equal to *Nothing* and then use. To sum up this discussion, we would like to point out that when you initially declare an object variable, Visual Basic initializes it to null. To use this object variable you should set it to an instance of a declared class that will assign a reference to an object in memory to this object variable. When you are done with the object variable it is important to dereference it. Dereferencing will detach the object in memory from the object variable and will guarantee that the former will be destroyed by the GC. To dereference an object variable, simply set it to *Nothing*. For example:

```
If Not objStreamRdr Is Nothing Then
      'Use the object variable
      'When done set it to null
      objStreamRdr = Nothing
Else
      'Handle the error.
End If
```

Variable Scope

A variable scope concept is used to handle two aspects of a variable: its visibility and lifetime. The way you declare a variable will determine how long it will live in the program and whether other procedures in that program can see and use it. Thus, when you declare a variable you have to decide what scope it needs.

Variable Scope Flavors:

> ➢ Block scope
> ➢ Procedure scope
> ➢ Class scope
> ➢ Global scope

Note:

Think about variable scope as something similar to how far your variable declaration is heard and honored. Whenever you create a variable, you need to project its level of visibility and lifetime. You can determine this by selecting a declaration location and using an appropriate access modifier.

Variable Accessibility and Lifetime

Variable scope may be compared with a train ticket expiration time and valid zones, where time is equal to code execution duration and zones are similar to code blocks, procedures and modules. Therefore, a variable is in scope as long as code where it was declared is being executed. If it is a class variable it will be in scope until the class code is running. A block variable is in scope only while the block code is being executed. It will be out of scope as soon as the execution reaches the end of the block. Similarly, a procedure variable will be in scope until the *End Sub* or *End Function* is reached. Variable accessibility is more about where and how far the variable is visible. It is determined by two factors: the declaration location or context and the use of the access modifiers. By location we mean where the variable is declared. For example, if it is declared in a class code, it is a class level variable, which is accessible from anywhere within that class. If it is declared in a procedure, then it is a procedure variable visible within that procedure only. Access modifiers can be used with class variables only. We will talk about them later in this chapter.

Why do you need to know about the variable scope? The time a variable is kept in memory is determined by its scope. The variable scope is dependent on its accessibility range. The wider the range, the longer the scope. Theoretically, whenever the variable goes out of scope .NET runtime is supposed to delete any data associated with it and release the memory used by it. Thus, variable scope considerations are important to better manage your application resources.

Now let's look at how variable scope can be applied to value and reference types. With value type variables, things are more or less simple because these variables are destroyed as soon as they go out of scope. Things are totally different when it comes to managing memory used by reference type variables. An object variable lifetime is dependent on its scope and .NET runtime Garbage Collection. Let's now consider types of variable scope in more detail.

Block Scope

If you declare a variable within *If ...End If* block or within *For ... Next, While ...End While, Do While...Loop* and other execution control structures, it will have a block scope. The visibility of such variables will be limited to that block only. When code execution reaches the end of the block the variable will go out of scope. Apparently, the block scope is the most limited scope and this should always be kept in mind when you declare such variables. Here's an example of a block variable:

```
Dim strArrValues() As String
ReDim strArrValues(5)
For i As Int32 = 0 To strArrValues.Length - 1
    Dim bln As Boolean
    If bln = True Then
        strArrValues(i) = "0"
        bln = False
    Else
        strArrValues(i) = "1"
        bln = True
    End If
Next
```

What happens if you try to access a block scope variable outside the block? Visual Basic compiler is smart enough not to compile such code. Here's a modified version of the above code:

```
Dim strArrValues() As String
ReDim strArrValues(5)
For i As Int32 = 0 To strArrValues.Length - 1
    Dim bln As Boolean
    If bln = True Then
        strArrValues(i) = "0"
        bln = False
    Else
        strArrValues(i) = "1"
        bln = True
```

```
    End If
Next
'The next line will not compile
bln = True
```

The above code will not compile. Visual Basic 2005 compiler will simply deny the existence of this variable by stating: "Variable 'bln' is not declared." Visual Basic 2003 compiler will generate a more elaborate error message like the following: "Variable 'bln' hides a variable in an enclosing block."

Note:

With block scope variables, you should remember the following: the scope of such variables is limited to the time until the code executes in the block. Thus, variables declared within *If End If, For...Next* and other loops cannot be referenced outside such blocks.

Procedure Scope

Procedure scope has a higher visibility than block scope. It means a variable declared anywhere in a procedure except within the flow control blocks will be visible anywhere in that procedure. For example:

```
Private Sub TestProcedure()
    Dim blnIsOpen As Boolean
    'Procedure code
End Sub
```

The scope of procedure variables is limited to the time until the procedure code is executing. Note that procedure level variables are the most inexpensive in terms of using application resources and so they are the most recommendable type of variables. Most importantly, all procedure level variables except object variables are deleted immediately after the procedure is complete. It is highly recommended to declare all procedure variables at the beginning of the procedure. It will help you to better manage your variables and avoid some errors.

Class Scope

Variables declared in the class namespace area will assume class level scope. They have one important difference from block and procedure variables—they can use access modifiers, which can provide additional variable scope granularity. Thus, class variables can use the following access modifiers: Private, Protected, Friend, Protected Friend, Public.

The Variable Access Modifiers:

- Private
- Protected
- Friend
- Protected Friend
- Public

Let's sum up. First, class variables can have a greater range of scope as they can apply access modifiers. Second, for class variables a lot depends on from where you try to access them: from inside or outside the class. Inside the class all class variables are accessible from anywhere in the class. From outside the class accessibility is dependent on accessibility locations:

Variable Accessibility Locations:
- ➢ From another class in the same assembly
- ➢ From another class in a different assembly
- ➢ From derived class

Class variable accessibility is a result of two factors: access modifiers and variable accessibility location. If we look at class variables from this perspective, we may distinguish the following accessibility categories:

- **From another class in the same assembly**

This is a case when we have two or more classes within one assembly. Thus, from outside these classes only Public, Friend and Protected Friend variables are visible.

- **From a derived class**

A class that inherits from another class is called a derived class and the inherited class is called a base class. In a derived class only Public, Protected and Protected Friend variables of the base class are visible.

- **From another class in a different assembly**

When you try to access any class member from a class in a different assembly, the visibility is limited to Public variables only. Now let's look at some examples.

(We assume that the following two classes are in one and the same assembly.)

```
Public Class Class1
      Private strPassword As String
      Public strLastName As String
      'Class code
End Class
```

```
Public Class Class2
      Private Sub TestProcedure()
            Dim strTmp As String
            Dim myClass1 As New Class1
            strTmp = myClass1.strLastName
      End Sub
End Class
```

The above code is an example of the same assembly accessibility location where two classes reside in one and the same assembly. In Class1, we have declared one public and one private class variable. In the TestProcedure of Class2, we created a Class1 object variable that allows it to access public variables in that class.

Note:

> Class variables may have different scope depending on what access modifiers are used to declare them. Ideally, a class variable may have five scopes, one for each access modifier. However, the variable scope can be modified by accessibility locations listed above.

We will discuss class variables in more detail in Chapter 10.

Global Scope

Visual Basic .NET has a special item in its arsenal—module. It is a legacy that is carried forward from VB 6 Standard Module. A module in Visual Basic .NET is actually a specialized version of class, in which any public variable or method will automatically acquire a global scope within your project. This means that you can reference such variable or method directly without using the module name from anywhere in your application. You can add a module to your project by choosing Add Module on the Project menu and selecting the Module template. In this event a module file will be added to your project, which you can code like any other class.

```
Module Module1
      Public g_strModelDesc As String
      Public g_strModelSerialNum As String
End Module

Public Class ClassA
      Private Sub GetModelData()
            Dim strSerialNum As String
            Dim strModelDesc As String
            strSerialNum = g_strModelSerialNum
            strModelDesc = g_strModelDesc
      End Sub
End Class
```

In the above code, we declared two public variables in Module1 module that will have global scope. We reference them directly from ClassA class GetModelData subroutine.

Summary

In this chapter, you have learned how to handle variables in your program. Variables are used in an application as temporary data storage devices. A variable declaration statement determines what data can be stored by the variable. Variable scope reflects its visibility and lifetime and may help to better manage application resources. Class variables utilize a wide range of scopes because they can use the access modifiers. Object variables should be properly instantiated to avoid object reference errors.

Lab 5: The Funny Labels Project

Funny Labels

In this Project:

You will create the Funny Labels project, in which you will practice using labels, arrays, the timer component and the execution flow control structures to create simple animation effects. This lab will help you to consolidate your knowledge of using variables and data types.

Create a New Project

- ➤ Create *Lab5* project folder.
- ➤ Open Visual Studio .NET.
- ➤ Create a new Windows Application project.
- ➤ Set the project Location to C:\Labs\Lab5.
- ➤ Set the project Name to *FunnyLabels*.

Design User Interface

Add Controls

Add form controls and set their properties as specified in Table 1.

Table 1. The FunnyLabels form controls.

Control Type	Property Name	Value
Form	Text	Funny Labels Program
GroupBox	Text	Crawl and Jump
-/-	BackColor	RoyalBlue
Label 1 to 20	Text	--
-/-	BackColor	RoyalBlue
Label 21 to 24	Text	1-,2-,3-,4-
RadioButton	Name	radioCrawl
-/-	Text	Crawl
RadioButton	Name	radioJump
-/-	Text	Jump
Button	Name	btnClose
-/-	Text	&Close

When you add controls, pay attention to the following. You will use the GroupBox to frame labels. Resize the GroupBox to form a rectangle that fits the size of your form. Then add 20 label controls. All labels should keep the default names, such as Label1, Label2 and so on. Set their BackColor property to RoyalBlue. Position labels in such a way that they would build a serpentine-like line. Make sure that you add labels to the chain in an incremental order. This is important because at runtime we access each label properties and our logic assumes that labels are ordered according to the numbers in their names.

Four labels are used to display static data. These labels will hold hard-coded values; for example, "1-," and will range from Label21 to Label24. Set each of these four labels ForeColor to Red, FontStyle to Bold and FontSize to 11. They should be placed on the left-hand side of the form. Names are not important so you may keep the default names. Set the Text property of each label to 1-, 2-, 3- and 4- correspondingly.

Add other controls. In the other controls group you should add two RadioButtons at the bottom of the form outside the GroupBox, and one button. Resize them and set their properties according to Table 1. Notice that when you add the Timer component it will appear on the component tray beneath the form. The Timer properties will be set at runtime.

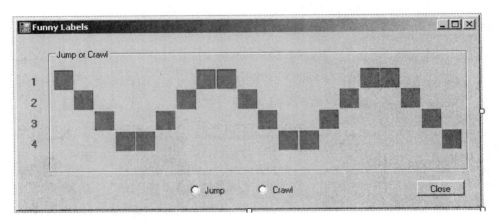

Figure 1. The FunnyLabels form.

When you complete the design of the form, it should look like the one shown in Figure 1.

Write Code

In this project, you will practice declaring class level and local procedure level variables, read and write to variables at runtime and manipulate label properties. You will learn how to use the Timer component, how to manage array of controls and create subroutine procedures. The Timer component role in this project is to run a certain action in a certain time interval. It suits this task because it is designed to do one simple thing: fire Tick events at a certain time interval set in its Interval property. Note that we do not set the Interval property at design time. We do it at runtime. The entire application code is shown in Listing 1.

Listing 1. The FunnyLabels program code.

```
Public Class Form1
        'Declaration of class variables:
        Private arrLabels(20) As Label
        Private intCounter  As Integer
Private Sub Form1_Load(ByVal sender As Object, _
ByVal e As EventArgs) Handles MyBase.Load
        arrLabels(0) = Label1
        arrLabels(1) = Label2
        arrLabels(2) = Label3
        arrLabels(3) = Label4
        arrLabels(4) = Label5
        arrLabels(5) = Label6
        arrLabels(6) = Label7
        arrLabels(7) = Label8
        arrLabels(8) = Label9
        arrLabels(9) = Label10
```

```vb
        arrLabels(10) = Label11
        arrLabels(11) = Label12
        arrLabels(12) = Label13
        arrLabels(13) = Label14
        arrLabels(14) = Label15
        arrLabels(15) = Label16
        arrLabels(16) = Label17
        arrLabels(17) = Label18
        arrLabels(18) = Label19
        arrLabels(19) = Label20
        Timer1.Enabled = True
        Timer1.Interval = 70
        GroupBox1.BackColor = Color.RoyalBlue
End Sub


Private Sub Timer1_Tick(ByVal sender As Object, _
ByVal e As EventArgs) Handles Timer1.Tick
    If radioJump.Checked = True Then
        Jump()
    Else
        Crawl()
    End If
End Sub


Private Sub btnClose_Click(ByVal sender As System.Object, _
ByVal e As System.EventArgs) Handles btnClose.Click
        Me.Close()
End Sub
```

```
Private Sub Jump()
'Turn the current label's BackColor to Blue
'And the next one to Red
If intCounter  < 20 Then
      arrLabels(intCounter ).BackColor = Color.RoyalBlue
      If intCounter  <= 18 Then
            arrLabels(intCounter  + 1).BackColor = Color.Red
      End If
      intCounter  += 1
Else
      intCounter  = 0
End If
End Sub


Private Sub Crawl()
'Change the BackColor of each next label
If intCounter  < 20 Then
      colLabels(intCounter ).BackColor = Color.Red
      intCounter  += 1
Else
      intCounter  = 0
      CleanUp()
      End If
End Sub
Private Sub CleanUp()
Dim i As Int32
For i = 0 To 19
      arrLabels(i).BackColor = Color.RoyalBlue
```

```
Next
End Sub
End Class
```

We will now walk you through the code in each procedure. Code in Listing 1 features the following major parts: declaration of class variables; three event handler procedures such as the Form_Load, the Close button click event procedure and the Timer1 Tick event procedure and three worker subroutine procedures: Jump, Crawl and Cleanup.

Declare Class Variables

Declare two class level variables at the top of the class code. The *arrLabels* array of labels will be used to hold 20 label controls. The *intCounter* integer variable will be used to hold the index. These variables will be accessed from various procedures in this class so we need to make them visible anywhere in this class. Using the *Private* access modifier suits this purpose perfectly. Please type these variable declarations at the beginning of class code.

Write the Form Load Event Procedure

Write code in the form load event procedure. Double-click any free space on the form. The code editor will open an empty form load event procedure. Type code shown in Listing 1. In this procedure you will populate an array of labels with 20 labels that you placed on the form. Then set the Timer1 Enabled and Interval properties as follows:

```
Timer1.Enabled = True
Timer1.Interval = 70
```

At the end of this procedure, set the BackColor property of GroupBox1.

Write the Timer1 Tick Event Procedure

The Timer component that you added to the project is designed to fire Tick events. You can use this event to perform some repeated actions. The frequency of these actions will be set through the Timer Interval property. Note that the Timer engine starts as soon as you set its Enabled property to true. To stop the Timer you need to set it back to false. In this project you will create two actions: Jump and Crawl. These actions will be called from the Timer Tick event procedure. If the user checks the Crawl radio button then the Crawl action is called, and if the Jump is checked the Jump action is performed. Locate the Timer1 Tick event procedure code in Listing 1 and type it. To write code in the Close button click event procedure, double-click the Close button and type:

```
Me.Close()
```

Write the *Jump* and *Crawl* Procedures

The main task of the Jump procedure is to dynamically reset the BackColor property of the current label to Blue and set the next label's BackColor property to Red. Note that this action will be performed at each Timer tick event and should produce an illusion that the label is jumping. Since you set the Timer interval to 70 ms, this color manipulation action will occur once in every 70 ms. Note that in the Jump procedure you should keep only one label red by always resetting the current label's BackColor to its original color and setting the next label to red. Type this procedure code into your project.

In the Craw procedure, your task is to make all labels move from left to right. The main difference from the Jump procedure is that you should gradually display all labels until you get to the 20th label. This can be achieved by not resetting the BackColor property of labels back to their original color until you reset all 20 labels. When the index count reaches 19, you should stop and call the CleanUp procedure. Why 19 and not 20? That's because the array's first subscript index starts with 0 and as a result the twentieth label will have subscript 19. Please enter this procedure code into your project.

Write the *CleanUp* Procedure

The CleanUp procedure is designed to reset all labels' BackColor property to original color, which you set at design time. Since you have to deal with multiple labels, you should use the *For ...Next* loop reset each label in the array. Please type this procedure code into your project.

Test the Application

To run the application in the debug mode, click on Start or press F5. If everything is OK, Visual Studio will run the application and show the form. Test the following program features. Check the Crawl radio button. Does the program perform the crawl action? Do the same with the Jump radio button.

Congratulations, you successfully completed this project!

Part IY Windows Forms Programming

Windows Forms Programming

Chapter 6: Windows Forms Properties

Windows Forms Properties

In this Chapter:

You will learn Windows forms properties. Dealing with Windows forms is an essential part of a user interface application development. To successfully program Windows forms applications you should understand the form class functionality. In this chapter, you will consider the Windows forms properties and their uses.

Chapter 6 at a Glance

- ➤ Windows Forms Properties
- ➤ Design Time vs. Runtime
- ➤ The Form Class Property Categories
- ➤ The Form Appearance Properties
- ➤ The Form Design Properties
- ➤ The Form Class Behavior Properties
- ➤ The Form Designer Layout Properties
- ➤ The Windows Style Properties
- ➤ Other Form Properties

The Form Class Properties

The form class properties can be viewed from at least three perspectives: form design, form appearance and form behavior. Therefore, all form properties can be grouped into the following categories: form appearance properties, form designer properties, form designer layout properties, Windows style properties and other properties.

The form that you used in all previous labs to create the application user interface is a pre-defined Visual Basic .NET class. Like any other class it defines properties, methods and events. With the form class these three features are even more important because they determine the appearance and the behavior of your application window. In this chapter, we will take a look at the most often used form properties and will show you how to make the most of them. Before we start we would like to introduce two terms: design time and runtime. The form and other control properties can be set in two ways: at design time, i.e. when you develop a program; and at runtime, i.e. when a program is running. The latter can also be called a programmatic method since you would modify properties by executing code. In the next section we will explain how these notions relate to the form properties.

Design Time vs. Runtime

First of all, understanding these terms will help you to learn the difference between some types of form properties that we will talk about later. When you create a user interface you can set the properties of the form using the Properties window or by writing and executing code. If you use the former, you are setting properties at design time. Using the latter will do the same at runtime or programmatically. Which method to choose may depend on the property type, project specifications and your preferences. However, some form properties can only be set at design time. They are called runtime *Read-Only*. For example, the form *Name* property is one of them. With this type of property you have no choice but to set it at design time. With all other properties, it is a matter of project requirements and your preferences. Thus, using a design or runtime method is not just about when or how you set a property, it is also about what type of property you are dealing with.

Note:

Most form properties can be set both at design and runtime. Some form properties are runtime read-only, which means they can only be set at design time. Setting a property at runtime can be done by writing and executing appropriate code.

The Form Property Categories

- ➢ Appearance Properties.
- ➢ Behavior Properties.
- ➢ Designer Properties.
- ➢ Layout Properties.
- ➢ Window Style Properties.
- ➢ Other Form Properties.

In the following sections we will briefly discuss these properties.

The Form Class Appearance Properties
- **Visible**

The Visible property is used to toggle the display of the form on the screen. Setting it to true will display the form and the opposite will hide it. This property is used by the *Show*, *ShowDialog* and *Hide* form methods to display or hide the form correspondingly. Therefore, setting this property false or calling the Hide method will produce the same effect.

- **Text**

The Text property accepts a string value and displays it on the form's title bar. This property is typically used as a descriptive name of the form. It may describe a form or a program in general. For example, in Lab 5 we used *Funny Labels Program* and in Lab 6 we will use *The Windows Form Properties Program*.

- **BackColor**

The BackColor property is self-explanatory. It is used to set or reset the background color of the form. If there are other controls on the form, you can set their BackColor property individually or let them assume the one used by the form. This property can be set both at design and runtime. To set it at design time, open the Properties window, locate the property and click on it. Then click on a tiny downward arrow and select a color from a color palette displayed in System, Web or Custom tab. To do the same at runtime you have to write code. When you do so be aware that the value assigned to any color-related property must be of *System.Drawing.Color* structure. To simplify things, you can choose a color defined in the *Color* structure; for example:

```
Me.BackColor = Color.Blue
```

If you want to set it using a string expression you can but you should convert it to the *Color* type first. For example, this can be done by using the *FromName* method as follows:

```
Me.BackColor = Color.FromName("LightBlue")
```

In the above statement we first convert a string color name to the *Color* type and then assign it to the form's BackColor property. Please find more details on this property in Lab 6.

- **Cursor**

The Cursor property can be set both at design time and runtime. Note that the design time setting can be reset at runtime. This technique is commonly used to send additional information to a user. For example, when you start a procedure that may run for some extended amount of time, it would make sense to set the cursor to *WaitCursor* (*Hourglass*) and when the procedure is complete set it back to the default.

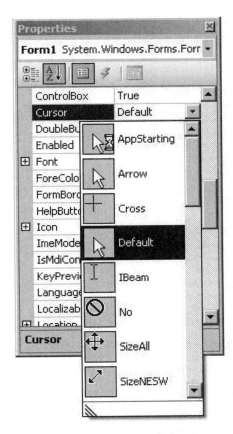

Figure 6.0 The Cursor property.

Here's another typical example. You may have noticed that when you move the cursor to the edge of the form it turns into *SizeWE* cursor (the arrows point both to West and East). If this happens, it signifies that the form can be resized. If it doesn't then the form borders are fixed and cannot be resized. To set the cursor at design time, open the Properties window and select a cursor from the dropdown as shown in Figure 6.0. The selected cursor will always be associated with the form if you do not reset it at runtime. To programmatically set the Cursor, you should use the *Cursors* structure that contains a collection of cursors; for example:

```
Me.Cursor = Cursors.Arrow
Me.Cursor = Cursors.WaitCursor
```

When you programmatically read the Cursor property value, you can either convert it to a string and write to a string variable or declare a Cursor variable and assign it to it. Your code may look like this:

```
Dim strCurrentCursor As String
Dim csCurrentCursor As Cursor
strCurrentCursor = Me.Cursor.ToString()
csCurrentCursor = Me.Cursor
```

- **Font**

The *Font* property allows setting the Font Family, Font Style and Font Size of the text displayed on the form. The relationship between the form font and the control font properties is exactly the same as for all other properties. By default, controls assume the related property setting of the form. However, if you reset a control property, it will overwrite the default. Thus, you can set the Font property of each control separately. The Font property of the form and other controls is runtime read-only. The following code can be used to read this property at runtime:

```
Dim sngFontSize as Single
sngFontSize = Me.Font.Size
sngFontSize = Button1.Font.Size
```

Note that code that attempts to write to the Font property will not compile.

- **ForeColor**

The *ForeColor* property is associated with the color of the text displayed on the form or controls. It can set or reset both at design and runtime. Please find more details on this property in Lab 6.

- **FormBorderStyle**

The *FormBorderStyle* property determines how the borders of the form look and also if the form can be resized at runtime. You can use one of the following constants as a setting value: *None, Fixed3D, FixedDialog, FixedSingle, Sizable*. Here is a brief description of each setting:

None - will make the form borders look flat. Also, you will lose the form title bar and the form size will be fixed, which means the user will not be able to resize it at runtime.

FixedDialog - the form will have a fixed size. The borders will have a dialog box style. It is a default setting.

Fixed3D - is the same as FixedDialog except that it adds a three-dimensional look.

FixedSingle - will produce a non-resizable form with single-line borders.

Sizable - is the only setting that allows resizing the form at runtime and also produces 3D-style borders.

The Form Design Properties

The following form properties are included in this category: *Name, Language, Localizable* and *Locked*. In Visual Studio 2003, the list is a little different and includes: *Name, Locked, GridSize, SnapToGrid* and *DrawGrid*. The Name property is read-only at runtime and is a programmatic name of the form object. The Language and Localizable properties are used when an international version of the application is created. The Locked property determines if the control can be moved or resized both at design and runtime. The GridSize is the size of the grid shown on the form. You can increase or decrease it according to your preferences. The SnapToGrid is used to position controls inline with one of the closet grids. The DrawGrid is used to toggle the grids display at design time.

The Form Class Behavior Properties

AllowDrop

The *AllowDrop* property determines if the form can accept data dragged and dropped by a user. If it is set to false, the form will not allow drop operation.

Enabled

The *Enabled* property may be used to enable or disable the form at runtime. When set to false, all controls on the form will be grayed and become inactive. In addition, all buttons in the ControlBox will also be disabled. This setting will actually freeze the form until this property is set back to true. It may be useful when you have multiple forms in a program and due to a certain event or condition need to temporarily disable a form.

ContextMenuStrip

The *ContextMenuStrip* property allows setting the context menu of the form to a specified menu object, which you need to create prior to setting this property. It's worth noting that the form and each control may have their own context menus. Normally, this is a context menu pop-up when you right-click a form or a control. Therefore, this property is used to wire a context menu to the form's right-click event.

The Form Layout Properties

Location

The *Location* property is used to set or get the X and Y coordinates of the upper left corner of the form. X is used to indicate the horizontal position and Y—the vertical position. This property accepts *System.Drawing.Point* variable. For example, the following code will reset the form's location:

```
Dim pntFormLocation As New Point(100, 100)
Me.Location = pointFormLocation
```

Note that in the above code we declare and instantiate a pntFormLocation Point variable and set its X and Y integer parameters to 100 points. Then we assign it to the form's Location property.

Size

The *Size* property is used to set or get the width and the height of the form. This property accepts the *System.Drawing.Size* type and can be set both at design and runtime. At runtime, it can be reset if the form is resizable; for example, executing code like this:

```
Me.Size = New Size(500, 700)
```

In the above code, we create a Size structure variable, pass 500 points as the width and 700 points as the height and assign it to the form. If you need to use the Size structure more than once or want to deal with each Size parameter separately, you may have to create a Size variable first and then assign it to the form. For example:

```
Dim FormSize As Size
```

```
Dim sngFormWidth As Single
Dim sngFormHeight As Single
sngFormWidth = 200
sngFormHeight = 200
FormSize = New Size(sngFormWidth, sngFormHeight)
Me.Size = FormSize
```

In the above code, we declared three variables: a Size variable and two Single variables. First we set the width and the height variable values and then create an instance of the Size structure and assign it to the form's Size property. If you need to know the current width and height of the form you can extract them from the form object:

```
sngFormWidth = Me.Size.Width
sngFormHeight = Me.Size.Height
```

StartPosition

The *StartPosition* property is used to control the form's positioning when it is displayed for the first time. This property takes one of the following constants: *Manual, CenterScreen, WindowsDefaultLocation, CenterParent* and *Windows-DefaultBounds*. The default is WindowsDefaultLocation. If this setting is used, the form is shown in the upper left corner of the screen. Other choices such as Manual, CenterScreen and CenterParent are self-explanatory. Note that CenterParent means the form will be centered within the parent form, which may be relevant when you open a child form within a parent form in an MDI application.

WindowState

The *WindowState* property helps to control the size of the form at runtime. You can use one of three pre-defined constants: *Normal, Minimized* and *Maximized*. If you choose Normal it will show the form in its design time size. The Maximized will enlarge the form to full screen mode. Minimized will hide the form and show its icon on the Windows taskbar.

MaximumSize

This property is used to control the maximum size of the form. It may prove useful when you have a requirement to limit the maximum size of the form to a certain size. This form feature will allow a user to change the size of the form but to a certain limit. Alternatively, you can use a fixed form, which will not allow resizing.

MinimumSize

The *MinimumSize* is the opposite of the MaximumSize. It can be used to prevent the user from decreasing the form to an inappropriate size that will make it unusable.

The Windows Style Properties

Icon

The *Icon* property is used to set the image displayed on the form's title bar. It accepts a path to an icon image file. By default, Visual Basic .NET uses the icon image that symbolizes a form. You may change it at design or runtime to make your form distinguishable from other forms.

ControlBox

The *ControlBox* consists of three tiny boxes that are displayed in the right-hand part of the form's title bar. These include the Minimize, Maximize and Close boxes. By default, this property is set to true and the ControlBox is displayed as shown in

Figure 6.1.

Figure 6.1 The ControlBox.

 If you set this property to false, the boxes and the form icon won't be displayed. The form also allows configuring the ControlBox further to determine which buttons should be displayed. Setting the MaximizeBox property to false will remove it from the ControlBox. Setting the MinimizeBox to false will hide the minimize box. The Close box cannot be removed; you need to disable the ControlBox to get rid of it.

As we mentioned earlier, the form is a container for other controls. Some controls are added to the form by default; for example, the title bar and the ControlBox. It's worth mentioning that the form's title bar besides displaying the caption and hosting the ControlBox exposes some additional functionality. For example, the color of the title bar indicates if the form is in focus. If it is blue the form is in focus. When the form loses focus it is grayed. Furthermore, you can use the title bar to move the form around. Move the mouse pointer to the title bar and holding the left mouse button down drag the form.

Other Form Properties

There are a few form properties that do not belong to any of the above-mentioned categories. Thus, they are listed in the Other Properties group. The form has two useful features that allow associating pressing of a certain key on the keyboard with a click of a certain button on the form. In particular, you can tie pressing of the *Enter* or *Esc* keys with any button on the form. This is achieved by setting the form's AcceptButton and CancelButton properties.

AcceptButton

The *AcceptButton* property allows associating the Enter key with a specified button on the form. A common practice is to wire the AcceptButton property with a frequently used functional button such as Run, Submit, Send and so on. Note that you need to add a button to the form and then select it from the dropdown provided by this property. Only one button can be tied up to the AcceptButton property.

CancelButton

The *CancelButton* property works the same way as the AcceptButton. The only difference is that it allows associating the Esc key with any specified button on the form. Typically, this feature is used to cancel a certain action, hence the name of the property. For instance, you may associate this property with such buttons as Cancel, Abort, Close and so on.

KeyPreview

The *KeyPreview* is a property that determines the order in which the *KeyPress* event is processed. The KeyPress event can be processed by the form and text processing controls such textbox and listbox. By using this property you can set the priority. If you set this property to true, the form takes precedence over controls. By default, this property is set to false, which means the form controls will process the above events before the form will.

Language

The *Language* property is used to indicate which localizable language the program will use. This property may be relevant when you create multiple versions of an internationally used application.

Summary

In this chapter, you have been introduced to Windows form properties. The form is a powerful, pre-defined class that can be used to create application windows. The form properties may be grouped into several categories that describe different aspects of the form such as appearance, design, layout and behavior. Most of the form properties can be set at both design and runtime but some are runtime read-only and should be set at design time.

Lab 6: The Windows Forms Properties Project

Windows Forms Properties

In this Project:

You will create the Windows Forms Properties application. This project will allow you to consolidate your knowledge of form properties and practice using them in a demonstration program.

Create a New Project

- ➢ Create *Lab6* project folder.
- ➢ Open Visual Studio .NET
- ➢ Create a new Windows Application project.
- ➢ Set the project Location to C:\Labs\Lab6.
- ➢ Set the project Name to *WinFormProperties*.

Design User Interface

Add Controls

Add controls to the form and set their properties according to Table 1.

Table 1. The *frmWinFormProperties* form controls.

Control Type	Property Name	Value
Form	Name	frmWinFormProperties
-/-	Text	Windows Form Properties Program
-/-	StartPosition	CenterScreen
-/-	AcceptButton	btnChangeText
-/-	CancelButton	btnCancel
Label	Text	Select Color:
ComboBox	Name	cboColors
Label	Text	Select Cursor:
ComboBox	Name	cboCursors

Label	Text	Select Window State:
ComboBox	Name	cboWindowStates
Label	Text	Type Text:
TextBox	Name	TextBox1
Button	Name	btnCancel
-/-	Text	Cancel
-/-	BackColor	Blue
Button	Name	btnClear
-/-	Text	Cl&ear
-/-	BackColor	Blue
Button	Name	btnClose
-/-	Text	&Close
-/-	BackColor	Blue
Button	Name	btnBackColor
-/-	Text	Change BackColor
Button	Name	btnForeColor
-/-	Text	Change ForeColor
Button	Name	btnCursor
-/-	Text	Change Cursor
Button	Name	btnWindowState
-/-	Text	Change Window State
Button	Name	btnChangeText
-/-	Text	Change Text

Set Controls Properties

Note for all buttons set the Font Style to Bold and the Font Size to 10, ForeColor to Blue or White depending on the BackColor. Set the form's AcceptButton and CancelButton properties after you placed the ChangeText and Cancel buttons. Notice how each property is used and if necessary review Chapter 6 for additional details. You need to properly resize all controls when you place them on the form. In Visual Studio 2005, the AutoSize property of labels is set to true by default, which won't allow you to resize them at design time. Set it to false if you want to adjust their size. To get help in positioning multiple controls on the form you may use the formatting functionality available in the Format menu.

When you set the BackColor and ForeColor properties use the Custom color tab, which offers more colors than the System tab. In Visual Studio 2003, the ComboBox and Textbox Text property default values should be deleted. Keep the default names in all labels and textboxes.

Set the Form Properties

To change the default form file name, in the Project Explorer right-click Form1.vb, choose Rename and type *frmWinFormProperties.vb*. In Visual Studio 2005, you will see a message that reads: "You are renaming a file. Would you also like to perform a rename in this project of all references to the code element 'Form1'?" Click Yes. In Visual Studio 2003, there is no such friendly service. So you need to reset the form class name and then reset the project Startup Object in the Project Property Pages to the new form name.

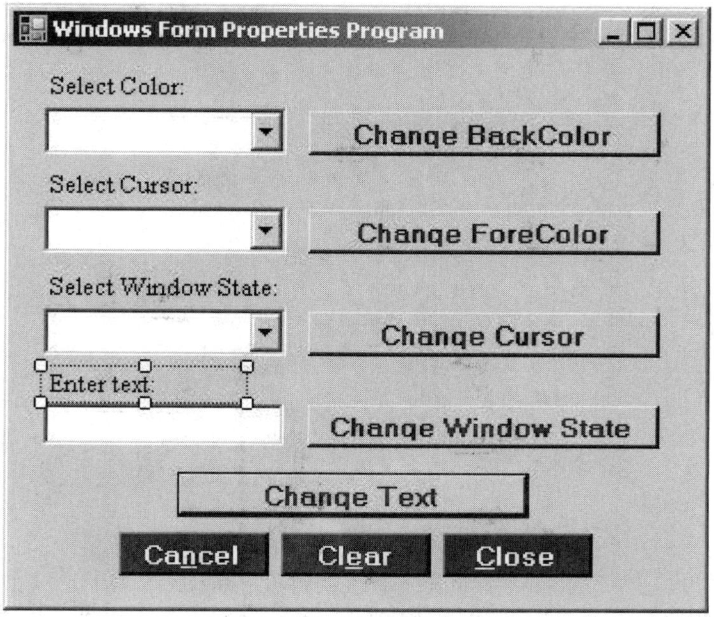

Figure 1. The WinFormProperties form.

As previously mentioned, the StartPosition property allows positioning the form on the screen or a parent window. Set it to CenterScreen, which will center it on the screen. Set the AcceptButton property to a button of your choice; we suggest the btnChangeText button. Set the CancelButton property to the btnCancel button. Save your work. When you complete design work your form should look like the one presented in Figure 1.

Write Code

Declare Form Variables

Write code to declare two form variables. You will need them to store the initial values of the form's BackColor and Text properties. Your code should look like this:

```
Private m_FormText As String =
                    "Windows Form Properties Program"
Private m_FormBackColor As Color = Me.BackColor
```

Write Private Procedures

In this lab, you will populate three ComboBoxes with the values used for BackColor, ForeColor, Cursor and FormWindowState properties.

Listing 1. Populate procedures.

```
Private Sub PopulateCursors()
        cboCursors.Items.Add(Cursors.Cross)
        cboCursors.Items.Add(Cursors.Hand)
        cboCursors.Items.Add(Cursors.IBeam)
        cboCursors.Items.Add(Cursors.WaitCursor)
        cboCursors.Items.Add(Cursors.HSplit)
        cboCursors.Items.Add(Cursors.Help)
        cboCursors.Items.Add(Cursors.NoMove2D)
        cboCursors.Items.Add(Cursors.PanNorth)
        cboCursors.Items.Add(Cursors.SizeAll)
        cboCursors.Items.Add(Cursors.SizeWE)
End Sub

Private Sub PopulateColors()
        cboColors.Items.Add(Color.BlueViolet)
        cboColors.Items.Add(Color.Chocolate)
        cboColors.Items.Add(Color.Cornsilk)
        cboColors.Items.Add(Color.Blue)
```

```
        cboColors.Items.Add(Color.LightBlue)
End Sub


Private Sub PopulateWindowStates()
        cboWindowStates.Items.Add(FormWindowState.Normal)
        cboWindowStates.Items.Add(FormWindowState.Minimized)
        cboWindowStates.Items.Add(FormWindowState.Maximized)
End Sub
```

Locate PopulateCursors, PopulateColors and PopulateWindowStates procedures in Listing 1 and type them into your project.

Write the Form Load Event Procedure

Write code in the form load event procedure. Open the form designer and double-click any free space on the form. Your code editor window will open an empty Form_ Load event procedure. Type three lines of code to call the populate procedures, which you wrote earlier. Your code should look like the following:

```
Private Sub Form1_Load(ByVal sender As System.Object, _
            ByVal e As System.EventArgs) Handles MyBase.Load
    PopulateColors()
    PopulateCursors()
    PopulateWindowStates()
End Sub
```

Note that the form load event procedure is used to invoke the populate procedures so that when the form is displayed all ComboBoxes are loaded.

Write the Click Event Procedures

You have placed a number of buttons on the form. Now you need to associate their click events with certain action procedures. For each button you will write a corresponding click event procedure. Please find Change BackColor, Change ForeColor, Change Cursor, Change Text, Change WindowState, Cancel, Clear and Close buttons click event procedures in Listing 2 and type them into your lab project.

Listing 2. Click event procedures.

```
Private Sub btnBackColor_Click(ByVal sender As Object, _
      ByVal e As EventArgs) Handles btnBackColor.Click
      Me.BackColor = cboColors.SelectedItem
End Sub


Private Sub btnForeColor_Click(ByVal sender As Object, _
      ByVal e As EventArgs) Handles btnForeColor.Click
      Me.ForeColor = cboColors.SelectedItem
End Sub


Private Sub btnCursor_Click(ByVal sender As Object, _
      ByVal e As EventArgs) Handles btnCursor.Click
      Me.Cursor = cboCursors.SelectedItem
End Sub


Private Sub btnChangeText_Click(ByVal sender As Object, _
      ByVal e As EventArgs) Handles btnChangeText.Click
      Me.Text = TextBox1.Text
End Sub
```

```
Private Sub btnWindowState_Click(ByVal sender As Object, _
     ByVal e As EventArgs) Handles btnWindowState.Click
     Me.WindowState = cboWindowStates.SelectedItem
End Sub
Private Sub btnClear_Click(ByVal sender As Object, _
     ByVal e As EventArgs) Handles btnClear.Click
     TextBox1.Text = ""
End Sub


Private Sub btnClose_Click(ByVal sender As Object, _
     ByVal e As EventArgs) Handles btnClose.Click
     Me.Close()
End Sub


Private Sub btnCancel_Click(ByVal sender As Object, _
     ByVal e As EventArgs) Handles btnCancel.Click
     ResetProperties()
End Sub
```

Write the ResetProperties Procedure

This procedure is designed to reset all properties to their initial or default values. You declared and initialized two form variables to store the initial settings of the form's BackColor and Text properties. In this procedure, you will read these values and assign them to the corresponding form properties. Then call this procedure from the Cancel button click event procedure. The procedure code should look like this:

```
Private Sub ResetProperties()
     Me.WindowState = FormWindowState.Normal
     Me.Cursor = Cursors.Default
```

```
    Me.BackColor = m_FormBackColor
    Me.ForeColor = Color.Black
    Me.Text = m_FormText
    TextBox1.Text = ""
End Sub
```

You have completed coding. Great job! Please save your work.

Test and Debug

Now it's time to test the application. Remember, before you begin testing check if your code does show any red or blue wavy lines. If you find any, hover the mouse pointer over the underlined word and read the error message and try to fix the problem. Also, before actually running the program it is useful to try to compile it by running the Build Solution or Rebuild Solution method in the Build menu.

Test the Application

To test the application, click on Start or press F5. Perform the following functionality testing.

.

- Select any color in the Select Colors dropdown and click on the Change BackColor button. Does the form's background color change accordingly? Click on the Cancel button. Does it reset the BackColor?
- Select any color in the Select Colors dropdown and click on the Change ForeColor button. Does all labels text color change accordingly? Click on Cancel to rollback the changes.
- Select any cursor in the Select Cursor dropdown and click on the Change Cursor button. Does the form's cursor change to the selected cursor? Click on Cancel to reset the property.

- Select any window state property from the Select Window States dropdown and click on the Change Window State button. Does the window state change?
- Type any text in the Type Text textbox and click on the Change Text button. Does the text appear in the form's title bar? Click on Cancel to reset the property.
- Repeat text typing and press Enter. Does the text in the form's title bar change? Press Esc. Does it restore the default text?
- Type any text in the textbox and click on the Clear button. Does it delete the text?
- Using the above testing routine change the form's BackColor, ForeColor and Cursor and then press Esc. Did it reset all changed properties to the default?
- Click on the Close button. Does the application close?

If you get errors, check your code and fix them. You may get errors related to typos and spelling. Congratulations! You have successfully completed this project!

Extra Credit Task

For those of you who would like to try to solve a more challenging task, here's an extra credit assignment. As we mentioned earlier, the program is not protected from the events when user clicks a button without selecting any value in a dropdown box. Fortunately enough, this will not cause the program to fail because Visual Basic .NET partially handles such situations for us. However, the program will fail to complete the requested action. Hence, it would be nice if you write code that would verify user input and remind users that they have to select a value first.

To write code that will implement the so-called user input validation you need to check if the value that is going to be assigned to a certain form's property is valid. Here comes a little complication. To do this properly you need to know what data type is expected by the property and if it is a value type or a reference type. If it is a value type, for example, a string, you may want to check if the length of the string variable is greater than 0. One of the following tests should work:

```
If strTestValue.Length = 0 Then
If strTestValue = "" Then
If strTestValue = String.Empty Then
```

But if the value is a reference type, a different approach should be used. You should first verify if the object variable is not null. Remember that trying to use the object variable that is not instantiated will cause a notorious "Object reference is not set to an instance of an object" error. Hence, you need to test if the object reference is null. Note that in all ComboBoxes you are reading the *SelectedItem* property that returns an object. This means you need to check if the returned object is referencing null. Your if statement may look like this:

```
If Not cboColors.SelectedItem Is Nothing Then
      Me.BackColor = cboColors.SelectedItem
Else
      MessageBox.Show("Please select a color first.")
End If
```

Write similar code for each property used in this lab. Good Luck!

Chapter 7: Windows Forms Methods and Events

Windows Forms Methods and Events

In this Chapter:

You will learn the Windows forms methods and events. To create a powerful program you need to know how to control the form's behavior at runtime. For instance, how to hide the form and then show it again, disable a button or a set of controls or pass parameters from one form to another. Also, to make a program more efficient and user friendly you may want to validate user input, handle key press events and if necessary notify a user how to correct errors. To do all this and much more you need to learn how to program the form methods and events. In this chapter, we will show you how.

Chapter 7 at a Glance

- ➤ Windows Forms Methods
- ➤ Exploring the Form Class
- ➤ Using a Form Object
- ➤ The Show Method
- ➤ The ShowDialog Method
- ➤ The Close Method
- ➤ The Hide Method
- ➤ The Form Class Events
- ➤ The Form Load Event
- ➤ The FormClosing Event
- ➤ User Triggered Events
- ➤ The KeyPress Event
- ➤ The MouseDown Event
- ➤ The KeyDown Event
- ➤ The MouseEnter Event

Exploring the Form Class

The form is a class and as any class it can have properties, methods and events. Properties determine the form's appearance and methods are used to implement its behavior. As for events, they are similar to notifications that are broadcast by the form to whoever might be using it and is subscribed to receive them. In Chapter 6, we discussed the form properties and here we will show you how to program the form's methods and events to manage the form behavior at runtime.

The Form Class Declaration

When you add a new form to the project, you do not create the form from scratch. Instead, you build your custom form class on top of the base form class that resides in *System.Windows.Forms* namespace. If you examine the declaration of the form class you should notice the inheritance statement like the following:

```
Public Class Form1
              Inherits System.Windows.Forms.Form
```

In Visual Studio 2005, the form class code is distributed between two partial classes that are contained by two separate files: the user code file, where you are expected to write all your code, and the form designer code file. The "user code" in this context means the code written by you. This file normally bears the form name; for example, Form1.vb. Here the form class declaration does not contain the inheritance statement. The second form file is automatically generated by the form designer and contains the word *Designer* in its name; for example, Form1.Designer.vb. In this file, the form is defined in a partial class and the inheritance statement is here. Obviously, you can name the form class as you wish and add your own methods, properties and events. In most cases you would start with changing the form class name. You may have many reasons to do so, for example, to make it more meaningful, but you cannot change the *Inherits* statement unless you intend to write your own form class from scratch. Note that all code that is to be used in the "Windows Form Designer Generated Code" region is now in this file. Code in this file is called a "Non-User code." This division of form code allows separating the form designer code, which you are not encouraged to modify, from user-developer code. If you convert a Visual Studio 2003 application into Visual Studio 2005, the designer file will not be created and all your form code including the designer code will be in a single form file.

Using a Form Object

When you add a form to your project, its *Name* property automatically becomes the name of the form class. If you do not change it, the default Form1 name will be used. Furthermore, the form class file name will carry the same name with the filename extension ".vb"

To reference any form class used in the project, you need to create a corresponding object variable. This means you need to declare and instantiate a form class object variable as you would normally do with any other reference type. The good news is that this is already done for you by Visual Basic .NET. Remember the keyword *Me*. It is an alias of the form object variable internally created by Visual Basic. This is done by the following hidden form object declaration:

```
Public WithEvents Form1 as New Form1
```

Of course, you can create your own form object variables whenever you need them. For instance, in the following code we declare and instantiate the form class object variable and then use it to call its Show method.

```
Dim objForm As New frmWinFormProperties
objForm.Show()
```

The following two lines of code are equally legal and can perform the same job.

```
Me.Hide()
objForm.Hide()
```

However, the form object variable alias *Me* has a private scope and is visible inside the form class only. You cannot use it from outside the form. Besides, if you do try to use it in another form in your project, it will actually point to that form. Therefore, if you need to manipulate multiple forms in a project, you have to create corresponding form object variables. This becomes even more important when you want to use form methods or subscribe to its events.

The Form Methods

The Show Method

The main mission of the *Show* method is to display the form. If you have one form in your project, it will be shown automatically when you start the application. But if you have multiple forms and, for example, want to show Form2 from Form1, you need to instantiate Form2 and call its Show method. Let's look at a scenario where two or more forms are involved.

If you create a new Windows application project, which we recommend you to do to test the main points of our discussion, you will have one form by default. To add another form to the project, on the *Project* menu, choose *Add Windows Form* and then in the *Add New Item* dialog box, select *Windows Form* and click Open. Keep all default settings so you will have less typing work. Add a button to Form1, name it btnShow and for the Text property type "Show Form2." Double-click the button to create a click event procedure and type in the following code:

```
Private Sub btnShow_Click(ByVal sender As System.Object, _
        ByVal e As System.EventArgs) Handles btnShow.Click
        Dim objForm2 As New Form2
        objForm2.Show()
End Sub
```

Press F5 to run the application and click Show Form2. This should display Form2.

Note:

In the Form class methods, events and properties are interrelated. When you call a certain form method it may change a certain form property, which generates a property change event. Then the property change event does some work that may be associated with the method and the property. Also, when events fire they may pass some useful information to event handlers by using special objects that contain the words events and arguments in their names. For instance, when you call the form's *Show* method, it will change the form's *Visible* property, which will cause the *VisibleChanged* event to fire.

However, you will receive events only if you subscribe to them. For example, to process the form events you need to create corresponding callback subroutine procedures and bind them to the form events. Most of this work is again done for you by Visual Basic. All you need to do is write code in the corresponding event handler procedures, which we will show you later in this chapter.

Note an event handler procedure is normally named after the form class name or an object name plus the event name; for example: Form2_Load, From2_ Acticated or btnShow_Click and so on. To see the form events in action do the

following. In your test project that you created earlier, add a Label control to Form2.
Double-click Form2 and type this line of code in Form2_Load event handler:

```
Private Sub Form2_Load(ByVal sender As Object, _
         ByVal e As EventArgs) Handles MyBase.Load
    Label1.Text = "Form2_Load event: " & DateTime.Now
End Sub
```

Press F5 to run the application and click on the Show Form2 button. Notice that
Label1 should display the message and the time when the form load event occurred.
Do the same with the Activated event. Right-click Form2, select Properties. At the
top of the Properties window, click on the Events button. This should show all form
events. Find the Activated event and double-click it. The Form2_Activated event
handler procedure should be opened in your code editor window. Type one line of
code as shown below:

```
Private Sub Form2_Activated(ByVal sender As Object, _
         ByVal e As EventArgs) Handles MyBase.Activated
    Label1.Text = "Form2 activated at: " & DateTime.Now
End Sub
```

Press F5 to run the application and click on the Show Form2 button. Label1 should
display the Activated event message. Keep in mind that the form load event will fire
before the activated event but they will run so fast that you will not notice the change
of text in Label1. To fix this problem, replace the above code with the following
MessageBox.Show method call:

```
MessageBox.Show("Form2 activated at: " & DateTime.Now)
```

Run the application and click on the Show Form2 button again. You should see both event messages. Some events that accompany methods are not just notifications. They act as a two-way communication between the form and the client and even allow interfering with the method execution or aborting it. A good example is the *FormClosing* event that passes a Cancel property in its event arguments object. If you set this property to true, the form close procedure will be aborted.

Events associated with the Show method:

> ➢ HandleCreated
> ➢ Invalidated
> ➢ Load
> ➢ VisibleChanged
> ➢ Activated
> ➢ Shown
> ➢ Paint

So far we considered the main aspects of the Show method. However, there is one thing that we did not talk about yet. The Show method opens a form in the so-called modeless mode, which means the form may yield its active status to other forms in the same application. This feature allows users to have multiple forms open and switch between them in any desired order. But there may be situations when you would like to give a form an exclusive application-wise control so that no other form can be opened before it is closed. This can be achieved by using the *ShowDialog* method.

The ShowDialog Method

The main difference of the *ShowDialog* from the *Show* method is that it will display the form in the modal mode. If the form is opened in a modal mode the users are not allowed to open or work on any other form in the same application until they close the modal form. The ShowDialog method has the following features:

> ➤ It shows the form in modal mode.
> ➤ Does not allow switching to other forms in the same application.
> ➤ It returns the *DialogResult* type.

To experiment with this method you need to modify Form1. Add another button, name it btnShowDialog and type "Show Dialog" for its Text property. Double-click the newly created button and type the following code in its click event procedure:

```
Private Sub btnShow_Click(ByVal sender As Object, _
          ByVal e As.EventArgs) Handles btnShow.Click
          Dim objForm2 As New Form2
          objForm2.ShowDialog()
End Sub
```

To test the ShowDialog method, press F5 and click on the Show Form2 button. When Form2 is displayed, try to click on Show Form2 button again or do something else. You should not be able to do anything else until you close Form2.

Note:

The *ShowDialog* method shows the form in a modal mode, which means no other form in the same application can be opened or activated until it is closed. How is this effect achieved? Code execution after a call to the ShowDialog method will not continue until this method call returns, which will happen only when the form is closed. The ShowDialog method returns a DialogResult value that can be used to identify user activity on the form. To use this feature you need to set the DialogResult property of corresponding buttons on the called form.

To practice using the DialogResult enumeration, modify your test application code. Write the following code in the Show Form2 button click event procedure:

```
Private Sub btnShow_Click(ByVal sender As Object, _
        ByVal e As EventArgs) Handles btnShow.Click
        Dim frm2 As New Form2
        Dim DialogResultValue As DialogResult
        DialogResultValue = frm2.ShowDialog()
        Label1.Text = DialogResultValue.ToString
End Sub
```

In Form2, add two buttons named btnOK and btnCancel and set their DialogResult properties to OK and Cancel correspondingly. Note that you don't have to write any code in Form2. Press F5 and click on the Show Form2 button. When Form2 is displayed, click on the OK button. This action will automatically close Form2 and you should see OK displayed in Label1 in Form1, which represents the value returned by the ShowDialog method. Repeat the test with the Cancel button.

The Close Method

Functionality wise, the *Close* method is the opposite of the *Show* method. It is designed to trigger a series of actions such as change the Visible property, deactivate the form, destroy the window handle and finally dispose the form object. It begins its destructive work with changing the form's Visible property, which erases the window image from the screen and raises the VisibleChanged event. Then the FormClosing event is fired followed by the FormClosed, Deactivated, HandleDestroyed and Disposed events. Thus, the Close method will not only remove the form image from the screen but it will also unload the form object from memory.

Using the FormClosing Event

The *FormClosing* event is an early notification that the form is in the closing process. As previously mentioned, this event may be used for a number of practical tasks. For example, it can be used to abort the form close action and do some custom cleanup. Its event handler procedure accepts a *FormClosingEventArgs* object, which along with many other things has the Cancel property. In Visual Studio 2003, it is called *CancelEventArgs*. If this property is set to true, the close process will be stopped and the form won't be closed. Here's the code written in the FormClosing event handler that shows a message box asking the user if she or he really wants to close the form. By the way, the MessageBox's Show method is displayed in modal mode and returns a DialogResult enumeration. So if it returns DialogResult.Cancel value the close action is rolled back. Here's the code that does it:

```
Private Sub Form1_FormClosing(ByVal sender As Object, _
ByVal e As FormClosingEventArgs) Handles MyBase.FormClosing
    If MessageBox.Show("Do you want to close?", "Test", _
    MessageBoxButtons.OKCancel) = DialogResult.Cancel Then
        e.Cancel = True
```

```
        End If
End Sub
```

Why should you consider the *FormClosing* event or worry about preventing the Close method from doing its job? This may be relevant when you may want to make a program user-friendly. Sometimes a user may accidentally hit the close button and only then realizes that she did not save her valuable work but it's too late. Therefore, you can use the *FormClosing* event to show a message box asking if the user really wants to shut down.

In Visual Studio 2005, the FormClosing event uses an enhanced version of CancelEventArgs object, which is now called FormClosingEventArgs. This object carries a new and very useful property called *CloseReason*, which can be used to find out what caused the close action or who initiated it. CloseReason enumeration contains the following values:

- FormOwnerClosing
- ApplicationExitCall
- TaskManagerClosing
- MdiFormClosing
- WindowsShutDown
- UserClosing

If you look at the list of CloseReasons, you may realize that in five out of six cases it won't make sense to ask a user if she or he wants to shut down, simply because the action is not initiated by a user. More importantly, inserting a MessageBox into a non-user initiated closing process may cause problems. The following is a modified version of the above FormClosing event handler:

```
Private Sub Form1_FormClosing(ByVal sender As Object, _
```

```
ByVal e As FormClosingEventArgs) Handles MyBase.FormClosing

If e.CloseReason = CloseReason.UserClosing AndAlso _
    MessageBox.Show("Do you want to close?", "Test", _
    MessageBoxButtons.OKCancel) = DialogResult.Cancel Then
    e.Cancel = True
End If
End Sub
```

Note that in the above code we check both the reason for closing the form and also the *MessageBox.Show* method return value before we confirm that the form should closed.

Events Associated with the Close method:

- VisibleChanged
- FormClosing
- FormClosed
- Deactivated
- HandleDestroyed
- Disposed

Note:

The form's *Close* method first changes the form's Visible property, which hides the form and causes the VisibleChanged event to fire. Then the FormClosing event is raised. At this stage the form is still fully and easily recoverable and the Close method can be aborted by just setting the FormClosingEventArgs object's Cancel property to true. When the FormClosed or Deactivated events are raised, the form cannot be revived but the form object is still in memory. The HandleDestroyed event signals that the form's window handle is released. When the Disposed event is raised, the form object is destroyed.

The Hide Method

The *Hide* method is used to stop displaying the form window on the screen. This is achieved by setting the Visible property of the form to false, which in its own turn causes the VisibleChanged event to fire. Thus, the Hide method triggers a chain of events that result in erasing the form image from the screen while the form object is still loaded in memory and can be re-painted by simply setting its Visible property back to true or by calling the Show or Activate methods. Thus, to toggle the form's visibility you can do one of the following:

```
m_frm.Show()
m_frm.Visible = False
m_frm.Activate()
m_frm.Hide()
m_frm.Visible = True
```

One of the practical uses of the Hide method is that instead of closing the form you may hide it and when necessary display it again. This will drastically improve performance and save resources. For example, if you want to allow the user to switch between two or more forms you may use the Hide, Show and Activate methods interchangeably.

The Form Events

The form events can be classified into two main categories: the form class generated events that we discussed in previous sections and user triggered events, such as button click, key press or mouse actions. In this section, we will consider user triggered events.

User Triggered Events

The form class can receive and process Windows events generated by peripheral devices such as the keyboard and the mouse. A list of events that can be handled by the form class is very long. Here we will limit our discussion to: KeyPress, KeyDown, KeyUp, MouseDown and MouseEnter events.

The KeyDown Event

The *KeyDown* event is raised when the user presses a key on the keyboard. When the key is released, the *KeyUp* event is generated. Each key is assigned a unique integer *KeyCode*, which is used to identify a pressed key.

Figure 7.0 The KeyEventArgs object properties.

The KeyCode and other key event properties shown in Figure 7.0 are carried by the *KeyEventArgs* object. The KeyCode and KeyData properties store the Keys enumeration that can be used to identify the key for both KeyDown and KeyUp events. The *KeyValue* property represents the value of the KeyCode. From a practical perspective, the KeyDown and KeyUp events allow you to control processing of the user key strokes. You can identify which key was pressed by using the KeyCode and take a necessary action. For example, if your project requires disabling the Escape key you can do so by writing code in the KeyDown event handler like this:

```
Private Sub Form1_KeyDown(ByVal sender As Object, ByVal e
                      As KeyEventArgs) Handles Me.KeyDown
    If e.KeyCode = Keys.Escape Then
        MessageBox.Show("Escape key is disabled")
        Exit Sub
    End If
End Sub
```

Remember, for the above code to work, you need to set the form's KeyPreview property to true. In a real-world project you may not need to do this because you would use the control's key events instead. Note that we use the *Keys* enumeration to find out the key name from the KeyCode. This relieves us from a necessity to translate key codes. To experiment with key codes, add a Label to your test project and name it lblKeyCode. Write the following code in the form's KeyDown event handler:

```
Private Sub Form1_KeyDown(ByVal sender As Object, ByVal
                 e As KeyEventArgs) Handles MyBase.KeyDown
    lblKeyCode.Text = e.KeyValue.ToString()
End Sub
```

Run the application and press any printable key. For instance, if you press "a" you should see 65, "b" – 66. Now press any non-printable key. For example, F1 should produce 112, F2 – 113.

The KeyPress Event

The *KeyPress* event handler accepts two parameters: object sender and KeyPressEventArgs object. Note that in Visual Studio 2005, the KeyPress event is raised for both printable and most non-printable keys with a few exceptions. For example, it is not generated for such keys as Enter, Backspace and Tab. In Visual Studio 2003, this event is generated for printable keys only. Note that this could be an issue when you convert a project from Visual Studio 2003 to Visual Studio 2005.

When you process key events, you may need to translate the KeyCode into a character if it is a printable key or a functional key name. To identify the character value of a printable key you can use the *KeyChar* property of KeyPressEventArgs object. This property conveniently returns the corresponding key character. For non-printable keys use the KeyCode and the Keys enumeration as we did in the above examples.

As you may realize, many user triggered events are common for both the form and the controls. The question is when the user causes an event that is going to receive and process it first, will it be the form or the control? The dilemma is solved by setting the form's *KeyPreview* property. If it is set to false, only the control's KeyPress event handler is executed. The form's KeyPress event handler is not executed. If you set the KeyPreview to true, the form's KeyPress event handler is executed first and then the one of the control. By default, the KeyPreview is set to false, which guarantees that only related controls will receive these events. To practice using the KeyPress event, write the following code in your test Form1 form KeyPress event handler:

```
Private Sub Form1_KeyPress(ByVal sender As Object, ByVal
        e As KeyPressEventArgs) Handles MyBase.KeyPress
    'For this to work set the form's
    'KeyPreview property to True
    lblKeyCode.Text = e.KeyChar.ToString()
End Sub
```

Press F5 to run the application. Press any printable key and notice what is displayed in the lblKeyCode label. If you try a non-printable key, either its KeyCode should be displayed or nothing. As we mentioned earlier, no KeyPress event is generated for Backspace, Enter and Tab.

The MouseDown Event

The *MouseDown* event is generated when the user presses any mouse button. Detailed information about the mouse event is contained in the MouseEventArgs object, which is shown in Figure 7.1.

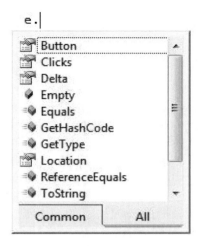

Figure 7.1 The MouseEventArgs object properties.

This object is passed to all mouse event handlers. Thus, to handle a mouse event all you need to do is read the MouseEventArgs object and use the information to process the event. For example, the *Button* property can be used to identify which button was pressed. The *Clicks* integer property signifies how many clicks were made. Theoretically, you may write a program that would handle one, two, three and more mouse clicks differently. The X and Y properties indicate the horizontal and vertical positions of the mouse pointer at the time when the mouse event such as MouseDown or MouseUp occurred. In most situations you will first need to determine which mouse button was pressed. Note that you can use the *MouseButtons* enumeration to assist you with this task. To practice handling mouse events, do the following. In your test application, create a Form1 MouseDown event handler and type in the following code:

```
Private Sub Form1_MouseDown(ByVal sender As Object, _
     ByVal e As MouseEventArgs) Handles MyBase.MouseDown
     Dim msButton As MouseButtons
     msButton = e.Button
```

```
        Label1.Text = "The " & msButton.ToString & _
        " button was clicked."
End Sub
```

Run the application to test which button was clicked. Note that the first clicks may not be shown, so move the mouse over the form and try again.

The MouseEnter Event

Mouse movements over the form area, excluding any control real estate, can produce a number of mouse-related events, such as *MouseEnter, MouseLeave, MouseHover* and others. If necessary, you may write event handlers to use these events in your program. For example, it is a common practice to change the cursor type when the mouse enters a button area. This should be followed by changing the cursor back to default when the MouseLeave event occurs. To practice writing code for these mouse events, in your test application create Form1 MouseEnter and MouseLeave event handler procedures and type the following code:

```
Private Sub Form1_MouseEnter(ByVal sender As Object, _
        ByVal e As EventArgs) Handles MyBase.MouseEnter
        Label1.Text = "The mouse entered the form area."
End Sub
Private Sub Form1_MouseLeave(ByVal sender As Object, _
        ByVal e As EventArgs) Handles MyBase.MouseLeave
        Label1.Text = "The mouse left the form area."
End Sub
```

Run the application. Move the mouse to enter and then leave the form area and check if the label's text reflects mouse movements accordingly.

Summary

In this chapter, you've learned how to program the form class methods and events. The form class methods give you the ability to control many aspects of its behavior at runtime. By using the form methods you can show, hide, activate or close the form. The form can be opened in normal mode using the Show method or modal mode using the ShowDialog method. The form events may be classified into two categories: events that are raised by the form class and events triggered by user actions. The former typically accompany form method execution or property change processes and allow tracking and if necessary imposing additional code execution control. The latter are used to process user actions performed through peripheral devices.

Lab 7: The Using Windows Forms Project

Using Windows Forms

In this Project:

You will create a Windows forms application and practice using the form class methods and events to exchange and process data in a multiple forms application environment. This lab will help you consolidate the knowledge acquired in Chapter 7 and practice using the form methods and events.

Create a New Project

- ➢ Create the *Lab7* project folder.
- ➢ Open Visual Studio .NET
- ➢ Create a new Windows Application project.
- ➢ Set the project Location to *C:\Labs\Lab7*.
- ➢ Set the project Name to *UsingWinForms*.

Design User Interface

In this project, you will have three Windows forms. The frmMain form is used as the main form and as a startup object while Form1 and Form2 will be used to demonstrate the form events and the use of the DialogResult property. Please pay attention to how to record and display the form Open and Close events sequence in the frmMain and Form1.

Design the frmMain Form

This is the first form in the project. Change the form Name and Text properties. Right-click the form and select Properties. In the Properties window, find the Name property and type *frmMain*, scroll to the Text property and type *Windows Forms Program*. Add controls to the form according to Table 1.

Table 1. The frmMain form controls.

Control Type	Property Name	Value
Form	Name	frmMain
-/-	Text	Windows Forms Program

Label	Name	lblEvents
-/-	Text	Events:
Label	Name	lblUserAction
-/-	Text	User action:
Label	Name	Label2
-/-	Text	Enter any date:
Textbox	Name	txtDate
Label	Name	Label3
-/-	Text	Returned date:
Textbox	Name	txtReturnedDate
Button	Name	btnShowForm1
-/-	Text	Show Form1
Button	Name	btnShowForm2
-/-	Text	Show Form2

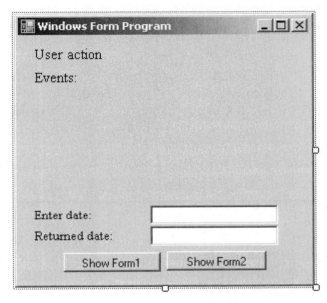

Figure 1. The frmMain form design view.

When you complete the design work, your form should look like the one shown in Figure 1.

Add the Form1 Form

Add another form to the project. Place controls and set their properties according to Table 2.

Table 2. The Form1 form controls.

Control Type	Property Name	Value
Form	Name	Form1
Label	Name	Label1

Button	Name	btnShowOpenEvents
-/-	Text	&Show Events
Button	Name	btnOK
-/-	Text	&OK
-/-	DialogResult	OK
Button	Name	btnCancel
-/-	Text	&Cancel
-/-	DialogResult	Cancel

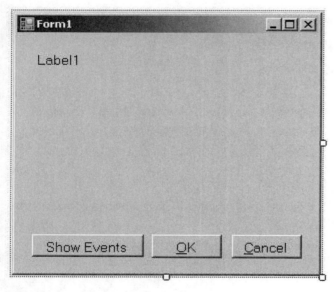

Figure 2. The Form1 form design view.

Your complete Form1 should look like the one shown in Figure 2.

Design the Form2 Form

Add one more Windows form to the project with the default name Form2. Design it according to Table 3.

Table 3. The Form2 form controls.

Control Type	Property Name	Value
Form	Name	Form2
Label	Name	Label1
-/-	Text	Form2 events:
Button	Name	btnClose
-/-	Text	&Close

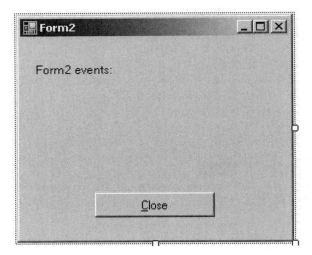

Figure 3. The Form2 form design view.

The Form2 form layout is shown in Figure 3.

Write Code

In this project, you will code three forms: frmMain, Form1 and Form2.

Code the frmMain Class

Since you are going to manipulate two other forms from the main form, you need to declare two form level object variables. Please type the following code:

```
Private frm1 As Form1
Private frm2 As Form2
Public strCloseEvents As String
```

Write the Form Load Event Procedure

Code in form load event procedure reads the value of the *strCloseEvents* variable and assigns it to Label1:

```
Private Sub frmMain_Load(ByVal sender As Object, _
         ByVal e As EventArgs) Handles MyBase.Load
    lblEvents.Text = strCloseEvents
End Sub
```

Write the Show Form1 Button Event Handler

The "Show Form1" button is used to display Form1. Please type the following code into your project:

```
Private Sub btnShowForm1_Click (ByVal sender As Object, _
     ByVal e As EventArgs) Handles btnShowForm1.Click
     Dim dlgResult As DialogResult        'Line 1
```

```
frm1 = New Form1                          'Line 2
dlgResult = frm1.ShowDialog()             'Line 3
lblUserAction.Text = "Form1 action user clicked " & _
dlgResult.ToString()                      'Line 4
End Sub
```

In the above button click event procedure, you declare the DialogResult variable (line 1) and instantiate frm1 object variable as Form1 (line 2). Then you call the ShowDialog method to show Form1 in modal mode (line 3). When the ShowDialog method call returns you read its return value and assign it to the DialogResult variable (line 3). Then a DialogResult value is converted into a string and assigned to the lblUserAction label (line 4).

Write the Show Form2 Button Event Handler
This procedure is similar to the one above but here you show Form2 using the Show method and also perform user input validation.

```
Private Sub btnShowForm2_Click(ByVal sender As Object, _
        ByVal e As EventArgs) Handles btnShowForm2.Click
    frm2 = New Form2
    If txtDate.Text.Length > 0 Then
        frm2.dtInputDate = Date.Parse(txtDate.Text)
        frm2.Show()
    Else
        MessageBox.Show("Please enter a date")
    End If
End Sub
```

To check the user input you use the *if* statement that verifies if the length of the value entered in the *txtDate* textbox is greater than zero. If the test fails, you show a message box prompting the user to enter a value. To avoid a conversion error this should be done before you try to convert the string value to Date. This value is then exported from frmMain to Form2. This is done by assigning it to a public variable *dtInputDate* in Form2.

Write the frmMain Activated Event Procedure

You will use the *Activated* event procedure to obtain data from Form 1 or Form 2 and display it in the frmMain form every time there is a switch between the forms. Please type the following code:

```
Private Sub frmMain_Activated(ByVal sender As Object, _
      ByVal e As EventArgs) Handles MyBase.Activated
      If Not frm1 Is Nothing Then
            lblEvents.Text = "Form1 events: " & _
            frm1.strCloseEvents
      End If
      If Not frm2 Is Nothing Then
         Label3.Text = frm2.SendBackData()
      End If
End Sub
```

In the first *if* block, you check if frm1 variable was instantiated to avoid object reference not set error. Then you read the Form1 form public *strCloseEvents* variable and assign its value to Label1. In the second *if* block, you do the same with Form2 form. If this test returns true, you use the frm2 object variable to call the *SendBackData* method created in Form2. This method is designed to export data from Form2 to frmMain. If you open and then close Form1, you will get the *Close* method events recorded in that form and then passed to frmMain.

Code the Form1 Class

In Form1, you will make use of several form variables, which are accessible from various procedures inside and outside the form. Your code should look like the following:

```
Private intOpenOrder As Integer
Private intCloseOrder As Integer
Public strCloseEvents As String
Public strOpenEvents As String
```

Write the Form Event Handlers

Your task here is to write the names of events associated with the Open and Close methods to the *strOpenEvents* and *strCloseEvents* string variables. Beside the event names you write the incremental order number that should indicate the order in which these events fired. Note that each record ends with the *vbCrLf* constant that is equal to writing a carriage return and line feed commands. Please type code presented in Listing 1 into your project:

Listing 1. The Form1 form event handlers.

```
Private Sub Form1_HandleCreated(ByVal sender As Object,
        ByVal e As EventArgs) Handles MyBase.HandleCreated
    intOpenOrder = intOpenOrder + 1
    strOpenEvents += vbCrLf & "Event " & intOpenOrder & _
    ": HandleCreated event."
End Sub
```

```
Private Sub Form1_Load(ByVal sender As Object, ByVal e As
                    EventArgs) Handles MyBase.Load
    intOpenOrder = intOpenOrder + 1
    strOpenEvents += vbCrLf & "Event " & _
    intOpenOrder & ": Form load."
End Sub

Private Sub Form1_Shown(ByVal sender As Object, ByVal e As
                    EventArgs) Handles MyBase.Shown
    intOpenOrder = intOpenOrder + 1
    strOpenEvents += vbCrLf & "Event " & _
    intOpenOrder & ": Form shown."
End Sub
Private Sub Form1_Activated(ByVal sender As Object,
    ByVal e As EventArgs) Handles MyBase.Activated
    intOpenOrder = intOpenOrder + 1
    strOpenEvents += vbCrLf & "Event " & intOpenOrder & _
    ": Activated event."
End Sub
Private Sub Form1_Paint(ByVal sender As Object,
        ByVal e As PaintEventArgs) Handles MyBase.Paint
    intOpenOrder = intOpenOrder + 1
    strOpenEvents += vbCrLf & "Event " & intOpenOrder & _
    ": Paint event."
End Sub

Private Sub Form1_Invalidated(ByVal sender As Object,
ByVal e As InvalidateEventArgs) Handles MyBase.Invalidated
```

```
        intOpenOrder = intOpenOrder + 1
        strOpenEvents += vbCrLf & "Event " & intOpenOrder & _
        ": Invalidated event."
End Sub


Private Sub Form1_VisibleChanged(ByVal sender As Object, _
        ByVal e As EventArgs) Handles MyBase.VisibleChanged
        intOpenOrder = intOpenOrder + 1
        strOpenEvents += vbCrLf & "Event " & intOpenOrder & _
        ": VisibleChanged event."
        intCloseOrder = intCloseOrder + 1
        strCloseEvents += vbCrLf & "Event " & intCloseOrder _ &
        ": VisibleChanged event."
End Sub


Private Sub Form1_Deactivate(ByVal sender As Object,
        ByVal e As EventArgs) Handles MyBase.Deactivate
        intCloseOrder = intCloseOrder + 1
        strCloseEvents += vbCrLf & "Event " & intCloseOrder &_
        ": Deactivate event."
End Sub


Private Sub Form1_FormClosing(ByVal sender As Object,
        ByVal e As CancelEventArgs) Handles MyBase.FormClosing
        intCloseOrder = intCloseOrder + 1
        strCloseEvents += vbCrLf & "Event " & intCloseOrder &_
        ": FormClosing event."
End Sub
```

```
Private Sub Form1_FormClosed(ByVal sender As Object,
     ByVal e As EventArgs) Handles MyBase.FormClosed
     intCloseOrder = intCloseOrder + 1
     strCloseEvents += vbCrLf & "Event " & intCloseOrder & _
     ": FormClosed event."
End Sub


Private Sub Form1_HandleDestroyed(ByVal sender As Object,
     ByVal e As EventArgs) Handles MyBase.HandleDestroyed
     intCloseOrder = intCloseOrder + 1
     strCloseEvents += vbCrLf & "Event " & intCloseOrder & _
     ": HandleDestroyed event."
End Sub
Private Sub Form1_Disposed(ByVal sender As Object,
     ByVal e As EventArgs) Handles MyBase.Disposed
     intCloseOrder = intCloseOrder + 1
     strCloseEvents += vbCrLf & "Event " & intCloseOrder & _
     ": Disposed event."
End Sub


Private Sub btnShowOpenEvents_Click(ByVal sender As Object,
         ByVal e As EventArgs) Handles btnShowOpenEvents.
Click
     Label1.Text = strOpenEvents
End Sub
```

In the Form1 form you use the btnShowOpenEvents button to display the value of the strOpenEvents variable in Label1.

Code the Form2 Class

Write the following code in the Form2 form class:

```
Public dtInputDate As Date
Private Sub Form2_Load(ByVal sender As Object,
    ByVal e As EventArgs) Handles MyBase.Load
    Label1.Text = "It happened on " & dtInputDate
End Sub
(Listing 1 continues)
Private Sub btnClose_Click(ByVal sender As Object,
    ByVal e As EventArgs) Handles btnSubmit.Click
    Me.Close()
End Sub
```

Write the SendBackData Function

Type the following function into your project:

```
Public Function SendBackData() As String
    Return dtDatePassed.ToString()
End Function
```

The *SendBackData* procedure is a function. It returns the value of the form variable dtDatePassed. This function is called from frmMain to import data from this form. Congratulations! You completed coding this lab project.

Test the Application

Test the application. To start the application, click on Start or press F5. Perform the following functionality tests:

- Run the application. Click on the *Show Form1* button. Is Form1 displayed?
- In Form1 click on the *Show Events* button. Does Label1 display the events associated with the Open method? Click OK. Form1 should be closed.
- Back in frmMain. Does the lblUserAction label display "User clicked OK"?
- Repeat the test with the Form1 Cancel button.
- After Form1 is closed, check if frmMain displays Form1 events?

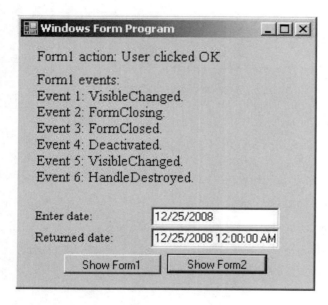

Figure 5.   The frmMain form at runtime.

- In the frmMain form type any date in the *Enter Date* textbox and click on the Show Form2 button. The date should be displayed in Label1 of Form2. Click on the Close button.
- Check if the date returned by Form1 is displayed in frmMain Returned Date textbox.

Congratulations! You have successfully completed this project.

Part V   Error Handling and Debugging

Error Handling and Debugging

Chapter 8: Application Errors

Application Errors

In this Chapter:

You will learn what application errors are. Applications may produce errors of various types at any stage of development, testing or usage. Understanding errors and recognizing their main characteristics will help you both prevent them while developing a new application or troubleshooting existing ones. In this chapter, we will show you what errors may occur in applications and how to avoid them.

Chapter 8 at a Glance

- ➤ Application Error Types
- ➤ External Errors
- ➤ Internal Errors
- ➤ Type Casting Errors
- ➤ Preventing Type Casting Errors
- ➤ Advanced Type Casting
- ➤ Logical Errors
- ➤ Dealing with Overflow Errors
- ➤ Numeric Precision Errors
- ➤ Using Application Compile Options

Application Error Types

Errors can happen at any time and anywhere. In the digital universe they represent a totally unique phenomenon. They are a mixture of human mistakes and unpredictable or hard to trace machine errors, although it well may be that those unpredictable machine errors are just hidden human faults. In this chapter, we will talk about the former. The human errors that may cause an application to malfunction, produce wrong output, lie, gaffe, bluff, bungle, blunder, fail, freeze or crash.

For purposes of this discussion, all potential application errors will be classified into several categories. The first two general categories are unknown and known errors. The former belongs to a group for which we do not have enough information and can't address accordingly. If you saw error messages like "Unknown error" or "Internal error" or "Unexpected error" that do not specify the nature of the problem, it may be one of those errors. The latter represents a category where each error has a distinct description, potential source of error and even recommendations of how to fix it.

All known errors are generalized into exception types. At runtime, the CLR tries to map a concrete error to a best matching exception type. Therefore, when a known error occurs the system identifies what exception type it could be assigned to and then throws that exception. Of course, if runtime fails to map the error, it will throw a general exception with a vague error description such as "Unexpected error" or "Unknown error." When you develop software, you should prepare your application to handle both known and unknown errors by diligently handling all exceptions. In the rest of this chapter, we will discuss some of the main known error types that you should be aware of when you write your own code. All potential application runtime errors can also be classified according to their location and type. From the location perspective, there are two main sub-categories: external and internal errors. External errors may be caused by outside conditions that cannot be controlled by the application. For example, file not found, unknown host, database or network not available errors belong to this category. It is difficult or impossible to prevent such errors but the application can be designed to properly handle them.

Internal errors are a completely different issue. They are typically rooted in the application logic and are simply caused by programming mistakes. In the following sections, we will describe some of most typical application errors and show you how to avoid them. Let's start with external errors.

External Errors

External errors are typically caused by unexpected or unforeseen outside conditions. For instance, the user may direct the program to read a file from a floppy disk while no disk is inserted. A program may attempt to read a file that has accidentally been deleted or moved to another directory. In other cases the application user may be denied access to a file because of insufficient privileges. Also, the application may attempt to process a file of a wrong format or type.

In addition, a number of external errors may be related to application infrastructure or enterprise network and database status. For example, the application server, the network or the database may be down or busy. Although these errors are out of the application's control, you can program the application to handle them properly. Can these types of errors be debugged? Yes, they can, if you manage to recreate them in the development or test environment. Again, you cannot prevent external errors but you can handle them if you write appropriate error handling code similar to what we will discuss in Chapter 9.

Internal Errors

Essentially, any application code fault or inaccuracy may be a source of an internal error. It could be anything from incorrect calculation formula or wrong execution flow to inadequate decision making or invalid data processing. Obviously, this topic is huge and somehow we need to narrow it to fit the scope of this book. Thus, we will discuss a few error types that we consider useful to understand the nature of most typical internal application errors. So in the rest of this chapter we will consider the following error types: logical errors, type casting errors and numeric errors.

Logical Errors

Logical errors may be caused by a variety of programming mistakes. Let's first look at errors related to improper use of logical operators and *if* statement condition evaluation faults. For example, some relatively simple errors may be caused by an inadequate *if* statement condition evaluation sequence. Code presented in Case 1 is an example of wrong condition evaluation sequence:

Case 1:

```
Dim intAmount As Integer
If intAmount > 0 Then
      'The If block code
ElseIf intAmount < 201 Then
      'The If block code
ElseIf intAmount > 1000 Then
      'The If block code
End If
```

In the above if block, *intAmount < 201* and *intAmount > 1000* conditions will never evaluate to true because both are greater than 0 so they will always fall into the first condition (> 0). To fix the problem you need to change the sequence and place more restrictive conditions before less restrictive ones. For example:

```
Dim intAmount As Integer
If intAmount < 0 Then
      'Amount is negative.
ElseIf intAmount < 201 Then
      'Amounts from 0 to 200
ElseIf intAmount > 1000 Then
      'Amounts from 1001 and up
Else
      'Amounts from 201 to 1000
End If
```

Alternatively, the above *if* block can be implemented using the *And* logical operator. For example:

```
If intAmount < 0 Then
      'Amount is negative or 0
ElseIf intAmount >= 0 And intAmount < 201 Then
      'Amounts from 0 to 200
ElseIf intAmount > 200 And intAmount < 1001 Then
      'Amounts from 201 to 1000
ElseIf intAmount > 1000 Then
      'Amounts from 1001 and up
End If
```

Another frequent source of errors is a compound condition, which is a combination of a test condition with a mathematical operation. First, we would not recommend using mathematical operations in the *if* conditions. However, if you think that you cannot avoid using compound conditions, then you should be aware of the following potential errors. In many cases, using compound conditions in *if* statements may cause errors especially if you use a compound condition along with a simple condition in one *if* statement. For example, if a division operation is used in a compound condition, a division by zero error may occur. This event is presented in Case 2:

Case 2:

```
Dim intAmt As Integer = 0
Dim intAmt2 As Integer = 9
Dim intAmt3 As Integer = 7
If intAmt3 < intAmt2 And intAmt3 < (intAmt2 \ intAmt) Then
      'The If block code
End If
```

The above code will compile but may cause a runtime error because the rightmost condition may generate a *DevideByZeroException* if the denominator is zero. This may not be caught by unit testing, if zero value occurs rarely. Theoretically, to avoid this error you should validate variable values and make sure that the value of the denominator is not zero before performing a division operation.

Case 3:

```
Dim objSales As Sales
If Not objSales Is Nothing And objSales.Total > 0 Then
      'The If block code
End If
```

Case 3 is a variation of Case 2, in which both conditions of the *if* statement work with an object variable. And, of course, when you deal with an object, it is important to check if it is instantiated to prevent a NullReferenceException or object variable not instantiated to an instance of an object error. In other words, you need to check if the object variable is *Nothing*, which you may want to do in the leftmost condition. But sometimes we may also want to check a certain object property value, which may be done in the rightmost condition. This scenario is presented in Case 3. In this code you want to run the body of the *if* block only if both conditions evaluate to true.

The main problem with Case 3 is that it presents a high risk of "Object reference not set to an instance of an object" exception. Because even though the leftmost condition may evaluate to false, the *And* operator will always execute the rightmost condition too, which may cause an exception if the object variable is not set. The first and, probably, the simplest solution is to have a nested *if* statement like the following:

```
Dim objSales As Sales
If Not objSales Is Nothing Then
        If objSales.Total > 0 Then
                        'The If block code
        End If
End If
```

In this case, the second condition, which tries to access the object variable, will be executed only if the first condition evaluates to true. However, there is good news. As you may know Visual Basic .NET offers two new logical operators: *AndAlso* and *OrElse* that can do some fantastic work for you. They are designed in such a way that they will not execute the rightmost condition if the leftmost condition evaluates to false.

Case 4:

```
Dim objSales As Sales
```

```
If Not objSales Is Nothing AndAlso objSales.Total > 0 Then
      'The If block code
End If


If Amt3 < Amt2 AndAlso Amt3 < (Amt2 \ Amt) Then
      'The If block code
End If
```

The code snippet presented in Case 4 uses the *AndAlso* operator, which can help to effectively eliminate potential errors described in Case 2 and Case 3. The AndAlso logical operator behavior is known as short-circuiting. It will short-circuit on the leftmost condition if it evaluates to false, which will guarantee that the rightmost condition will not be tested.

Type Casting Errors

The term *Type Casting* means practically the same as type conversion. Therefore, errors that we are going to talk about may happen when you try to convert one type to another. Remember we briefly discussed this topic in Chapter 4. Type casting can be performed by explicitly calling a certain conversion function; for example, *CType*. This is called *explicit* casting. Alternatively, you may try to simply assign one type to another and see if Visual Basic will do the conversion for you. This is known as *implicit* casting.

In the explicit casting, you are the one who controls the process and decides what conversion functions to use and if the conversion is valid and so on. In the implicit casting, you rely on Visual Basic to make all decisions for you and actually perform the operation. Let's now look at a couple of type casting scenarios that may cause potential errors.

Listing 1. Invalid type casting scenario.

```
Public Class ClassA
      'Class code
End Class


Public Class ClassB
      'Class code
End Class
Public Class Consumer
      Public Sub Test()
            Dim clsA As New ClassA
            Dim clsB As ClassB
            'The following will not compile
            clsB = CType(clsA, ClassB)    'Explicit casting
            clsB = clsA                           'Implicit
      casting
      End Sub
End Class
```

Listing 2. A valid type casting scenario.

```
Public Class ClassA
        Inherits ClassB
      'Class code
End Class
Public Class ClassB
      'Class code
```

```
End Class
Public Class Consumer
     Public Sub Test()
          Dim clsA As New ClassA
          Dim clsB As New ClassB
          'Both will compile
          clsB = CType(clsA, ClassB)     'Explicit casting
          clsB = clsA                              'Implicit
     casting
     End Sub
End Class
```

In Listing 1, we presented an invalid type casting scenario where ClassA object cannot be converted to ClassB because they have nothing in common and simply belong to different types. As you may see from our comments in code, both explicit and implicit casting attempts will not even compile.

Why should we talk about type casting if we cannot convert different types? Is it possible to convert different types? Yes, it is. In a very simplified explanation, type casting is possible if the target type bears some similarity to the destination type. For example, if one type inherits another type's implementation they become related and will have something in common. Code in Listing 2 is a modified version of Listing 1. In this case both explicit and implicit casting of ClassA to ClassB will compile and work fine because now ClassA inherits from ClassB. We can say that ClassA and ClassB are now related and bear similar digital genes. But they are not identical because ClassA may still have its own implementation, which may not be present in ClassB. This discussion should lead you to the following conclusion. When type casting is performed you need to make sure that the target type can be converted into a destination type. The implicit type conversion rules are stricter than those of the explicit casting. That's why when in certain cases the implicit casting is not permitted you can try to use the explicit casting to do the job.

Note:

There are at least three things that you need to keep in mind when you perform type casting:
- ➤ Check if the target type can be converted into the destination type.
- ➤ Verify if the objects are properly declared and istantiated.
- ➤ Check if the implicit casting can be used.

The type casting errors are a typical example of internal errors. They can cause runtime exceptions or data loss. These errors can be easily avoided if you pay enough attention to how you program your type conversion procedures. In most cases, the source of such errors can be minimized by doing appropriate type checking, type planning and, of course, proper type conversion.

After this brief introduction to the type casting errors let's consider a few examples. The first one is related to data exchange between controls and variables. You may have noticed that in Visual Basic .NET some control properties are defined as object. This makes them more flexible and actually allows assigning practically any data type to them. However, this flexibility comes with a price—type casting chores.

Let's take a *ComboBox* control as an example. Its *Items* collection property accepts an object. So when you assign a new value to it you should first convert it to an object. For example, if you want to add a string value you need to convert it to an object. And when you select that item you should convert it back from an object to a string. Thus, when data travels from one control to another or from a variable to a control you have to convert it twice if the type is different, first from a specific type to an object and then from an object to a specific type. We will illustrate this in two examples. Let's consider two data exchange tasks in which we will show the details of data transfer and type casting. The first task is to add *System.Drawing.Color* type to ComboBox's Items collection. The second task is to assign an item selected in a ComboBox to the form's BackColor property.

Populating a ComboBox

Theoretically, to add a Color type to a ComboBox you should do the following:

1. Declare an object variable. For example:

```
Dim objGeneric As Object
```

2. Convert a Color type to an object using the CType function:

```
objGeneric = CType(Color.Coral, Object)
```

3. Add the item to a ComboBox Items collection:

```
cboColors.Items.Add(objGeneric)
```

Alternatively, you can do it all in one statement as follows:

```
cboColors.Items.Add(CType(Color.Coral, Object))
```

But do you always have to do the above work? No, you don't. As usual there is good Visual Basic news. Visual Basic does all this work for you behind the scenes. Remember when you added items to a ComboBox in Lab 6? Here's the code:

```
cboColors.Items.Add(Color.BlueViolet)
cboColors.Items.Add(Color.Chocolate)
```

In the above code, you assigned two Color types to the ComboBox's *Items* collection directly leaving all the casting work to Visual Basic. Now let's look at the second process.

Assigning Values to a Form's BackColor Property

The second task in this type casting practice is to assign appropriate values to the form's BackColor property. This property is defined as *System.Drawing.Color* so trying to assign anything else should cause an error. If it's true then how were we able to successfully compile and run this code:

```
Me.BackColor = cboColors.SelectedItem
```

We think you know the answer. Yes, Visual Basic does implicit casting for you again. In this case, the *SelectedItem* property returns an object, which must be converted to a Color type. For comparison sake, we would like to point out that in C# the above code will produce a design time error: *"Cannot implicitly convert type 'object' to 'System.Drawing.Color'"* and will not compile. If you answered the above question can you also figure out how Visual Basic does the conversion? Note that the ComboBox's SelectedItem property returns an object. Therefore, all you need to do is convert an object to a Color type. And if you want to perform casting yourself then here's one of the ways to do it using the CType conversion function:

```
Me.BackColor = CType(cboColors.SelectedItem, Color)
```

So far, we covered some of the potential "what if" questions. But this discussion won't be complete if we leave out two more cases: null value and wrong type errors. We will discuss them in the next section and will also show you how to write code that can protect your application from invalid type casting errors.

Preventing Type Casting Errors

In the second data transfer task shown above, we assigned a value to the form's BackColor property, which expects *System.Drawing.Color* type. When we do so, we should be aware of two more cases that may cause invalid casting errors: null and wrong type values. What if the assigned value is Nothing (null)? As we already mentioned, variables must be initialized or instantiated. For example, if you use an object variable, which was not instantiated, you should get an error. Theoretically, in this case a NullReferenceException should be thrown. Remember, in Lab 6 you were asked to test a case when a user clicks on the *Change BackColor* button while nothing is selected in the ComboBox. If you performed that test, you should know that no error occurs because Visual Basic again does a lot of work for us.

How does Visual Basic handle this situation? First, it initializes all your variables at the time when you declare them. All value types are initialized to a default value. For example, *Integers* are set to 0, *Decimals* - to 0.0 and so on. All object variables are set to *Nothing*. Remember that an object variable initialized to *Nothing* holds a *null* reference and if you reference it in code a *NullReferenceException* will occur. But what if a wrong type value is assigned? For example, what happens if a user selects a string expression from the ComboBox and it is assigned to a form's BackColor property? Finally, Visual Basic will throw an *InvalidCastException*. Because no matter how powerful and patient it is, it cannot convert a String into a Color type. The error message should say: "Specified cast is not valid."

Let us remind you that in the non-.NET version of Visual Basic, in VB 6, this was defined as a *Type Mismatch* error. It is worth mentioning that *Type Mismatch* was the one-for-all error stamp used to describe conversion errors. Fortunately enough, in Visual Basic .NET you won't see it. The *InvalidCastException* is more specific and describes the error as an invalid cast. And although it does not pinpoint why the cast is invalid, it gives the following useful troubleshooting tips: "When casting from a number, the value must be a number less than infinity. Make sure that source type is convertible to destination type." The last tip is, probably, more important and can help you to investigate the source of the error.

Advanced Type Casting

Explicit type casting can be performed by direct or defined type casting. In the former you convert apples to apples. In the latter a conversion is performed according to a defined casting between the expression and the target type. To prevent errors in direct casting, you need to make sure that both the expression and the object parameters belong to exactly the same type. To check the expression type, you can use the *Type Of...Is* operator or the *GetType* method.

Listing 3. Direct casting.

```
Private Sub ConvertDataSet(ByVal objDS As Object)

    Dim objDataSet As DataSet
    If TypeOf objDS Is DataSet Then
            objDataSet = DirectCast(objDS, DataSet)
    Else
            'Handle the error
    End If
End Sub


Private Sub ConvertDataSet(ByVal objDS As Object)

    Dim objDataSet As DataSet
    Dim strTypeName As String
    strTypeName = objDS.GetType.FullName
```

```
If strTypeName.Equals("System.Data.DataSet") Then
      objDataSet = CType(objDS, DataSet)
Else
      'Handle the error
End If
```

```
End Sub
```

In Listing 3, we presented two versions of a subroutine procedure that accepts an object parameter, which is assumed to be a DataSet object. We use *CType* and *DirectCast* functions to perform type casting. For this type of conversion, both functions can be used. The only difference is that DirectCast is faster. To check the expression and the object parameter types we use the *TypeOf...Is* operator and the *GetType* method. These procedures illustrate a scenario where some class methods use object parameters, which should be converted into certain assumed types.

Listing 4. Defined casting.

```
Public Class Automobile
    Public Auto1 As String = "Auto"
    'Class code
End Class
```

```
Public Class SUV
      Inherits Automobile
      Public SUV1 As String = "SUV"
      'Class code
End Class
```

```
Public Class Dealer
    Public Sub TradeOff()
        Dim objSUV As New SUV
        Dim objAutomobile As New Automobile
        'Narrowing conversion. Compiles and runs
        objAutomobile = DirectCast(objSUV, Automobile)
        objAutomobile = CType(objSUV, Automobile)
            'Widening conversion.
        'Compiles but causes a runtime cast exception
        objSUV = CType(objAutomobile, SUV)
        objSUV = DirectCast(objAutomobile, SUV)
    End Sub
End Class
```

In defined casting, you convert based on the assumption that both the runtime expression object and the type object contain the casted type definition. However, both the source and the target may represent different types. We illustrated defined casting in Listing 4, which should bring you to the following conclusion: You can convert a derived type into a base type because the former contains the latter. In our example the SUV class contains a definition of the Automobile type. But you can't do the opposite. We will talk more about type casting in Chapter 11. In the following sections, we will discuss two types of numeric errors: overflow and precision errors.

Overflow Errors

Typically, an overflow error is a result of exceeding the numeric data type range capacity. Let's first look at when and how an overflow may occur. As we already mentioned, each numeric type is designed to hold a certain range of values. If you try to assign a value larger than the maximum amount, an overflow will occur. In other words, an *OverflowException* is thrown whenever you try to assign a numeric value that exceeds the value range of a corresponding numeric data type. For instance, a *Short* is designed to hold the maximum number of 32767. If you try to assign 32768 you will get an overflow error. Take a look at the code below:

```
Dim intNumber1 As Short
Dim lngNumber2 As Long
lngNumber2 = 32768      'Line 1
intNumber1 = 32767      'Line 2
intNumber1 = 32768      'Line 3
intNumber1 = lngNumber2 'Line 4
```

In the above code snippet, we declared two variables and assigned values to them. Note that a Short's maximum is 32,767 and a Long can store up to 2,147,483,647. Can you tell what's wrong with the above code? Lines 1 and 2 are fine. Line 3 will produce a compilation error. You may read this error message in the IntelliSense. It should run as follows: "Constant expression is not representable in type Short." This message may sound confusing but it actually means an overflow. It says that the specified numeric value cannot be represented by this type. Line 4 will compile fine but will produce an overflow error at runtime. You should see an *OverflowException* error message with the additional information saying "Arithmetic operation resulted in an overflow." You can identify and prevent overflow errors if you carefully plan and select your data types according to the principles discussed in Chapter 4. Although data type planning alone may eliminate most of the possible overflow errors you can additionally protect your application by performing maximum/minimum value checks before assigning values to variables. When you select a numeric data type you should make sure that the selected type is able to represent the expected value range. As for maximum/minimum value checking, you don't need to remember or search for numbers anywhere. Each numeric value type has MaxValue and MinValue properties, which can be used in test statements like these:

```
If intNumber1 > Short.MaxValue Then
        'Error handling code
End If
```

Or

```
If intNumber1 < Short.MinValue Then
        'Error handling code
End If
```

Numeric Precision Errors

Numeric precision errors may often occur when an application performs calculations with large numbers. The worst thing about these errors is that they are not detected before the application starts producing wrong calculation results. Precision errors may be caused by inadequate data type planning, loss of data in invalid conversions or data formatting. It could be a combination of the following: inadequate use of integers and decimals, wrong choice of decimal types, invalid number formatting and finally use of insufficient precision. Thus, in most cases the source of error may be classified into the following categories:

> ➤ Incorrect data type selection.
> ➤ Inadequate number formatting.
> ➤ Invalid numeric conversion.

In the first category, we deal with cases where integer data types are wrongly used to represent decimals. A loss of data will occur at the time when you assign a fractional numeric value to any integer type variable. The number will be rounded, which may further cause invalid calculation. If such variables are used in any arithmetic operations, the results may show a considerable fluctuation. Here's a simple example:

```
Dim intAmount As Integer
Dim intNewRate As Integer
Dim decResult As Decimal
Dim decOldRate As Decimal
intAmount = 24500
decOldRate = 7.85
intNewRate = decOldRate          'Line 3
decResult = intAmount * intNewRate    'produces 196,000.0
decResult = intAmount * decOldRate    'produces 192,325.0
```

In the above code, we declared four variables: two integers and two decimal types. This code will compile and run but will fail to produce correct calculation results. The problem lies in line 3, which swaps the rate values and while doing so rounds the value stored in a *decOldRate* variable to 8. As a result, calculations with the new and old rates will show a significant difference. Inadequate use of decimal data types may occur if the selected data type cannot represent the expected numeric precision. In other words, the type cannot hold enough decimal places. In Visual Basic there are three numeric data types that can represent decimals: Single, Double and Decimal. Single can hold 7, Double can store 15 and Decimal can represent 28 decimal places. This should be taken into consideration when you plan your data types.

Some numeric precision errors may be caused by inadequate number formatting. In Visual Basic number formatting functions, such as *Format*, *FormatCurrency* and *FormatPercent,* can be used to change the way numbers are displayed. For example, you can add a thousands separator, dollar or other currency signs and so on. When formatting numbers you may accidentally reduce the number of decimal places. That's where numeric precision errors can get into calculation. For instance, you may either by mistake or because of wrong instructions decide that you need only 4 out of 7 decimal places carried by a variable and run a formatting procedure that would truncate the rest. Type the following code into your test procedure and run it:

```
Dim sngNumber1 as Single
Dim sngNumber2 as Single
sngNumber1 = 375.8785639
sngNumber2 = Format(sngNumber1, "###.####")
```

After formatting the *sngNumber2* variable will store 375.8786. Pay attention that the above formatting statement not only truncates decimal places but also rounds the number.

Compile Options

We will conclude this chapter with recommendations of when and how to use project compile options to automatically detect errors, which we discussed in this chapter. Enabling these options may help you catch many unwanted errors at compilation time.

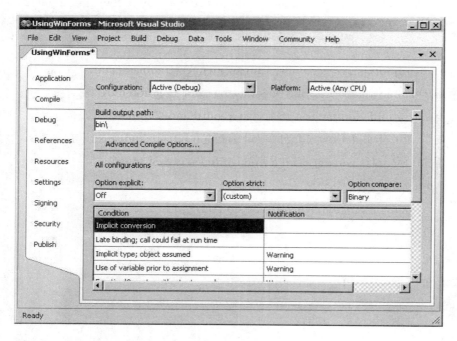

Figure 8.0 Visual Studio 2005 project Compile settings.

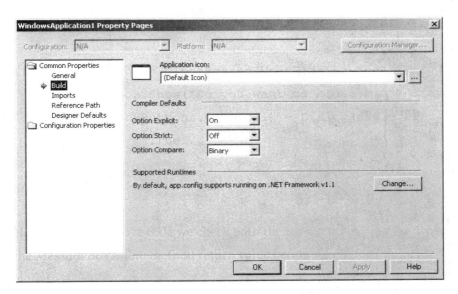

Figure 8.1 Visual Studio 2003 project Build settings.

Option Explicit

The *Option Explicit* setting forces you to explicitly declare all your variables. If undeclared variables are used, a compilation error will occur. It can also help you avoid spelling errors in variable names and confusions in variable scope. Also notice that with the Option Explicit turned off all your undeclared variables will default to an Object type. By default, Option Explicit is on.

Option Strict

Visual Basic's implicit conversion rules are liberal and allow a wide range of conversions. Some narrowing conversions, which we talked about in this chapter, where one data type is converted to another with less precision or smaller capacity may cause data loss or runtime errors. Many implicit conversion and type casting errors can be avoided by turning Option Strict on. Option Strict is almost like your internal QA department. It helps to enforce strong typing and disallows late binding. We will talk about late binding in Chapter 11. Furthermore, Option Strict improves overall performance and is strongly recommended. Note that by default, Option Strict is off.

Option Compare

Option Compare specifies the string comparison method, which can be *Binary* or *Text*. The default is Binary. In a very simplified explanation, setting Option Compare to Text will treat "BB" and "bb" as equal while Binary will treat and order them as different.

Note:

Compile options can be set in the following locations: in class code, in project property pages and in Visual Studio IDE.

In class code – write the option directives before the class code.
In project property pages – set options in Compile or Build sections.
In Visual Studio 2005 IDE – open Tools/Options/Projects and Solutions/VB Defaults.
In Visual Studio 2003 IDE – open Tools/Options/Projects/VB Defaults.

Keep in mind that you can set all compile options at the class, project or Visual Studio IDE level. Setting in Visual Studio IDE will make them effective for all projects. Setting in project property pages will spread them to all classes in the project. Finally, you can set or override compile options by including the corresponding directives in each class code.

Summary

All application errors may be classified into two main groups: internal and external errors. External errors may be caused by invalid user actions, application dependencies, infrastructure issues, enterprise environment conditions such as file systems, database and network status and so on. An application cannot prevent external errors but you can write code that will properly handle them. Internal errors are the result of programming mistakes, flaws in logical decisions, improper data type planning and type casting. Understanding application runtime errors may help to avoid them altogether or properly handle them. You can automatically filter out a lot of errors before or at compilation time by using compile options such as Option Explicit and Option Strict.

Lab 8: The SlideShow Project

SlideShow

In this Project:

You will create the SlideShow program that allows users to view pictures pre-grouped into albums. This lab will allow you to consolidate your skills in programming a PictureBox, ComboBox, populating and reading arrays and using control anchoring methods to provide dynamic resizing of controls at runtime.

Introduction

The goal of this project is to create a virtual picture album, which will allow users to continuously view images in a selected album using the Next and Previous buttons. To test the program, you need to create a few child folders under the main picture folder. It is assumed that each sub-folder inside the parent folder will represent a single photo album. When the program starts, it needs to know where the main picture folder is located. It then searches that folder and builds a list of sub-folders, which it loads into a *cboAlbumns* ComboBox. When a user selects an album from the dropdown menu, the images in the corresponding folder are enlisted internally and thus made ready for viewing.

Create a New Project

- ➢ Create the *Lab8* project folder.
- ➢ Open Visual Studio .NET
- ➢ Create a new Windows Application project.
- ➢ Set the project Location to C:\Labs\Lab8.
- ➢ Set the project Name to *SlideShow*.

Design User Interface

Add Controls

Add controls to the SlideShow form and set their properties according to Table 1.

Table 1. The SlideShow form controls.

Control Type	Property Name	Value
Form	Text	Slide Show Program
-/-	StartPosition	CenterScreen
GroupBox	Text	Slide Show
-/-	Anchor	Top, Left, Right, Bottom
Label	Text	Select Album:
-/-	Anchor	Top, Left
ComboBox	Name	cboAlbums
-/-	Anchor	Top, Left
Button	Name	btnPrev
-/-	Text	&Previous
-/-	Anchor	Top, Right
Button	Name	btnNext
-/-	Text	&Next
-/-	Anchor	Top, Right
PictureBox	Name	PictureBox1
-/-	Anchor	Top, Left, Right, Bottom
Label	Name	Default
-/-	Text	Status:
-/-	Anchor	Bottom, Left
Label	Name	lblStatus
-/-	Text	Not Ready
-/-	Anchor	Bottom, Left
Button	Name	btnClose
-/-	Text	&Close

-/-	Anchor	Bottom, Right

When designing the SlideShow form, keep in mind that in this project you will code for dynamic resizing of controls as a response to form resizing. This is done by using the control's Anchor property, which is discussed in the next section.

Anchoring Controls

The *Anchor* property allows tying the control to one or more sides of the form. When the form is resized the anchored control will keep the same distance from the side (or sides) it is bound to at design time.

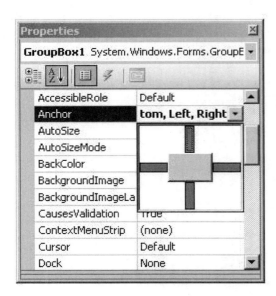

Figure 1. The GroupBox Anchor property.

You can anchor a control to a form or any other container control; for example, a GroupBox or a Panel. Various anchoring combinations will either fix a control to a certain form corner or stretch it. For example, if you anchor to the Top and Left, the control is "glued" to the top-left corner. If you anchor to the Left and Right, the

287

control will be stretched when the form is expanded width-wise. Note that by default, the Anchor property is set to Top and Left, which makes it tied to the upper left corner of the form. In Figure 1, you can see a GroupBox control, which is used in this project, anchored to all four sides.

Anchoring Effects

When setting the Anchor property you may want to divide all of your controls into two categories: fixed size and expandable. Normally, all your Buttons, Checkboxes, and Radio Buttons should belong to a fixed size category, meaning you don't want them to expand if the form is enlarged. All containers such as GroupBox, PictureBox, TabControl, SplitContainer, FlowLayoutPanel, TableLayoutPanel and Panel should be in the expandable category.

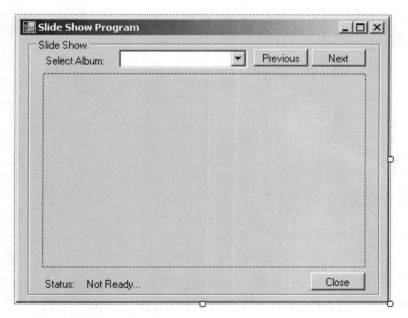

Figure 2. The SlideShow form.

If you examine the SlideShow form controls properties presented in Table 1, you will find that almost all controls on the form are fixed and anchored to a certain form corner except the GroupBox and the PictureBox. You want these two controls to resize in response to form resizing. Your complete SlideShow form should look like the one shown in Figure 2.

Write Code

Write the imports directive and declare the form variables as shown below.

```
Imports System.IO
Private m_objDicAlbums As New Dictionary(Of String, String())
Private m_intCurrentImage As Integer
Private m_strImgArrCurrent As String
Private m_strMyAlbumsFolder As String
```

Write Initialization Procedures

In this project, you have three initialization procedures: the *PopulateAlbum-Collection, CreateAlbumFiles* and *PopulateAlbumsDropDown*. The PopulateAlbum-Collection procedure reads the path to the parent images folder and extracts the albums list. Then it calls the CreateAlbumFiles procedure to populate a string array with image file paths. The PopulateAlbumsDropDown procedure populates the ComboBox with folder names that would represent virtual albums. Please create the "Initialization Procedures" code region and enter code shown in Listing 1.

Listing 1. Initialization procedures.

```
#Region "Initialization Procedures"
Private Sub PopulateAlbumCollection(ByVal
```

```
                         strAlbumFolderName As String)
   Dim objImgDirectory As DirectoryInfo
   Dim objDirArr As DirectoryInfo()
   Dim objDirInfo As DirectoryInfo
   Dim j As Integer
   Dim strArr As String() = Nothing
   Dim strFoderName As String
   Dim i As Integer, k As Integer
Try
   objImgDirectory = New DirectoryInfo(strAlbumFolderName)
   objDirArr = objImgDirectory.GetDirectories()
   For j = 0 To objDirArr.Length - 1
      objDirInfo = objDirArr(j)
      CreateAlbumFiles(objDirInfo.FullName, strArr)
      i = objDirInfo.FullName.LastIndexOf("\")
      k = objDirInfo.FullName.Length
      strFoderName = objDirInfo.FullName.Substring _
      (i + 1, k - i - 1)
      m_objDicAlbums.Add(strFoderName, strArr)
   Next
Catch ex As Exception
   MessageBox.Show(ex.Message)
End Try
End Sub
Private Sub CreateAlbumFiles(ByVal strAlbumFolderName As _
                   String, ByRef strArrFiles As String())
   Dim objDirInfo As DirectoryInfo
   Dim arrFilesInfo() As FileInfo
```

```vb
    Dim objFile As FileInfo
    Dim j As Integer
    Dim strArr As String()
Try
    objDirInfo = New DirectoryInfo(strAlbumFolderName)
    arrFilesInfo = objDirInfo.GetFiles()
    j = arrFilesInfo.Length
    ReDim strArr(j)
    For j = 0 To arrFilesInfo.Length - 1
        objFile = arrFilesInfo(j)
        strArr(j) = objFile.FullName
    Next
    strArrFiles = strArr
Catch ex As Exception
    MessageBox.Show(ex.Message)
End Try
End Sub


Private Sub PopulateAlbumsDropDown()
Try
    Dim objDicKeys As Dictionary(Of String, _
    String()).KeyCollection = m_objDicAlbums.Keys
    For Each s As String In objDicKeys
        cboAlbums.Items.Add(s)
    Next
Catch ex As Exception
    MessageBox.Show(ex.Message)
End Try
```

End Sub
#End Region

Write Private Methods

Create the "Private Methods" code region and type code shown in Listing 2.

Listing 2. Private methods.

```
#Region "Private Methods"
Private Function GetCurrentImage(ByVal strDirection
                             As String) As Integer
   Dim intCount As Integer
Try
   If m_strImgArrCurrent Is Nothing Then
      MessageBox.Show("Please select albom to view")
      Return -1
   End If
   intCount = m_strImgArrCurrent.Length
   Select Case strDirection
   Case "PREV"
   If m_intCurrentImage > 0 Then
   m_intCurrentImage = m_intCurrentImage - 1
   End If
   Case "NEXT"
   If m_intCurrentImage < m_strImgArrCurrent.Length - 1 Then
      m_intCurrentImage = m_intCurrentImage + 1
   Else
      m_intCurrentImage = 0
```

```
    End If
    End Select
Catch ex As Exception
    MessageBox.Show(ex.Message)
End Try


End Function
#End Region
```

Write the Form Event Handlers

Create the "Event Handlers" code region and enter code from Listing 3.

Listing 3. Form event handlers.

```
#Region "Event Handlers"
Private Sub btnClose_Click(ByVal sender As Object, ByVal _
                    e As EventArgs) Handles btnClose.Click
    Me.Close()
End Sub


Private Sub Form1_Load(ByVal sender As Object, ByVal _
e As EventArgs) Handles MyBase.Load
    m_strMyAlbumsFolder = "c:\Labs\Lab8\MyAlbums"
    PopulateAlbumCollection(m_strMyAlbumsFolder)
    PopulateAlbumsDropDown()
End Sub
Private Sub btnNext_Click(ByVal sender As Object, ByVal _
                    e As EventArgs) Handles btnNext.Click
```

```
        If GetCurrentImage("NEXT") = -1 Then
            Exit Sub
        End If
        PictureBox1.ImageLocation = m_strImgArrCurrent _
                                    (m_intCurrentImage)
End Sub


Private Sub btnPrev_Click(ByVal sender As Object, ByVal _
                   e As EventArgs) Handles btnPrev.Click
        If GetCurrentImage("PREV") = -1 Then
            Exit Sub
        End If
        PictureBox1.ImageLocation = m_strImgArrCurrent _
                                    (m_intCurrentImage)
End Sub


Private Sub cboAlbums_SelectedIndexChanged(ByVal sender _
                As Object, ByVal e As EventArgs) Handles _
                    cboAlbums.SelectedIndexChanged
Try
        m_intCurrentImage = 0
        m_strImgArrCurrent = m_objDicAlbums _ (cboAlbums.
        SelectedItem.ToString)
        lblStatus.Text = "Showing " & _        cboAlbums.
        SelectedItem.ToString
Catch ex As Exception
        MessageBox.Show(ex.Message)
End Try
```

```
End Sub
#End Region
```

Please remember that you need not type long event handler subroutine wrapper lines. You may use one of the methods shown in previous labs to have the Visual Basic code editor type them for you. For example, for all button click event handlers, double-click the corresponding button. For form load event handler, double-click an empty space on the form.

Test and Debug

To prepare the application for testing, you need to create a few album folders that should be placed in a parent folder called *MyPhotoAlbums*. Then copy a few images into each album folder. Hard code the path to the parent folder in the *m_ strMyAlbumsFolder* variable in the form load event procedure:

```
m_strMyAlbumsFolder = "c:\Labs\Lab8\MyPhotoAlbums"
```

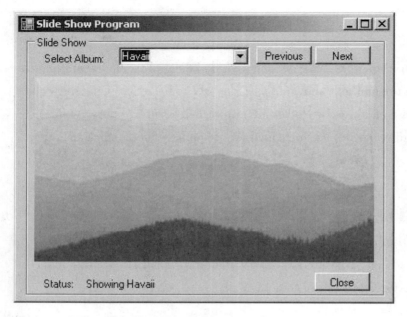

Figure 3. The SlideShow program at runtime.

Test the Application

- Press F5 to run the application. Check if the form initialization works as expected. Verify if the dropdown list box is populated with album folder names from the parent folder.

- Select an album and check if the status label displays the selected album name.

- Test the Next button functionality. If you successfully passed the first two tests you should be ready to test the Next button. Select any album and click Next. The first image in the selected album folder should be displayed. Continue clicking until you reach the end of the list. After the last image you should get one empty picture and then the first picture again.

- Test the Previous button. It is similar to the Next button except for one thing. When you reach the first picture in the list, further clicking should produce no effect.

- Test the form and controls resizing functionality. This is the coolest test in your project. Perform this only when an image is displayed. If you set the controls Anchor property correctly, you should get the following form behavior: When the form is enlarged, all fixed controls should stay attached to the corresponding form corners while the GroupBox and the PictureBox should get larger proportionally to the form expansion. If you try to make the form smaller you will see that at a certain point your controls will run onto each other and the form will become distorted. That's because the Anchoring functionality is not good enough to protect us from this effect. There is not much that can be done to remedy this issue except preventing the user from decreasing the form too much. This can be done by setting the form's minimum size. You should first find out the minimum size of the form at which the controls are displayed correctly. Try to resize the form in your Form Designer window and record the minimum acceptable width and height. In our test, the minimum width was 410 pixels and the minimum height - 130 pixels. Once you have the numbers, set the form's MinimumSize property accordingly.

Congratulations! You have successfully completed this project.

Extra Credit Task

You can enhance this program considerably by adding a browse button that will allow a user to navigate to a parent images folder that should contain the album folders. To implement this functionality you need to use an *OpenFileDialog* class to show the Open File Dialog box, then read the selected folder name and assign it to the m_ strMyAlbumsFolder string variable. Good luck!

Chapter 9: Error Handling

Error Handling

In this Chapter:

You will learn application error handling techniques. To deal with runtime errors, a program should have code that traps and properly handles them. This can save an application from crashing and at the same time may allow users to continue their work. However, if there are no error handlers a program failure is handled by the .NET runtime, in which case the application may be simply shutdown and the users won't have a chance to correct errors or save their work. In this chapter, we will show you how to code application error handlers.

Chapter 9 at a Glance

- ➤ The Role of Error Handlers
- ➤ How to Set Error Traps
- ➤ Understanding Exceptions
- ➤ Exception Types
- ➤ Exception Class Properties
- ➤ Coding Catch Blocks
- ➤ Nesting Error Handlers
- ➤ Locally Handling Errors
- ➤ Using Multiple Catch Blocks
- ➤ Using Finally Blocks

The Role of Error Handlers

When a program runs there is always a chance that something unacceptable or illegal can happen. A well-designed program should have protection from both expected and unexpected errors. In most cases this can be done by adding error handlers to application procedures. To better understand the role of error handlers, it is essential to know how .NET runtime reacts to errors. Whenever an error occurs, the CLR stops a normal execution process and investigates the problem. Then it performs the magic of mapping the error to the best matching exception type, which we briefly discussed in Chapter 8. It then wraps all information related to the error into a corresponding exception object. If a procedure where an error occurred happens to have an error handler, the exception object is passed to its Catch block where the information contained in it can be read and the error handled. However, if there is no error handler in the executing procedure, the CLR will check the calling procedure and will keep searching until it finds one. If none is found, the error will be handled by the CLR itself, which may result in showing a generic error message and shutting down the application.

As we mentioned earlier, exceptions come in a variety of flavors. The FCL contains numerous exception classes designed to represent various error types. For instance, errors related to database activities are packaged into *OracleException*, *OdbcException* or *SqlException* according to the database type. The *FileNotFoundException* will be thrown whenever you provide an invalid file name or file path to a file open procedure. If you try to assign a numeric value that exceeds the maximum value of a data type, you may get an *OverflowException*. We will discuss exception types in more detail in the Exception Types section.

Think of an exception as a type of accident that stops normal execution flow and requires immediate attention. Obviously, shutting down a program is a severe punishment. If you ask, can an application where an error occurred be given a chance to rehabilitate itself? The answer is yes, it can. Although an exception is always thrown whenever an error occurs, the CLR is smart enough to give an application a chance to correct the problem and if necessary continue running in normal mode. This mechanism is activated and enabled only if there are error handlers in the application code. Thus, to take advantage of this great feature, you need to write proper error handling code in each application procedure. Now let's look at how the error handlers should be coded.

How to Set Error Traps

A simple error handler may consist of two parts: the *Try* and the *Catch* blocks. Figuratively speaking, the try block may be viewed as an error trap and the catch block as a lightning rod or a send box that neutralizes the danger.

When you create an error handler, you actually do two things. First, you enclose your mischievous code in a special try block that signals to the runtime that code in this block is error aware. Next, you attach a special section of code called a catch block to it. Code written in the catch block will be executed only if an error occurs in any statement enclosed in the try block. Thus, the presence of Try-Catch blocks in a procedure sends a message to the CLR that says: if any error occurs in the try block, execute code in the catch block. What code you write in the catch block is entirely up to you. We will talk more about this in the Coding Catch Blocks section.

Note that after code in the catch block is executed, the CLR, figuratively speaking, washes its hands of all the problems related to the error. In fact, the application is considered out of error and back in normal status. Therefore, it may continue normal code execution. How the application behaves after the error largely depends on the code written in the catch block. You can show a message to the user and shut down the application or correct the error and continue as normal. Let's now look at a simple error handler, which is designed to process general exceptions.

Case 1:

```
Dim objProduct As Product
Dim intProductID As Integer
Try
      intProductID = objProduct.ProductID
Catch ex As Exception
          MessageBox.Show(ex.Message)
End Try
```

In Case 1, the try block contains a statement that attempts to access an object variable before it is instantiated, which should cause a NullReferenceException with the notorious error message: "Object reference not set to an instance of an object." When this happens, the execution will jump to the catch block, where the MessageBox's Show method is called to display the error message. This problem can be easily fixed by adding an object instantiation statement, in which case a modified code should look like the following:

Case 2:

```
Dim objProduct As Products
Dim intProductID As Integer
Try
      objProduct = New Products()
      intProductID = objProduct.ProductID
Catch ex As Exception
          MessageBox.Show(ex.Message)
End Try
```

The Case 2 code represents a general exception error handler. It is good to catch any type of exception thrown by the .NET runtime. But handling all errors in exactly the same way or executing the same catch block code may not always meet the specifications of your project. What if you need to handle each error type differently? In other words, can catch blocks be specialized to capture certain types of errors only? Yes they can and we will show you how in the next section.

Exception Types

In Visual Basic .NET, the exception generation mechanism is designed to shoot various errors with a relatively high level of precision. As we already mentioned, when an error occurs the runtime will do its best to match it with a known error type and then throw a corresponding exception. The question is can we create error traps that are specifically designed to catch certain exception types? Yes, we can. In fact, creating such specialized exception handlers is simple enough. All you need to do is declare a catch block exception object variable as a specific exception type. If you do so the catch block will "catch" exceptions of a certain type only. For example, we can rewrite the Case 2 error handler to specifically treat the NullReferenceException as follows:

Case 3:

```
Dim objProduct As Products
Dim intProductID As Integer
Try
      objProduct = New Products()
      intProductID = objProduct.ProductID
Catch ex As NullReferenceException
      MessageBox.Show(ex.Message)
```

```
End Try
```

In Case 3, we created an error handler, which is specialized to catch null reference exceptions only. However, in this case all other errors will be totally ignored and will automatically turn into unhandled errors, which is equal to not having an error handler. Of course, you want to avoid unhandled errors at any cost. This problem can be solved by always having one general exception catch block along with a specialized catch block. This way you may have any number of specialized catch blocks and one general exception catch block, which should handle errors that are not caught by specialized catch blocks. Case 4 is an enhanced version of Case 3, where both specialized and general catch blocks are implemented:

Case 4:

```
Dim objProduct As Products
Dim intProductID As Integer
Try
        objProduct = New Products()
        intProductID = objProduct.ProductID
Catch ex As NullReferenceException
        MessageBox.Show(ex.Message)
Catch ex As Exception
        MessageBox.Show(ex.Message)
End Try
```

Thus, to properly handle all errors you need to write appropriate error handling code in each catch block otherwise it will make no sense to have multiple catch blocks. We will talk about this in the Using Multiple Catch Blocks section.

To summarize what we've discussed so far, let's recap. You may code your application to deal with two general error categories: expected and unexpected errors. Unexpected errors are typically those that you cannot predict or anticipate. They should be handled by general exception catch blocks. Expected errors are those that you can foresee based on your analysis and the presence of code that may cause them. To properly handle these errors you may need to have specialized catch blocks. Now that you are armed with all the necessary tactical skills of how to trap and destroy errors, it's time to learn the exception class properties. You will certainly need them to get the error description, the error source and other error parameters.

Exception Class Properties

In .NET, all exception types derive from the base *Exception* class. Thus, normally you should expect each exception class to contain a set of common properties and a smaller number of exception-specific properties. For example, the *Message* and the *Source* properties are common to all exception types. However, the *FileName* property is present only in the FileNotFoundException class. To write smart error handlers, it may not be enough to include exception-specific catch blocks, you should also make use of exception properties that can provide additional error information.

For more advanced error handling, you may also need to know the source of the error, the call stack list and so on. All this information and much more can be obtained from the exception class properties. Let's look at some common exception class properties and their usage.

Message Property

The *Message* property gives a general error description and is most often used. Normally, it carries enough information about what went wrong. For example, if the file not found exception is thrown, it will return an error message like this: *Could not find file: FilePath*. It means that the error description contains the actual file path and name. In case of a division by zero error, the error message will run like this: "Arithmetic operation resulted in an overflow." You can add all examples of type casting errors to this that we discussed in Chapter 8.

TargetSite Property

The *TargetSite* property uses the *System.Reflection* classes to provide detailed information about the method where the error occurred. This includes the method name, attributes, arguments, scope and much more. The *TargetSite.DeclaringType* property goes even further: it gets the class name that declared the method.

```
Private Sub GetData()
    Dim intAmount As Int16
    Dim lngAmount As Int64
Try
    lngAmount = 32798
    intAmount = lngAmount
Catch ex As Exception
    Dim strModuleName As String
    Dim strMethodName As String
    Dim strClassName As String
    strModuleName = ex.TargetSite.Module.Name
    'Will return: WindowsApplication1.exe
    strMethodName = ex.TargetSite.Name
    'Will return: GetData
    strClassName = ex.TargetSite.DeclaringType.Name
    'Will return: Form1
End Try
End Sub
```

The catch block code in the code snippet above shows how you can extract the executing assembly name, the method name and the method class name from the exception object. It is assumed that the application and the form bear the default names: WindowsApplication1 and Form1.

Source Property

The *Source* property can be used to get the application name where the error occurred. This property may be useful in a multiple applications environment or when you need to get the application.

StackTrace Property

The *StackTrace* property is a string representation of frames on the call stack. It returns a list of all procedure names that were called prior to the procedure that caused the error. Note that the procedure where the error occurred will be shown at the bottom of the list.

HelpLink Property

This property can be used to get or set the help file name associated with the exception if you create such files. It can also be used to provide users with detailed help or FAQ information related to certain errors.

Coding Catch Blocks

A catch block is a place where the error is neutralized. The code you will write here will largely depend on your error handling strategy, project specifications and your preferences. Thus, there are no specific rules that may restrict your creativity. But for the purposes of this discussion, we will distinguish several catch block coding approaches that are shown in the following sections.

Exception Object Variable

Normally you will begin your catch block coding with the exception object variable declaration. Here you will have two options. As we mentioned earlier you can choose to declare a general exception or a specific exception type. The object variable name should confirm to normal variable naming rules. Note that when you type the keyword *Try* and press Enter, Visual Basic will complete the Try-Catch block declaration for you. By default, a general exception variable is created. From a tactical perspective, code written in a catch block can implement one of the following error handling approaches: locally handling errors, re-throwing the same exception or throwing a new exception.

Error Handling Tactics:

> ➤ Locally handling errors
> ➤ Re-throwing the same exception.
> ➤ Throwing a new exception.

Locally Handling Errors

If you decide to locally handle the error in your catch block, you would normally extract the error message and other necessary information from the exception object variable and make a decision as to how to handle the error. Your choices may differ. For example, you may show it to the user, send email alerts to a support team or log it. You may also direct a user to a help file associated with this particular type of exception if one exists. Of course, you may use a lot of other solutions. But the main outcome of this approach is that you actually suppress the error at its target site.

By doing so you help to move the application out of the exception status and allow the calling procedure and possibly the application in general to continue normal execution.

Re-Throwing the Same Exception

Alternatively, you may use your error handler to capture the exception and then re-throw it to the calling procedure. In this approach, you actually decline to take responsibility to handle the error and delegate this work to the calling procedure. If you feel that the terms calling and called procedure puzzle you, please find more information in Chapter 12. It is obvious that just re-throwing the same exception does not make much sense. In fact, by doing so you would waste application resources because the same exception would be thrown twice. However, it would make sense to do it if before re-throwing the exception you plan to do some cleanup and other critically important work. Case 5 is an example of re-throwing the same exception:

Case 5:

```
Public Sub TestProcedure()
Try
      'Procedure code
Catch ex as Exception
      Throw ex
End Try
End Sub
```

This code declares a general exception object variable *ex* and then calls the *Throw* method to re-throw it. How does the .NET runtime handle situations when the same exception is re-thrown? It will behave as if the exception was generated in the calling procedure and will execute its catch block code. When you use this approach please remember that re-throwing exceptions is a considerable performance hit..

Throwing a New Exception

The third error handling strategy is based on throwing a new exception. The use of this approach may be driven by a combination of two reasons. The first reason may be similar to the re-throw strategy where you do not want to take responsibility to handle the error and want to delegate this role to the calling procedure. The second motive may be determined by a number of factors; for example, it can simply be a necessity to add additional information to the original error message. Additionally, you may want to instantiate and throw a totally different exception type. Here's an example of throwing a new exception:

Case 6:
```
Private Sub ExecStoredProc(ByVal strStoredProcName As String)
      Dim strParam1 As String
Try
      ExecuteStoredProcedure(strStoredProcName, strParam1)
Catch ex As Exception
      Throw New Exception(ex.Message & " " & strStoredProcName
      & " " & strParam1
End Try
End Sub
```

We have thus far discussed the basic error handling techniques that you would most probably use very often. In the rest of this chapter, we will cover three more advanced error handling techniques: nested error handlers, serial task error handlers, multiple Catch blocks and the use of the *Finally* blocks.

Nested Error Handlers

The term nested in this context is used to denote cases where one error handler is placed inside the other. Why would you consider nesting error handlers? There can be a variety of reasons. Let's take the most typical one. In real-world projects, you may need to deal with certain expected errors on an individual statement or a block of code level rather then a procedure level. You can achieve this by enclosing a particular line of code or a block of code into a dedicated Try - Catch block.

This approach is typically used to handle some parts of code that have a high potential to cause an error. Also, it may be applied to some mission-critical procedure calls or when running other important parts of procedure code. Therefore, in this case you may end up having nested Try - Catch blocks in one procedure. By using nested Try - Catch blocks you actually created something known as an in-line error handler. Thus, any inner Try-Catch block in a nested error handler may be considered an in-line error handler because it will handle errors for certain lines or parts of code. An example of a nested error handler is presented in Case 7:

Case 7:

```
Private Sub TestProcedure()
Try
     'The outer try block code
     Try
          'The inner try block code
     Catch ex As Exception
          'The in-line error handling
     End Try
     'The outer try block code continued
Catch ex As Exception
```

```
      `Procedure level error handling
End Try
End Sub
```

In case 7, the Try – Catch blocks are nested. The outer try block is a procedure level error trap. If an error is generated in it, the procedure level catch block will be used to handle it. The inner try bock is an in-line error trap. Its catch block is designed to individually handle in-line errors. Thus, if an error occurs in the inner try block its own catch block will be used to process the error. The in-line error handlers allow to not only individually handle certain types of errors, but also continue code execution in the procedure.

Error Handling in Loops

There is a special case where in-line error handling may be very useful. If you need to process multiple records in a loop and want to keep on even if one or more records throw exceptions, because of bad data quality or other reasons, you may want to use an in-line error handler. Here's what may happen if you do not use an inner Try -Catch block in this case. If an exception is thrown in the loop the iteration will be halted and the procedure level catch block executed. This may cause a number of problems. First, you may not know where the loop stopped. Second, to complete the job you may need to start the loop from the beginning. Here's a simple example. Let's say you need to build a procedure that sends the same email message to a group of recipients and you want to make sure that even if exceptions are thrown the process is continued until the end of the list is reached.

Case 8:

```
Private Sub SendMessages(ByVal EmailList as String())
```

```
Try
    For i = 0 to EMailList.Length - 1
        Try
            SendEmail(EmailList(i))
        Catch ex As Exception
            LogError(ex.Message & " Invalid address " &

                    EmailList(i))
        End Try
    Next
Catch ex As Exception
    'Procedure error handling code
End Try
End Sub
```

Case 8 represents a subroutine that sends email messages calling the SendEmail
function in a loop using a pre-built list. If the function fails, the error is logged by
calling the *LogError* method and processing is continued. In this case we assume that
the *SendEmail* method will re-throw its exceptions.

Using Multiple Catch Blocks

The main reason why you would consider using multiple catch blocks is to be able
to individually handle each specific exception in a dedicated catch block. Typically,
multiple catch block error handlers are written on a procedure level. However, there
is nothing to stop you from using this technique in in-line error handlers as well.
Here's an example of a procedure level error handler that implements two specialized
and one general exception catch blocks:

Case 9:

```
Private Function TestProcedure(ByVal strFileName) As Boolean
     Try
             'Procedure code
             Return True
     Catch ex As NullReferenceException
             LogErr(ex.Message)
             Return False
     Catch ex As FileNotFoundException
             LogErr(ex.FileName & " " & ex.Source & " " &

                    ex.Message)
             Return False
     Catch ex As Exception
             Throw ex
End Try
End Sub
```

In the *TestProcedure* method shown in Case 9, there are two specialized and one general catch blocks. Both specialized catch blocks suppress the error, log the error description and return a failure code to the calling procedure. The general catch block re-throws the same exception. When you create multiple catch blocks, you should keep in mind that the order of catch blocks matter. A general exception catch block must always be the last because if you place it in front of others it will intercept all errors and leave no work for specialized exception blocks.

Using Finally Blocks

A Try-Catch block can be augmented by an optional *Finally* block. Code placed in a finally block is always executed irrespective if an error occurs or not. There may be at least two reasons why you would think about using the finally block:

> ➤ To handle situations when an exception is thrown from a catch block.
> ➤ To guarantee the execution of critically important code.

A Try - Catch mechanism is good to handle exceptions but it is not perfect. You can write any code in a catch block; for example, to log error details, cleanup, send alerts and so on. But what if your catch block itself throws an exception. If this happens, there is a good chance that part of your catch block error handling code will not be executed and the execution will leave the current procedure and jump into the calling procedure catch block. In this case you may fail to properly handle the error and do a necessary cleanup. The solution is simple: use the *Finally* block and put all of your critically important code into it.

Technically, the finally block is the third member of Try – Catch error handling mechanism. It is executed in any case whether an error in the corresponding procedure occurred or not. Hence, you can use it whenever it is necessary to guarantee code execution. What kind of code may be a good candidate for a finally block? It can be anything such as close database connections, file handles, data readers and so on. Case 10 is an example of a finally block that is used to guarantee database-related cleanup.

Case 10:

```
Imports System.Data.SqlClient
Private Sub ExecuteDateReader(ByVal strSqlQuery As String, _
```

```
                        ByVal strConString As String)
    Dim objSqlConn As SqlConnection = Nothing
    Dim objSqlCom As SqlCommand = Nothing
    Dim objSqlDataReader As SqlDataReader = Nothing
Try
    objSqlConn = New SqlConnection(strConString)
    objSqlConn.Open()
    objSqlCom = New SqlCommand(strSqlQuery, objSqlConn)
    objSqlDataReader = objSqlCom.ExecuteReader()
    'Use DataReader
    'Normal cleanup:
    objSqlDataReader.Close()
    objSqlDataReader = Nothing
    objSqlConn.Close()
    objSqlConn = Nothing
Catch ex As Exception
    LogErr("Application=" & ex.Source & " Method name=" & _
    ex.TargetSite.Name & " Error detail=" & ex.Message)
Finally
    If Not objSqlDataReader Is Nothing Then
        objSqlDataReader.Close()
        objSqlDataReader = Nothing
    End If
    If Not objSqlConn Is Nothing Then
        objSqlConn.Close()
        objSqlConn.Dispose()
        objSqlConn = Nothing
    End If
```

```
End Try
End Sub
```

In Case 10, we loaded the finally block with the database connection and data reader cleanup work. If you use a finally block, you may not need to write cleanup code twice, once in the try block and then in the finally block. If you take a close look at the code in Case 10, you may notice that cleanup is in both places. However, there is a little nuance in the code. In the try block cleanup, we set objects to null. Thus, in normal execution the finally block will not execute this code again because it checks the object variables status.

To complete our discussion of error handling we would like to point out that in Visual Basic .NET try blocks must have either a catch or a finally block. If neither is present your code will not compile and you will get an error like the following: *"Try must have at least one Catch or Finally."* In case you would like to experiment with Try-Catch-Finally blocks, please remember that although it is legal to replace catch blocks with finally, the absence of the former will cause a runtime error. After code in finally is executed, common language runtime will terminate the application. Furthermore, it is obvious enough that having a try block without a corresponding catch block doesn't make sense and is equal to not having an error handler in the procedure at all.

Summary

Error handling is a very important part of your application coding. If properly done, it allows you to overcome a critical situation gracefully. Executable code in each and every procedure in the application should have an appropriate error handler. In most cases it is sufficient to have general exception catch blocks that are good enough to respond to any type of exception thrown by the .NET runtime. Additionally, catch blocks may be configured to react to specific exception types. Using specialized catch blocks allows creating individual error handlers for each error type. Finally, nesting Try - Catch blocks gives additional power to capture errors caused by certain statements or blocks of code and creates the so-called in-line error handlers.

Lab 9: The Error Handlers Project

Error Handlers

In this Project:

You will consolidate your knowledge of error handlers discussed in Chapter 9. Your task will be to write error handlers for most procedures in one of the previous lab projects: the *WinFormsProperties* project.

Modify the Project

Here you will modify the project that you created in Lab 6. Therefore, first make sure that you have the project source code. If you did not do Lab 6, you need to create it first and then return to this lab. Open the WinFormsProperties project in Visual Studio. You will add error handling code to almost all existing application procedures.

Write Code

Error handlers that you will write in this project are divided into two categories. In form initialization procedures you will simply write all errors to a form level string variable. Since all form initialization procedures are called from the form load event, i.e., before the form is displayed to the user, it would not make sense to interrupt the process to show an error message at that time. In all button click event procedures you will show error messages as soon as the error occurs.

Form Initialization Procedures

Write general exception error handlers in the following form initialization procedures: *PopulateCursors*, *PopulateColors*, *PopulateWindowStates* and *Form1_ Load*. Also, add a form level string variable declaration to store errors. Please type code shown in Listing 1 into your project.

Listing 1. Error handlers in initialization procedures.

```
Private m_Errors As String
Private Sub PopulateCursors()
Try
        cboCursors.Items.Add(Cursors.Cross)
        cboCursors.Items.Add(Cursors.Hand)
```

```vb
        cboCursors.Items.Add(Cursors.IBeam)

        cboCursors.Items.Add(Cursors.WaitCursor)

        cboCursors.Items.Add(Cursors.HSplit)

        cboCursors.Items.Add(Cursors.Help)

        cboCursors.Items.Add(Cursors.NoMove2D)

        cboCursors.Items.Add(Cursors.PanNorth)

        cboCursors.Items.Add(Cursors.SizeAll)

        cboCursors.Items.Add(Cursors.SizeWE)

Catch ex As Exception

        m_Errors += vbCrLf & ex.Message

End Try

End Sub


Private Sub PopulateColors()

Try

        cboColors.Items.Add(Color.BlueViolet)

        cboColors.Items.Add(Color.Chocolate)

        cboColors.Items.Add(Color.Cornsilk)

        cboColors.Items.Add(Color.Blue)

        cboColors.Items.Add(Color.LightBlue)

Catch ex As Exception

        m_Errors += vbCrLf & ex.Message

End Try

End Sub

Private Sub PopulateWindowStates()

Try

        cboWindowStates.Items.Add(WindowState.Normal)

        cboWindowStates.Items.Add(WindowState.Minimized)
```

```
        cboWindowStates.Items.Add(WindowState.Maximized)
Catch ex As Exception
        m_Errors += vbCrLf & ex.Message
End Try
End Sub


Private Sub Form1_Load(ByVal sender As Object, _
        ByVal e As EventArgs) Handles MyBase.Load
Try
        Me.StartPosition = FormStartPosition.CenterScreen
        PopulateColors()
        PopulateCursors()
        PopulateWindowStates()
        If m_Errors.Length > 0 Then
            MessageBox.Show(m_Errors)
        End If
Catch ex As Exception
        m_Errors += vbCrLf & ex.Message
End Try
End Sub
```

Modify Click Event Procedures

In the following button click event procedures you will handle errors by calling the MessageBox's Show method to display the error message. You will also add the button and the event names to the exception error message. Please type error handlers into these procedures as shown in Listing 2. After this modification your code should look as follows:

Listing 2. Click event error handlers.

```vb
Private Sub btnWindowState_Click(ByVal sender As Object, _
        ByVal e As EventArgs) Handles btnWindowState.Click
Try
    Me.WindowState = cboWindowStates.SelectedItem
Catch ex As Exception
    MessageBox.Show(ex.TargetSite.Name & " error " & _
    ex.Message)
End Try
End Sub
Private Sub btnCursor_Click(ByVal sender As Object, _
        ByVal e As EventArgs) Handles btnCursor.Click
Try
    Me.Cursor = cboCursors.SelectedItem
Catch ex As Exception
    MessageBox.Show(ex.TargetSite.Name & " error " & _
    ex.Message)
End Try
End Sub
Private Sub btnBackColor_Click(ByVal sender As Object, _
        ByVal e As EventArgs) Handles btnBackColor.Click
Try
    If Not cboColors.SelectedItem Is Nothing Then
    Me.BackColor = cboColors.SelectedItem
    Else
        MessageBox.Show("Please select a color first.")
    End If
Catch ex As Exception
```

```
        MessageBox.Show(ex.TargetSite.Name & " error " & _
        ex.Message)
End Try
End Sub
```

Testing Error Handlers

Test if your error handlers work. To see error handlers in action you will have to simulate some errors. If you analyze code in the *PopulateColors* procedure, you will see that when you populate the ComboBox you use a Color structure. In the btnBackColor_Click event procedure the value selected in the ComboBox is assigned to the form's BackColor property. Since the BackColor property accepts a Color type, trying to assign a value of a different type should cause an error. That's exactly what you need to create a test case. Fortunately, or unfortunately, Visual Basic handles many errors and runs a lot of preventive code under the hood. That's why you won't get an error if you assign *Nothing* to the BackColor property. Try to click on the *Change BackColor* button when no color is selected and you will not receive an error. You need to modify the application to create an error condition. Your goal is to get an invalid cast exception.

Modify the PopulateColors Procedure

Modify the *PopulateColors* procedure to add a couple of string values instead of Color structures to the Colors ComboBox. Add two lines of code at the end of the procedure. The modified procedure should look like this:

```
Private Sub PopulateColors()
Try
        cboColors.Items.Add(Color.BlueViolet)
        cboColors.Items.Add(Color.Chocolate)
        cboColors.Items.Add(Color.Cornsilk)
```

```
        cboColors.Items.Add(Color.Blue)
        cboColors.Items.Add(Color.LightBlue)
        cboColors.Items.Add("Blue")
        cboColors.Items.Add("Red")
Catch ex As Exception
        m_Errors += vbCrLf & ex.Message
End Try
End Sub
```

Modify the BackColor Procedure

In this procedure, you will add an error handler that shows the error message from the catch block. Your modified procedure should look like the following:

```
Private Sub btnBackColor_Click(ByVal sender As Object, _
            ByVal e As EventArgs) Handles btnBackColor.Click
Try
        If Not cboColors.SelectedItem Is Nothing Then
            Me.BackColor = cboColors.SelectedItem
        Else
            MessageBox.Show("Select a color first.")
        End If
Catch ex As Exception
        Dim str As String
        str = ex.Source & vbCrLf
        str += ex.TargetSite.Name & vbCrLf
        str += ex.ToString & vbCrLf
        MessageBox.Show(str)
End Try
End Sub
```

Test Colors

Press F5 to run the application. Without selecting any color, click on the Change BackColor button. You should see a small dialog box prompting "Select a color first." Click OK to close the dialog box. This message is the result of data validation that you added to the procedure.

However, data validation is not enough to prevent the error that you are going to test. Select the "Red" color. Notice that the "Red" and "Blue" color items in the dropdown are not Color structures—they are strings. Click on the Change BackColor button. After a few seconds you should see a message box with this error message: "Specified cast is not valid." Finally, your procedure caught a *System. InvalidCastException*. More importantly, you should see the project name, procedure name and a full path to the directory from where it was run. You should also see the line of code that caused the error. This means your error trap works fine.

Here are some more comments as to what happened. Visual Basic comes to help you as usual and tries to implicitly convert a string data type to a Color structure, which is doomed to fail and causes an "InvalidCastException." You wrote an error handler that successfully processed the exception thrown by the NET runtime. Congratulations! You have successfully completed Lab 9.

Extra Credit Tasks

For those of you who were not really challenged by this simple project we have one extra credit task. Now that you know what exception type may be thrown in the above procedure, it would be a good idea to add another catch block that will catch this specific exception type. In this case it is an *InvalidCastException* exception. Within this catch block add an error message that shows which catch block was invoked. Remember that this specific exception catch block must precede a general exception catch block. Good luck!

Chapter 10: Application Debugging

Application Debugging

In this Chapter:

You will learn the art of application debugging. The process of making a new application work properly is typically not a simple one. One of the most difficult parts of this work is often not writing the application code but rather identifying the application errors or bugs. Finding the bugs is the first step in making the application error free. The second, much more complex issue is to locate the source of errors and correct them. In this chapter, you will learn how to debug your application, how to use breakpoints to stop processing and monitor code execution, how to step into code, execute code line by line, and how to use the IntelliSense, the QuickWatch, the Immediate window and other debugging tools.

Chapter 10 at a Glance

- Application Debugging
- Solution Build Configurations
- How to Insert Breakpoints
- The Leftbar Method
- The F9 Method
- The Context Menu Method
- A New Breakpoint Dialog Box
- A Breakpoints Window
- Debugging Methods
- Redirection of Execution
- Reading Variables Values
- Using the IntelliSense
- A QuickWatch Dialog Box
- QuickWatch Watch Windows
- Using the Immediate Window

Introduction

Application errors or inaccuracies may be caused by a variety of reasons such as incorrect calculation formulas, inadequate data processing sequence, wrong decision-making and many others. All these logical application programming faults have one general name—bugs. Bugs may cause unexpected application behavior and produce wrong or inadequate results. Apparently, spelling errors and typos cannot be qualified as bugs. Typically, a bug is a result of a programming logic error; for example, wrong sequence of actions in data processing, invalid runtime parameter values used in a formula or a wrong algorithm and so on. Thus, logical errors may produce wrong calculations or incorrect output. Once you identify such application bugs, you want to get rid of them as soon as possible. Note that wrong application output or incorrect calculations are not bugs. They are consequences of bugs. The roots of these bugs reside in the programming logic. To identify application logic errors you need to test the application according to a certain test plan like you did in previous lab projects.

Once you find a fault in the application functionality, you need to start looking for bugs in the application code, which means you have to debug the application. The term debug means both searching and liquidating application logic errors. To successfully destroy bugs you need to build an arsenal of debugging skills. The first step in this noble venture is to learn the basics of debugging techniques. In this chapter we will show you how.

Application Debugging

Detecting application runtime errors is not an easy task mainly because code execution is hidden from you and you cannot directly monitor calculation results, variable values and other application parameters. No matter how good you are in analyzing the code logic in your mind it will not compare to monitoring and analyzing a real code execution process. Fortunately, Visual Studio .NET allows you to run applications in the debug mode, which actually means that you can monitor the execution process in many different ways. More importantly, you can even stop code execution at any desired code line by placing breakpoints. You can also execute code line by line and check the values of variables or expressions. Additionally, Visual Studio offers a number of variable monitoring tools such as the IntelliSense, the Immediate Window and the QuickWatch that can be used to view the application parameters and variables at runtime, create items to watch, execute and modify code. To successfully debug an application, it is essential to learn the following debugging techniques:

> How to Insert Breakpoints
> How to Step Into Code
> How to Step Over Code
> How to Step Out of Code
> How to Run to Cursor
> How to Use the IntelliSense
> How to Use the Immediate Window
> How to use the QuickWatch

Debug Menu

The Debug menu is apparently the first place where you should begin learning the debugging functionality offered by Visual Studio .NET.

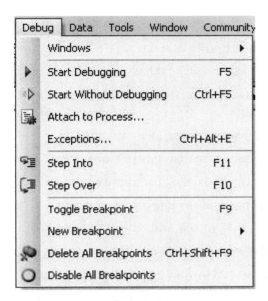

Figure 10.0 The Debug menu.

Spend some time to examine the Debug menu. Initially, you will largely rely on it to explore and invoke various debugging methods. Try to learn the hotkeys as soon as you can so that you will be able to execute the debug functions without actually using the Debug menu. A snapshot of the design time Debug menu is shown in Figure 10.0.

Let's begin with the first two menus: *Start* and *Start Without Debugging*. Start or F5 will run the application in the debug mode and if there are any breakpoints the execution will stop on them if they are in the execution scope. Start Without Debugging or Ctrl + F5 will run the application without debugging even though there are breakpoints in code. It means if you have breakpoints scattered all around the application you need not remove them to run the application normally, without breakpoints. Just press Ctrl + F5. It is extremely convenient and will save you a lot of time. To stop your debugging session, use the *Stop Debugging* menu or press Shift + F5.

Debugging Hotkeys:

F5	-	Run the application in the debug mode.
Ctrl + F5	-	Run the application without debugging.
Shift + F5	-	Stop debugging.

Notice that like many other Visual Studio menus, the debug menu is built dynamically at the time when you open it to make sure that only relevant menu items are displayed. That's why we will show you both design and runtime views of this menu. For example, *Clear All Breakpoints* and *Disable All Breakpoints* menus appear only if there are breakpoints in the project. And *Step Into*, *Step Over* and *Step Out* menus are displayed at runtime only. The *Debug/Windows* menu exposes a number of sub-menus, which can be used to open additional debugging windows such as the *Immediate* window, the *Breakpoints* window and some others. Remember, in order to be able to run the application in the debug mode you should first set the solution build configuration to Debug and have at least one breakpoint in the application code.

Solution Build Configurations

To run an application in the debug mode, you need to make sure that the project's build configuration is set to Debug.

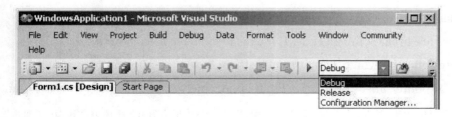

Figure 10.1 Solution build configurations.

In fact, this is the first thing that you need to know and check when you start debugging. You can do this by using the *Solution Configurations* dropdown shown in Figure 10.1. Note that Visual Studio .NET provides two pre-built configurations: *Release* and *Debug*. Of course, you can create your own configurations at any time by using the *Configuration Manager* utility. When you build a new project, its build configuration is set to Debug by default, so you don't have to do anything to start debugging your new project.

There are two things that you initially need to know about build configurations. The Debug build compiles your application code with the debugging symbols and will remember all of your breakpoints. This makes the debug version considerably bigger in size and will not allow code optimizations. The Release build does not include debugging symbols, will completely ignore all of your breakpoints and will apply optimization options. Therefore, if you compile a Release build and then later try to run the application in the debug mode your breakpoints won't be honored until you switch back to the Debug configuration.

Inserting Breakpoints

As with many other procedures, inserting a breakpoint can be done by using one of many different methods that we will describe in this chapter. In Visual Studio .NET, the following methods are available: the *New Breakpoint* dialog box, the *Breakpoints* window, the *F9* method, the *Leftbar* method and the *Context* menu method.

To run the application in the debug mode you need to place at least one breakpoint in the application code. Remember, this breakpoint should be within the execution scope, which means you should first map your code execution path and then place your breakpoint somewhere within that path. For example, a breakpoint can be placed at the beginning of a procedure or on any executable line of code. Code execution will halt on that particular line. Note that not all code can accept breakpoints. The rule is simple: only executable code will accept breakpoints. After all, it won't make sense to break on code that is not executed at runtime. For example, variable declarations are not executable code. However, if variable declaration is combined with variable initialization or instantiation then it becomes an executable code.

The Leftbar Method

The leftbar method is the simplest and, probably, more often used. It is based on using the left-hand side bar (leftbar) in the code editor window. To place a breakpoint, open your project code editor and click on the leftbar across a selected line of code.

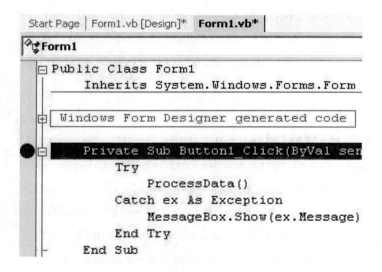

Figure 10.2 Inserting a breakpoint.

When you insert a breakpoint you should see a red circle on the leftbar and the entire line should be highlighted in the same color as shown in Figure 10.2. To remove the breakpoint simply click on the red circle again.

The F9 Method

This method utilizes the F9 functional key and the mouse cursor. The mouse cursor is used to select the line of code where you want to place a breakpoint. Hence, first you should move your mouse cursor to any place on a selected code line and then press F9. To remove the same breakpoint press F9 again or move the mouse cursor to the line where the breakpoint is and then press F9. Alternatively, you can use the *Toggle Breakpoint* menu to do exactly the same.

The Context Menu Method

The context menu method is a two-step procedure. First you need to right-click a code line where you wish to place a breakpoint. Then choose *Breakpoint* and select *Insert Breakpoint* or *Delete Breakpoint*. This will either insert or remove the breakpoint on the selected line of code.

A New Breakpoint Dialog Box

The New Breakpoint dialog box is different from all of the above-described methods. It is a user interface based tool that can insert a breakpoint in any place in your project code remotely, so to say. Thus, you don't need to open the definition of a function or move the mouse cursor to a certain code line. In other words, you need not access or see the actual code where the breakpoint will be inserted. The second, much more important, feature of the New Breakpoint dialog box is that it not only allows you to specify what function to break on but also what line of code or character it should start with. This method should be used when you want to create more sophisticated breakpoints.

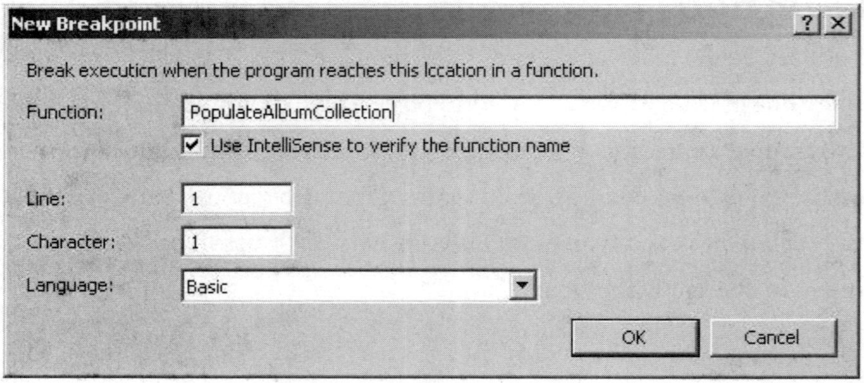

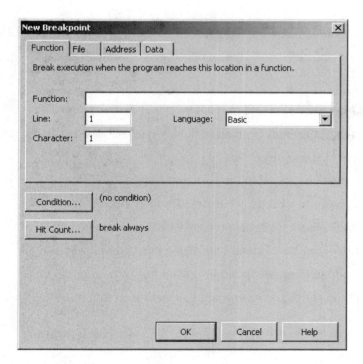

Figure 10.3 The Visual Studio .NET 2005 New Breakpoint dialog box.

Figure 10.4 The Visual Studio .NET 2003 New Breakpoint dialog box.

The appearance and functionality of this tool shown in Figures 10.3 and 10.4 is different in Visual Studio 2005 and Visual Studio 2003. In the latter there are four tabs: Function, File, Address and Data. These tabs provide some additional functionality. For example, you can use them to make the application stop execution when it reaches a specified memory address or when a specified variable value changes. Also, the *Condition* and the *Hit Count* buttons allow you to enter filter conditions and specify hit count after which the breakpoint should be disabled. Visual Studio 2005 has one new feature: *Use IntelliSense to Verify Function Name*, which turns on the IntelliSense to verify the function name before the breakpoint is inserted. There are two ways to open the New Breakpoint dialog box. You can use the Debug menu and choose *New Breakpoint/Break at Function*. Alternatively, you can open it from the Breakpoints window. On the Debug menu, choose *Windows/ Breakpoints*. Then in the Breakpoints window, click on the *New* menu and choose *Break at Function*.

A Breakpoints Window

The last but not least in the breakpoints tools collection is the Breakpoints window.

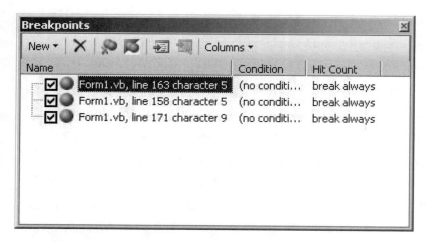

Figure 10.5 A Breakpoints window.

A Breakpoints window shown in Figure 10.5 can be used as a navigation tool to manage all of your project breakpoints from one place. Here you can view all breakpoints you have ever inserted in your project and may have totally forgotten about. This window is equipped with menus, buttons, checkboxes and the context menu, which will allow you to add or delete existing breakpoints, add or remove columns and disable breakpoints in the project. Remember, Visual Studio will store all of your breakpoints permanently. This means they will be available even after you close the project or shut down Visual Studio. So they will be there whenever you return and resume debugging or continue working on the project.

If breakpoints are not working:

➢   Set Active Solution Configuration to Debug.

➢   Check if breakpoints are within the execution scope.

We will conclude this part of the chapter by enumerating all methods that can be used to manipulate breakpoints.

Insert Breakpoint Methods:

- Click on the leftbar across a selected line of code.
- Select a line of code and press F9.
- Right-click a line of code and choose Insert Breakpoint.
- Use the New Breakpoint dialog box.

Debugging Methods

As we mentioned earlier, there are a number of advantages of using breakpoints. They allow you to stop code execution on a selected line of code. For instance, you can place a breakpoint at the beginning of the procedure that initiates a task or action and execute code line by line to the point where an invalid result is produced. Thus, the purpose of using breakpoints is multi-fold:

- Stop execution on a certain line of code.
- Execute code line by line.
- Modify and then execute code.
- Monitor application parameters and variables.

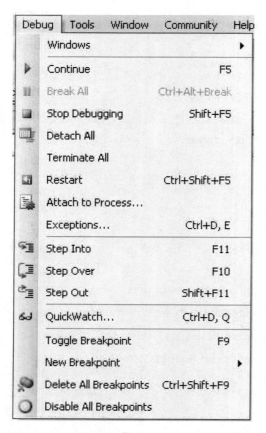

Figure 10.6 The Debug menu at runtime.

Once you started a debugging session, you can take advantage of executing code line by line and checking variable values. To make this process even more productive, Visual Studio .NET gives you four code execution methods to use. You can see these methods listed in the Debug menu shown in Figure 10.6. Basically, you have the following debug code execution choices. You can execute code line by line by using the *Step Into* method. Alternatively, you can execute a called procedure in one shot without stepping into its code by using the *Step Over* function. When you are done with debugging a particular procedure, you can step out of it by using the *Step Out* method. Also, you can re-run any particular line within the procedure by dragging the yellow arrow on the leftbar. Finally, you can jump to a selected line of code by using the *Run to Cursor* function. Let's now discuss each of these methods in more detail.

Using the Step Into Method

The Step Into method simply allows executing code line by line. To run this method, on the Debug menu, choose Step Into or press F11. If you encounter a call to another procedure the execution will jump into that procedure and you can continue line-by-line debugging there. Therefore, this method allows you to debug the application by stepping into each and every line of code within the execution scope.

The Step Over Method

The Step Over method has one important feature that makes it principally different from other debugging methods: It can execute code line by line like the Step Into method but it will not jump into a procedure code when a statement contains a call to another procedure. However, it will fully execute the called procedure on the fly without running into it. Thus, this method will execute a call to another procedure by stepping over it, so to say. For code that doesn't contain calls to other procedures, Step Over and Step Into will work the same way.

```
strProductID = "Sony 343"                             'Line 1
intModelNumber = 987601                               'Line 2
curPrice = GetPrice(strProductID, intModelNumber)     'Line 3
curDiscountPrice = curPrice * 0.9                      'Line 4
```

For example, in the above code snippet the first and the second lines will be executed similarly by both methods. The third line that calls the *GetPrice* procedure will be executed differently. The Step Into method will jump into the GetPrice procedure and will execute code line by line. The Step Over method will execute line 3 as a single statement. Thus, it will execute the GetPrice procedure code in one shot by stepping over it. Remember, stepping over does not mean that the procedure code that is stepped over is not executed. It is executed in a hidden mode without stepping into its code.

Using the Step Out Method

In some debugging sessions there will be times when you will want to stop line-by-line execution and return to the calling procedure or to the place where you started. This is where the *Step Out* method may be useful. The Step Out is a debugging method designed to interrupt line-by-line execution of code and leave the current procedure. So whenever you execute this method, you will exit only the current procedure and return to the point where you left the calling procedure. Notice that the Step Out menu won't be listed in the Debug menu until your application is running in the debug mode. How does this method work? When using the Step Out method you may have an impression that you are leaving a procedure on the line of code where you called the method without executing the rest of the procedure code. That's not exactly what happens. All code in the current procedure will be fully executed. This is done to ensure continuous code execution between the Step Into and Step Out points in the project code that will help to provide valid application results.

Essentially, the Step Out method allows you to stop line-by-line execution and exit the current procedure. The rest of the procedure code will be executed behind the scenes. This technique may be handy when you are debugging one or more procedures and at a certain point decide that you don't need to continue with the rest of the procedure and want to exit before you reached the end of it. Remember, this method works on a procedure level and will exit one procedure at a time. For example, if you started debugging in procedure #1 and stepped into procedure #2 and then into procedure #3. Somewhere in the middle of procedure #3 you choose Debug/Step Out. This action will return you to a line of code where you left procedure #2. If you execute Step Out again you will be returned to procedure #1.

Note:

The main difference between the Step Into and the Step Over methods is in how statements with procedure calls are executed. The Step Into always jumps into a called procedure and can then continue executing code line by line. The Step Over will execute such code as a single statement thus stepping over a procedure call embedded into a statement. The Step Out method will stop line-by-line execution and exit the current procedure while executing the rest of the procedure code in a silent mode.

Redirection of Execution

All the above-mentioned methods allow executing code in different manners but they cannot redirect code execution or skip execution of any selected part of code. However, this does not mean that you cannot do it. The only way to do it is by manually moving the execution point forward or backward. If you move the execution cursor backward, you will simply re-execute a certain part of code. However, if you move the execution cursor forward the skipped lines of code won't be executed.

Note:

To redirect code execution, drag the yellow execution pointer on the leftbar to the code line where you wish to continue debugging. By using this method you can move the execution point both forward and backward. Moving backward will result in re-executing code. Moving forward will leave some code unexecuted.

To practice using this method, try the following: Insert a breakpoint in any procedure that has multiple lines of code and run the application. When the execution stops on your breakpoint, place your mouse cursor on the leftbar across the executing line of code and then drag the yellow arrow downwards or upwards. Drop it right across the line of code that you want to execute. Once you are able to drag and drop the yellow arrow, you can continue debugging using one of the above-described methods.

Using the Run to Cursor

The Run to Cursor allows you to skip a certain portion of code within a procedure. For instance, if you debug a procedure and at some point want to skip a certain part of code that doesn't interest you, you can do so by calling the Run to Cursor method. Thus, this debugging technique is designed to allow you to stop line-by-line execution, skip a certain part of code and land at the line where you placed the cursor, and then if necessary continue line-by-line code execution. Note that the Run to Cursor method can only be used for forward execution. Also note that code between the current execution point and the cursor won't be skipped. It will be fully executed behind the scenes like in the Step Out method.

Figure 10.7 The Code Editor context menu.

The Run to Cursor method has no hotkeys and is only accessible from the code editor context menu shown in Figure 10.7. To run this method, start the application in the debug mode and select any line of code below the current execution point. This will be your run to cursor line. Right-click it and on the popup menu, choose *Run to Cursor*. Let's now practice using the above-mentioned methods in the execution context of three procedures presented in Listing 1.

Listing 1. Test procedures.

Procedure # 1

```
Private Sub Button1_Click(ByVal sender As Object, _
            ByVal e As EventArgs) Handles Button1.Click
```

```
Try
      ProcessData()
Catch ex As Exception
      MessageBox.Show(ex.Message)
End Try
End Sub


Procedure # 2
Private Sub ProcessData()
   Dim strReturnValue As String
   Dim strDesc As String
Try
   TextBox1.Text = RemoveChars(TextBox1.Text, "@")
Catch ex As Exception
   Throw ex
End Try
End Sub


Procedure # 3
Private Function RemoveChars(ByVal strDescText As String, _
               ByVal chrToRemove As String) As String
Try
   If strDescText.IndexOf(chrToRemove) > 0 Then
      Return strDescText.Replace(chrToRemove, "")
   End If
Catch ex As Exception
   Throw ex
End Try
```

```
End Function
```

Code in Listing 1 represents three test procedures. The button click event procedure is used to call the *ProcessData* subroutine, which in its own turn calls the *RemoveChars* function procedure. In this simple routine we expect that clicking on Button1 should remove the "@" character from the text typed in the TextBox1 textbox. Type this code into your test application and then place a breakpoint on the first line of the button click event procedure. Press F5 to start debugging. Type some text in the textbox and click on Button1. The execution should break on the first line in procedure #1. Run the first two lines by pressing F10 or F11. But when you get to the ProcessData() line, if you press F10 you will finish code execution and see the results in TextBox1. If you press F11, the execution will jump into the ProcessData procedure where you will execute three lines of code.

The same will happen if you press F11 on the RemoveChars() line. If you use the Step Out method while you are in procedure # 3, you will be returned back to where you were in procedure # 2. Similarly, if you call the Step Out from procedure # 2, you will be taken back to procedure # 1. If you use the Step Out method while you are in procedure # 1, all in scope code will be executed and the debugging session will end. In the next section we will talk about how to read variable values.

Reading Variable Values

Now that you know how to insert breakpoints and execute code in the debug mode, you need to learn how to monitor the application runtime parameters. You will do this by reading and analyzing various application variables. The ability to read variable values will allow you to examine the application input and output and find out where and why the application produces erroneous results.

Methods of Reading Variable Values:

- ➤ Using the IntelliSense
- ➤ Using the Immediate Window
- ➤ Using the QuickWatch

The IntelliSense

Using the IntelliSense is perhaps the easiest method to access variable values when you are debugging an application. This is an instant variable value monitor tool that will display a variable value in a tooltip box. To read the current value of any variable, just hover the mouse pointer over the variable. In Visual Studio 2003 and earlier, this method worked for value type variables only. Therefore, to access object variable properties you had to use the QuickWatch or the Immediate window. In Visual Studio 2005, the IntelliSense functionality has grown considerably. Not only can you now view the object variable properties but also drill down to object class members and view their properties. Let's consider the following two new features of enhanced IntelliSense functionality.

Figure 10.8 Object variable class members and properties.

For object variables the IntelliSense provides the ability to view the derived and base class members and their properties. To view object class members, just hover the mouse pointer over the object variable and then expand the tool tip. To see

348

the members of the base class, expand the base class section at the top of the list. For objects that may contain tabular data such as a DataSet or a DataTable, the IntelliSense provides a data *Visualizer* tool. Notice in Figure 10.8 that there is a checkmark after the *tblMovies* variable name. If you click on it the Visualizer button (DataTable Visualizer) will popup. Clicking on it will display the DataSet Visualizer window like the one shown in Figure 10.9.

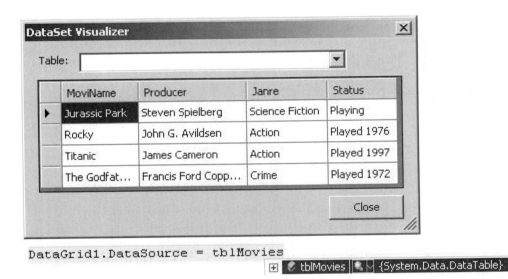

Figure 10.9 The DataSet Visualizer window.

By using a data Visualizer tool you can instantly view the data contained by the underlying object. Note that unlike the IntelliSense tool tip box, the Visualizer allows you to view the result set as long as you need and close it when you are done.

The QuickWatch

The QuickWatch, in spite of its name, is actually a static variable value monitoring tool. It can be used as a persistent storage of application watch parameters, variables and expressions that you may need to monitor repeatedly or frequently during the entire project development cycle. You will especially appreciate the QuickWatch when you need to frequently watch the same set of application variables and method return values especially when these parameters change dynamically or get modified in multiple loops. And of course, you can use the QuickWatch both for value and reference type variables. The QuickWatch employs two tools: a QuickWatch dialog box and a QuickWatch Watch window that can be used in interrelated or independent modes.

Using a QuickWatch Dialog Box

It will make sense to begin entering your watch items in the QuickWatch dialog box. Once you have one or more items entered, you may use the Watch window to monitor, edit or remove them. Let's start with a QuickWatch dialog box. Place a breakpoint somewhere in the project code; for example, at the beginning of the Form_Load procedure. Press F5 and wait for the application to stop on the breakpoint. Right-click anywhere in the code editor window and select *QuickWatch*. Alternatively, you can open the *Debug/Windows/QuickWatch* menu. You should see a window like the one shown in Figure 10.10. The dialog box is resizable so you can adjust it to your liking as we did.

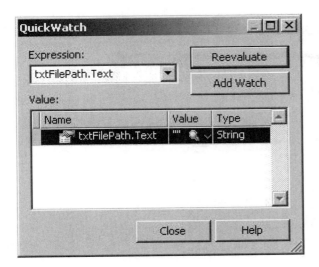

Figure 10.10 A QuickWatch dialog box.

To test this debugging tool, type in a valid variable name or expression and click Recalculate or press Enter. This will bring up the most recent value of the variable or property if the corresponding code that initializes it has been executed. The results should be shown in the *Value* pane, which normally includes the item's name, current value and the data type.

QuickWatch Watch Windows

Part of the QuickWatch functionality is implemented in QuickWatch Watch windows. Visual Studio will pre-build four Watch windows for you. Normally the Watch 1 window will be first used to store any watch items entered by you through the QuickWatch dialog box.

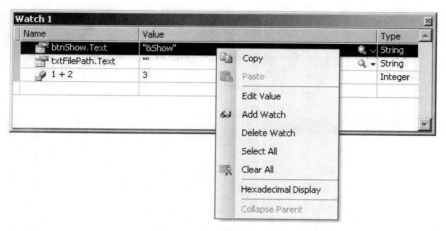

Figure 10.11 QuickWatch Watch window context menu.

A Watch 1 window shown in Figure 10.11 should be automatically displayed when you click on the Add Watch in the QuickWatch dialog box. By default, it will be shown docked to the bottom of your Visual Studio IDE screen. You can undock and resize it according to your liking. A great thing about the QuickWatch is that it allows you to enter and permanently store multiple watch items. You enter them once and they will be stored in this utility until the project files exist. You can reuse them as many times as you need. Once you have entered one or more watch items you can access the Watch windows by using the *Debug/Windows/Watch* menu shown in Figure 10.12.

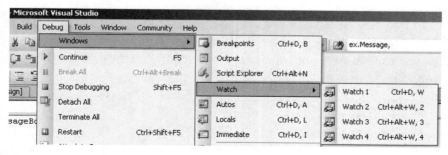

Figure 10.12 QuickWatch Watch menu.

Note that all functionality provided by the QuickWatch can be invoked from Watch windows as well. Here you can view watch item values, their data types, enter new ones and delete existing ones. This will prove to be a great help when you debug large projects and have to examine the same application parameters over and over again.

Note:

By using a QuickWatch you can read variable values, execute statements and monitor any application variables. Note that both a QuickWatch dialog box and a Watch window are not accessible until you run your application in the debug mode.

Using the Immediate Window

The Immediate window is a much more simplified but still a very powerful debugging tool. It does not have all the bells and whistles of QuickWatch but it will allow you to read variable values and modify and execute statements. It won't identify the variable data type but it will store all variables and expressions entered between project or Visual Studio shutdowns. The technique of reading variable values in the Immediate window is simple enough. Type a question mark (?) followed by the variable name and press Enter. The current variable value should be displayed on the next line as shown in Figure 10.13.

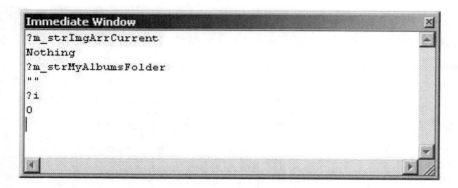

Figure 10.13 The Immediate Window.

You can open the Immediate window by using the *Debug/Windows/Immediate* menu or a hotkey Ctrl+D+I or Ctrl+Alt+I. Remember that when you read or write to a variable, it must be in the execution scope otherwise the response will be *Nothing*, which means that the variable is either out of scope or has not been initialized. Here's a short summary of what you can do in the Immediate window:

> ➢ Read variable values.
> ➢ Write to variables or object properties.
> ➢ Execute methods.
> ➢ Run methods with new input parameters.
> ➢ Type in and execute additional code.
> ➢ Use the IntelliSense.
> ➢ Use the Auto Data Tip.

Note that the Immediate window supports the IntelliSense and the Auto Data Tip functionality, which means you can use it exactly the same way as in the code editor window. Most importantly, in the Immediate window, you can execute application functions or subroutines. For example, for debugging purposes you can execute certain methods with new input parameters. This may prove even more helpful in Visual Studio 2003 where you cannot modify code and then re-run it while in the debug mode.

The most important thing about the Immediate window is that it allows both reading and writing to variables. You can execute practically any piece of code in this utility. Apparently, this opens up a lot of additional debugging avenues and makes it a really powerful debugging tool. Also note that you can bring the Immediate window up at any time, even when the application is not running. But, of course, to get any valid application data you need to run the application in the debug mode.

Summary

In this chapter, you have learned the fundamentals of application debugging. Obviously, debugging is a fundamental application development skill. Runtime errors are inevitable especially at the early stages of the application design. Technically, debugging is first used when you perform the so-called unit testing to check if each procedure in your application is able to perform its task in an isolated environment as a unit of code. At this level of debugging you are expected to catch most of your bugs. The next phase of debugging may be done during the so-called system integration testing. This is when you try to run your application from within a larger system and integrate it with other applications or sub-systems. This type of debugging is much more complex and time consuming. Remember that good debugging skills will save you a lot of development and testing time and will certainly help you to make your applications error free.

Lab 10: The MoviExporer Project

MoviExporer

In this Project:

You will create a MoviExplorer program that should be designed as a tool to view movie titles. The application functionality is very simple. It provides the capability of viewing text files that contain information about movies. This project will allow you to practice and consolidate your debugging skills learned in Chapter 10 and will also show you how to open and read files, use a DataSet, a DataTable and a DataGridView to display tabular data.

Create a New Project

- ➢ Create the *Lab10* project folder.
- ➢ Open Visual Studio .NET
- ➢ Create a new Windows Application project.
- ➢ Set the project Location to C:\Labs\Lab10.
- ➢ Set the project Name to *MoviExplorer*.

Design User Interface

Right-click any free space on the form and choose Properties. In the Properties window find the Text property and type *The Movie Explorer*. Add controls and set their properties according to Table 1.

Table 1. The MoviExplorer form controls.

Control Type	Property Name	Value
Form	Text	The Movie Explorer
GroupBox	Text	Enter movie file path:
TextBox	Name	txtFilePath
Button	Name	btnShow
-/-	Text	&Show
Button	Name	btnClose
-/-	Text	&Close
GroupBox	Text	Movies List:

DataGridView	Name	Default
OpenFileDialog	Name	Default

Since you are using GroupBox controls, remember that you should always place them first and then add other controls. The first GroupBox is used as a movie source file frame. The second one builds a contour around the DataGridView control that is used to display the data retrieved from the source file. In this application you will use an OpenFileDialog component, which allows the user to navigate to and select a file.

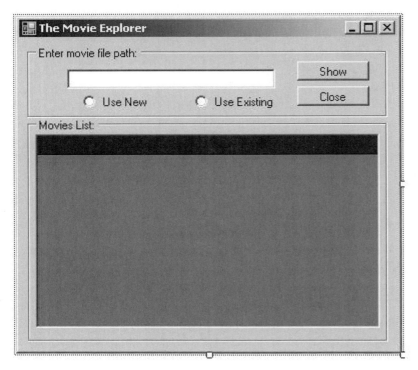

Figure 1. The MoviExplorer form.

When you complete your design work your form should look like the one shown in Figure 1.

Write Code

In this project, you will write a relatively small amount of code to implement the main application task to display movie titles stored in a special text file that is called a movie source file. Using a text file allows you to create a solution without using a database. You will use a database solution after we have covered ADO.NET in Chapter 12. Begin coding with writing the imports directives and declaring form level variables as follows:

```
Imports System.IO
Imports System.Data
Public Class Form1
Private m_objStreamReader As StreamReader
Private m_strMovieFilePath As _
                String = "C:\Labs\Lab10\Movie.txt"
```

Write the CreateAndDisplayDataTable Function

This is the main procedure in the project. Its mission is to read data from the source text file and populate a DataTable object, which is used to create a portable tabular data source that can further be used as a data source for a DataGridView control. Please find the CreateAndDisplayDataTable function code in Listing 1 and type it into your Form1 class.

Listing 1. The CreateAndDisplayDataTable, OpenFile and CloseFile functions.

```
Private Function CreateAndDisplayDataTable() As Boolean
```

```
    Dim tblMovies As New DataTable
    Dim row As DataRow
    Dim clmMoviName As New DataColumn
    Dim clmProducer As New DataColumn
    Dim clmType As New DataColumn
    Dim clmStatus As New DataColumn
    Dim strRowData As String
    Dim arrColumns As String()
    Dim i As Integer
Try
    'Add columns to DataTable
    clmMoviName.Caption = "Movie Name"
    clmMoviName.ColumnName = "MovieName"
    tblMovies.Columns.Add(clmMoviName)
    clmProducer.Caption = "Producer"
    clmProducer.ColumnName = "Producer"
    tblMovies.Columns.Add(clmProducer)
    clmType.Caption = "Janre"
    clmType.ColumnName = "Janre"
    tblMovies.Columns.Add(clmType)
    clmStatus.Caption = "Status"
    clmStatus.ColumnName = "Status"
    tblMovies.Columns.Add(clmStatus)
    'Open data source file
    If OpenFile() = False Then
        MessageBox.Show("Source file not found.")
        Return False
    End If
```

```
    'Populate DataTable
    Do While Not m_objStreamReader.EndOfStream
        strRowData = m_objStreamReader.ReadLine
        row = tblMovies.NewRow
        arrColumns = strRowData.Split(CChar("|"))
            For i = 0 To arrColumns.Length
                row(i) = arrColumns(i).ToString
            Next
        tblMovies.Rows.Add(row)
    Loop
    CloseFile()
    'Set DataGridView1 DataSource property
    DataGrid1.DataSource = tblMovies
    Return True
Catch ex As Exception
    MessageBox.Show(ex.Message)
End Try
End Function


Private Function OpenFile() As Boolean
Try
    If txtFilePath.Text.Length > 0 Then
        objStreamReader = New StreamReader(txtFilePath.Text)
    Else
        MessageBox.Show("Please select source file")
    End If
    Return True
Catch ex As Exception
```

```
    MessageBox.Show(ex.Message)
    Return False
End Try
End Function
Private Function CloseFile()
Try
    If Not objStreamReader Is Nothing Then
        objStreamReader.Close()
        objStreamReader = Nothing
    End If
Catch ex As Exception
    MessageBox.Show(ex.Message)
End Try
End Function
```

Review the CreateAndDisplayDataTable procedure after you type it in. Here's a brief interpretation of its code that should help you understand its logic.

First: You create DataTable columns. Note that when you use a DataAdapter to fill a DataSet the latter internally creates a DataTable and automatically generates columns using data types and field names in the result set retrieved from the database. In this case you will have to do it manually because you will populate the DataTable with data imported from a text file. Thus, you have to make up column names and assign values to them based on the order of fields in the source file.

Second: You call the OpenFile procedure to open a text file selected by a user. If this operation fails you should exit because if you can't open a file there's no sense to continue.

Third: You use a StreamReader object to read the text file line by line until the end of the stream is reached. Note that when the *EndOfStream* property becomes true, the loop will stop automatically. Then using the pipe (|) character as a separator you will split each text line into fields and load them into a string array called *arrColumns*.

Fourth: You start a For loop and feed the content of the array to DataTable row objects. The following code does it:

```
For i = 0 To arrColumns.Length - 1
    row(i) = arrColumns(i).ToString
Next
```

Fifth: Once you are done with a row object you assign it to the DataTable's rows collection. When the end of the file is reached it is closed by calling the CloseFile method.

Sixth: Finally, you assign the *tblMovies* DataTable object to the DataGridView's DataSource property.

Write File Functions

These two methods are helper functions. Here the code is branched into two separate procedures to make them reusable and to better control the file manipulation process. For instance, in the CreateAndDisplayDataTable procedure you call the OpenFile function and if it returns false you have to exit the function. Note that in almost all procedures you should use Try - Catch blocks. These are the error handlers that we discussed in the previous chapter. Please find the CreateAndDisplayDataTable, OpenFile and CloseFile procedures in Listing 1 and type them into your project.

Write Event Handlers

Write the Show and Close button click event procedures as shown in Listing 2.

Listing 2. Event handlers.

```
Private Sub btnShow_Click(ByVal sender As Object, _
                ByVal e As EventArgs) Handles btnShow.Click
Try
    If radioNewFile.Checked Then
        OpenFileDialog1.ShowDialog()
        txtFilePath.Text = OpenFileDialog1.FileName()
    Else
        txtFilePath.Text = MovieFilePath
    End If
    CreateDataTable()
Catch ex As Exception
    MessageBox.Show(ex.Message)
End Try
End Sub
Private Sub btnClose_Click(ByVal sender As Object, _
        ByVal e As EventArgs) Handles btnClose.Click
        Me.Close()
End Sub
```

Note that code in the btnShow_Click event procedure is designed to accomplish two things. First, to find out if a user wants to use a new or an existing source file. To do so check if the radioNewFile radio button is checked. If yes, show an Open File dialog box so that the user can select a file. Then write the file name returned by the *OpenFileDialog.FileName* property to the txtFilePath textbox. If the value is false then in the Else block you need to read the m_strMovieFilePath variable's value. When you are done with the source file name, call the CreateAndDisplayDataTable function that displays the data. In the Close button click event, call the form's Close method to shut down the application.

Before you begin testing, review your code for incomplete statements and undeclared variables. Once you are done with code review, try to Debug the application. This will allow you to identify all errors and warnings in the project. If errors are found they will be shown in the Error List or Task List dialog box like the one shown in Figure 2.

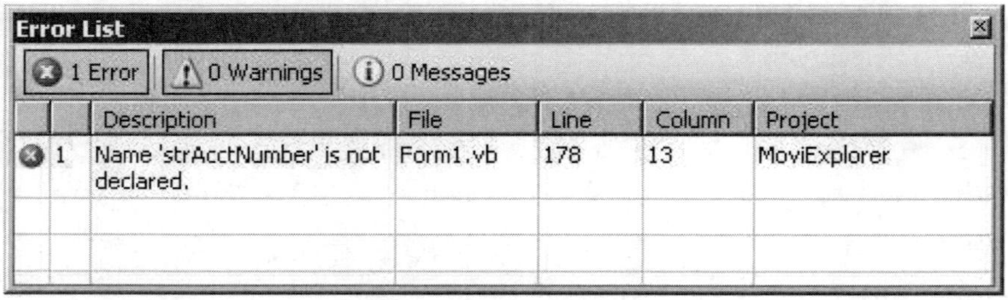

Error List					×
1 Error	0 Warnings	0 Messages			
	Description	File	Line	Column	Project
1	Name 'strAcctNumber' is not declared.	Form1.vb	178	13	MoviExplorer

Figure 2. The project Error List dialog box.

For example, in this project for test purposes we wrote a statement that uses an undeclared variable *strAcctNumber* and tried to compile the application. This is the only error shown in the Error List dialog box in Figure 2. If this happens in your project, check if the variable is declared. In most cases a simple spelling check can resolve the problem.

Tip:

To quickly access a line of code that causes an error listed on the Task List or Error List dialog boxes, just double-click the line. This will open the code editor and move the cursor to that line.

Test and Debug

Now you will test and debug the application. We planted two bugs in the application code. Your task is to test the application and identify the functionality flaws and then debug and fix them. Please perform the follow testing and debugging procedures.

Test the Application

To test the application, you need to create and save a simple text file that will be used as a data source. Open a Notepad and type data for a few movie titles. Each line should represent one movie and should be in the following format:

Title | Producer | Genre | Status.

For example:

> Jurassic Park|Steven Spielberg|Sc.Fiction|Playing
>
> Rocky|John Avildsen|Action|Played 1976
>
> Titanic|James Cameron|Action|Played 1997
>
> The Godfather|Francis Ford Coppola|Crime|Played 1972

Save the file as *Movies.txt* in C:\Labs\Lab10 directory. Perform the following tests. Open the application in Visual Studio .NET. Press F5 to run the application. Select "Use Existing" and click on the "Show" button. You should get a "File not Found" error displayed in the message box. You have discovered the first application runtime error. This is not the bug yet. To find the bug that causes this error you need to debug the application.

The First Bug

Open the application in Visual Studio .NET. Make sure that your solution build configuration is set to Debug. Open the code editor, find btnShow_Click event procedure and place a breakpoint at the first line. Press F5 to start debugging. Check the "Use Existing" and click on the Show button. The execution should break on the btnShow_Click event procedure. Press F10 to execute code line by line. When you reach a call to the *CreateAndDisplayDataTable* procedure, press F11 to step into that procedure. Then use F10 until you reach the *OpenFile* procedure call. Press F11 to jump into it. Continue executing code by pressing F10. When you execute this line of code:

```
objStreamReader = New StreamReader(txtFilePath.Text)
```

The CLR will throw an exception and code execution will jump into the catch block. Continue executing code until you get the message box with the error message that says "Could not find file: C:\Labs\Lab10\Movie.txt." The first thing to do is to check if the file name and path are valid and if the file really exists. Remember that you created the text file and saved it as Movies.txt. You saved the file as Movies.txt but hard-coded the file path as:

```
Private m_strMovieFilePath As String =
```

```
"C:\Labs\Lab10\Movie.txt"
```

Hence, the error is caused by an invalid file name hard-coded into the form level variable *m_strMovieFilePath*. Stop debugging by pressing Shift + F5. To fix the problem, find the variable declaration statement and change the file name to Movies. txt. Check if the bug is fixed. On the Debug menu, choose *Clear all Breakpoints* to get rid of all existing breakpoints. Then find the *OpenFile* procedure and place a breakpoint on this line of code:

```
m_objStreamReader = New StreamReader(txtFilePath.Text)
```

Press F5 to run the application, check "Use Existing" and click on the Show button. When execution breaks on the above line, press F10. Now this statement should execute fine and the file should be open. Congratulations! You have successfully detected and liquidated a bug. Notice that if you choose "Use New," this bug will be skipped but another one will popup.

The Second Bug

There is another more complex logical error in the application. This one is hiding in the *CreateAndDisplayDataTable* procedure. To see how this error manifests itself run the application normally without debugging. Press Ctrl + F5 select "Use Existing" and then click on the Show button. After a few seconds you should see a message box that says: "Index was outside the bounds of the array." In the *CreateAndDisplayDataTable* procedure you have two loops *Do While* and *For... Next*. The Do While loop iterates through the text lines in the source file. The For loop is used to iterate through the columns of the DataTable to populate them with data extracted from the file. To further investigate this issue you need to run the application in the debug mode and note which line of code causes an error. In the CreateAndDisplayDataTable procedure, place a breakpoint on this line of code:

```
arrColumns = strRowData.Split(CChar("|"))
```

Press F5 and then F10 to execute code line by line. Remember, when you reach the *For...Next* loop, start counting the number of iterations. On the fifth iteration the CRL will throw an exception complaining that the index was outside the bounds of the array. This is a typical error. In the source file you should have four values delimited by |. This means you should iterate only four times to read these fields and populate four columns in the DataTable object. Then why does the loop makes five iterations? Can you figure out? It is caused by this line of code:

```
For i = 0 To arrColumns.Length
```

The problem is that you are using the number of elements in the *arrColumns* array as the upper subscript index. But the array is 0-based, which means that its first element is stored under the index 0 and the index of the last item is equal to 3 not 4. So in your code you need to subtract 1 from the array length property to get a valid upper subscript index. Here's the bug fix:

```
For i = 0 To arrColumns.Length - 1
```

Alternatively, you can use the *GetUpperBound* built-in method like the following:

```
For i = 0 To arrColumns.GetUpperBound(0)
```

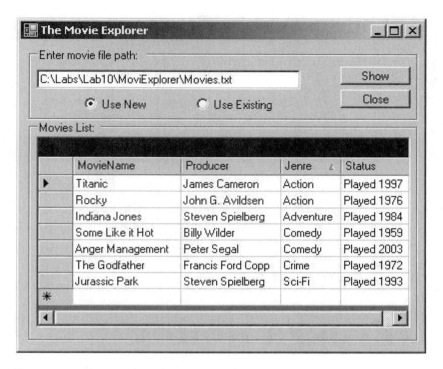

Figure 3. The MoviExplorer at runtime.

Please modify your code, remove all breakpoints and run the application again. The application should successfully display the source file data. Your screen should look like the one shown in Figure 3. Now test the "Use New" option. In this case, clicking on the Show button should display an Open File dialog box. Select a file that contains data in the format described above. As soon as the dialog box is closed the file data should be displayed. Check if the file content is displayed correctly. Congratulations! You have successfully completed Lab 10.

Part YI   Object-Oriented Programming

Object-Oriented Programming

Chapter 11: Classes and Objects

Classes and Objects

In this Chapter:

You will consider the main concepts of object-oriented programming. Visual Basic .NET is an object-oriented programming language so it is essential to understand the principles of object-oriented programming. You will learn how to write classes, class methods, properties and events, create object variables and use the .NET Framework Class Library (FCL).

Chapter 11 at a Glance

- ➤ Object-Oriented Concepts
- ➤ Class Programming
- ➤ Class Home Assembly
- ➤ Class Access Modifiers
- ➤ Class Design
- ➤ Class Members
- ➤ Class Constructors
- ➤ Creating Class Methods
- ➤ Creating Class Properties
- ➤ Programming Class Events
- ➤ Object Binding
- ➤ Early Binding
- ➤ Late Binding
- ➤ Advanced Late Binding
- ➤ Subscribing to Class Events
- ➤ Using Object Browser

Introduction

In previous chapters, we used the terms class and object quite often. The complexity of the underlying concepts was holding us from introducing them earlier. We hope that by now you had enough exposure to the context where they are used and ready to discuss the subject in a more systematic manner. Unlike its predecessor VB 6, Visual Basic .NET is an object-oriented programming language. This means that by programming in Visual Basic .NET you can take advantage of powerful features of object-oriented programming such as inheritance and polymorphism.

In this chapter, we will briefly touch upon the main concepts of object-oriented programming (OOP) since a more detailed discussion of the subject is beyond the scope of this book. Also, this will allow us to devote the main part of this chapter to a discussion of practical topics such as a class concept, programming class methods, properties and events and object binding.

Class in .NET

The more you progress in your study of Visual Basic and .NET in general, the sooner you will realize that every piece of code you are dealing with is either a class or part of a class. All of your programming creativity will be conducted in the world of classes. For instance, the Windows Form is a class and controls are classes too. Thus, a class is a major programming unit in the .NET universe. Therefore, understanding a class concept and learning how to program it is one the most fundamental skills in .NET programming.

Note:

Learning the principles of class programming is one of the most essential parts of .NET programming and object-oriented programming in general. Abiding to object-oriented principles helps to create powerful programs.

Object-Oriented Concepts

The first and, probably, the most important thing about a class is that it's a piece of highly reusable code. Classes are used as templates to create objects. Objects are classes in action. They are executable instances of a class and thus can be used to invoke class functionality. The same class can be used to create multiple objects with individual characteristics, which makes a class a factory of customizable objects.

You can use classes to create multiple objects in one or many different applications. Alternatively, if you were not using classes you would have to repeat the same code as many times as you need functionality provided by an object.

Encapsulation

A class is normally designed to implement some functionality and process related data. A class instance consists of two main parts: the implementation code and the instance data.

A class instance data can be anything from primitive data types such as numbers and characters to structured data such as database resultsets, collections and object data. Data can flow into a class instance through public class properties, variables and method parameters. Obviously, this happens when a client instantiates a class and assigns values to its properties or public variables and invokes its methods.

Class behavior is synonymous to class implementation, which is materialized in the actual class code. You would normally write this code to create class methods, properties and events. The term behavior is used to indicate the fact that this code will actually determine class actions. This may not always be true because class data may have enough power to impact class behavior as well.

Theoretically, class behavior, and ultimately functionality, is determined by code written in class methods. But this projected class behavior can be easily broken by bad or invalid data flowing into a class from the outside world. A class implementation can be programmed in such a way that it will strictly control what data is assigned to its instance members based on functionality requirements. This design principle helps to strictly control class instance data and protect it from unwanted access. If you look at a class from a client application perspective, you may know what functionality it can provide but you cannot see the implementation details. This ability of a class to expose functionality but hide internal implementation is known as **encapsulation**.

Inheritance

Classes live in a non-profit community. They can freely share each others intellectual property and demand no subscription fees. Thus, one class code may be reused by another class that inherits from it. This is one of the key features of object-oriented programming known as *inheritance*. It means a class can export or lend its code to another class. This is yet another way of increasing class code reusability by allowing other classes to inherit its implementation. From a practical perspective, inheriting another class' code is simple enough. You just add an inheritance statement immediately after the class declaration statement. For example, any Windows form that you have already used in your lab projects inherits from the *System.Windows. Forms.Form* base class. When one class inherits code from another class, their legal status is affected. A class that inherits from another class acquires a title of a **derived** class. A class that lends its code to other classes is promoted to a rank of a **base** class. However, if you look at this scenario from a more practical perspective, things may look simpler. You can say that a derived class simply extends the base class' functionality by either adding its own code to it or overriding the base class methods.

Polymorphism

The term *polymorphism* consists of two headwords: *poly,* which means many and *morph,* which denotes form. Thus, it can be translated as *many forms.* In programming, the term polymorphism denotes the ability of a code entity to automatically acquire multiple forms of implementation. This can work through method overloading or inheritance. The term overloading means that you can write two or more methods with exactly the same name but with different method signatures. A method signature includes a method return data type and method parameters. Thus, two overloaded methods must have either a different number of parameters or different parameter data types. Here's a simple example:

```
Public Sub GetOrderStatus(ByVal strCustomerName As String)
      'Procedure code
End Sub


Public Sub GetOrderStatus(ByVal intOrderID As Integer)
      'Procedure code
End Sub
```

In the above code, we presented two overloaded versions of the *GetOrderStatus* method, which use different parameter data types. Polymorphism can also work through inheritance. For example, in a derived class you can override the implementation of base class methods.

Listing 1. Method polymorphism.

A base class:

```
Public Class LegalEntity
      Public Overridable Sub CreateEntity()
         'Method implementation
      End Sub
End Class
```

A derived class:

```
Public Class Principal
      Inherits LegalEntity
      Public Overrides Sub CreateEntity()
        'Method implementation
      End Sub
End Class
```

A derived class:

```
Public Class CounterParty
      Inherits LegalEntity
      Public Overrides Sub CreateEntity()
        'Method implementation
      End Sub
End Class
```

Code in Listing 1 features three classes: a base class that defines and implements some functionality and exposes an overridable (virtual) method that can be enhanced or extended in a derived class. In this case, a base class *LegalEntity* is inherited by *Principal* and *CounterParty* classes, which override the *CreateEntity* base class method. A client using a derived class does not know whether a base class or a derived class method is executed. This is a point where inheritance and polymorphism shake hands.

Class Programming

Modeling Real-World Entities

A class is designed to perform a set of logically related tasks that are intended to automate a certain real-world process. Thus, a class may be used to model real-life entities and processes by creating programming abstractions. Typically, class functionality is focused on modeling a certain real-world entity actions and appearance. For instance, you can create a *Product* class with such properties as *Name, Type, Price* and *Size*. Then you can add a set of methods such as *AddProduct*, *DeleteProduct, SetProductPrice* and so on. You can use this class in an application to process a store or a warehouse inventory.

Class Home Assembly

A class must have a certain place to reside. When you compile your project code, a virtual home for your classes is created. It is called an assembly. .NET offers two types of class residential assemblies: DLL (dynamic link library) and EXE (executable). In the .NET world, any code that you create will end up in one of these assemblies. When you compile your application, each class in your project will be compiled into its own class module and placed into an assembly.

Theoretically, a class can live in any of these assemblies. For instance, you may create classes in a Windows forms application that will be compiled into an EXE assembly. Alternatively, you may create a set of classes in a class library application, which will be compiled into a DLL. Therefore, an assembly can host one or more classes in it. The visibility of classes that may live in one and the same assembly depends on the access modifiers used to define a class. We will discuss this topic in the next section.

Class Access Modifiers

A class access modifier is like a traveling permit. It determines if objects created from this class can travel outside their home assembly or just inside that assembly. In Visual Basic .NET, the following access modifiers are available:

Class Access Modifiers:

Public – Has no access limitations.

Friend – Is visible to other classes within home assembly.

Private – Is restricted to declaration context only.

Protected – Is accessible in the declaration context and a derived class.

Protected Friend – Combines features of Protected and Friend.

For example:

```
Public Class ClassA
Friend Class ClassB
Private Class ClassC
```

ClassA in the above class declarations can be exposed outside and inside its home assembly without any limitations. ClassB is visible anywhere inside home assembly only. ClassC is private, its visibility is limited to the declaration context only. If you create a stand alone private class it will be totally disconnected from other classes in the application and become useless. So the only way to expose a private class is to create a declaration context, which actually means declaring a private class within another more visible class. Listing 2 presents an example of a declaration context.

Listing 2. A declaration context accessibility.

```
Public Class OuterClass
    Private Class InnerClassA
        'Class implememtation
    End Class
    Private Class InnerClassB
        'Class implememtation
    End Class
End Class
```

In Listing 2, there are two inner private classes inside an outer public class. In this case the outer class serves as a declaration context for the inner private classes, which are now visible anywhere within the outer class. Why would you create such classes? A well known and typical use of such classes is as helper classes.

Tip:

Note that omitting a class access modifier in your class declaration is totally legal. However, if a class is declared without an access modifier, a default *Friend* modifier will be applied.

Inheritance Access Modifiers

Using the the inheritance access modifier or a combination of two modifiers allows you to create additional code accessibility flavors.

```
Public MustInherit Class ClassName
        'Class code
End Class
```

```
Public NotInheritable Class ClassName
        'Class code
End Class
```

The *MustInherit* access modifier creates an abstract class that should be inherited and cannot be directly instantiated. On the contrary, the *NotInheritable* modifier declares a class that cannot be inherited but can be used otherwise.

Class Design

As we mentioned earlier, when you create a class, you will most probably model a certain real-world entity; for example, a customer, a product, a trade, a calculation routine and so on. For example, you may program a class to perform a set of actions, such as Buy, Sell, CancelOrder and CreateOrder. Action procedures created in a class are called class methods and are implemented in subroutines or functions.

A class can define properties that describe characteristics of a modeled entity. For example, a trade order class may have such properties as OrderQuantity, ExecutedPrice, TradeID, ExecutedQuantity and others. To program such entity attributes, you need to create class properties. You may also program a class to send notifications or broadcast messages to whoever is using it. These notifications may contain information about changes of certain class parameters or how a certain class method completed its job and so on. To program such notifications, you need to create class events. In the following sections, we will discuss class members.

Class Members

When you use the Object Browser or MSDN help, you will often come across the term class member when you research a certain class structure. Thus, it will make sense to introduce this term now before we continue a discussion of this topic. All class methods, properties, events and class level variables irrespective of their accessibility level are class members. All local procedure variables will not acquire class member status and will only represent a class internal implementation.

Any further classification of class members is closely related to their scope. For example, public class members may represent the class outside the class. Private class methods, properties and variables represent private class members. Class member visibility is determined by access modifiers. Therefore, before you define any member of your class, you need to make a decision as to what visibility you want or need for that member. This decision should be driven by various factors but mainly by the level of exposure, the structure of the class and project specifications. For example, in a very simplified approach you would make all major functional procedures public and thus accessible from outside and all helper procedures private.

Class Constructor

A class constructor is a procedure that has a very specific mission—to assist CRL in building a class instance. It is always the first class method that is invoked by the CLR when a class object is created. That's why a constructor is the best place to do any class initialization work. Hence, a constructor is simply a class instance engine helper that has a special feature—it can be used to configure a class instance from inside the class. This mission is possible because a constructor is a class method that can internally determine how a class instance is built, typically, by doing the initialization work.

There are two general types of constructors: default and custom. The default constructor is supplied by the CLR. A custom constructor can only be created by you, if you decide that you need one. In other words, if you write a constructor procedure in your class it will be a custom constructor. If you don't write a constructor the CLR will generate a default one. What's the difference? The default constructor does not accept parameters and it won't do any class initialization work for you.

Custom Constructor 1

```
Public Class ClassA
    Public Sub New()
        m_strConfigFile = "C:\Files\ClassAConfig.xml"
        m_strLogFile = "C:\Logs\ClassALog.log"
    End Sub
    Private m_strConfigFile As String = ""
    Private m_strLogFile As String = ""
End Class
```

In the above code the *ClassA* class custom constructor does some simple initialization work. It initializes two class string variables m_*strConfigFile* and m_*strLogFile*.

Note:

There is nothing in the constructor itself that says it is a custom constructor. If you write any constructor in your class it will be a custom constructor. To take advantage of a custom class constructor, you have to write one and if necessary parameterize it.

As we already mentioned, custom constructors can accept parameters. In the above constructor code we initialized class variables by using hard-coded values. This isn't a good practice and normally should be avoided. We can fix this problem by using a parameterized constructor. This is how a parameterized ClassA constructor may look like:

Custom Constructor 2

```
Public Class ClassA
    Public Sub New(ByVal strConfigFile As String, _
                        ByVal strLogFile As String)
            m_strConfigFile = strConfigFile
            m_strLogFile = strLogFile
    End Sub
            Private m_strConfigFile As String = ""
            Private m_strLogFile As String = ""
End Class
```

Note that in the parameterized ClassA constructor we not only accept the corresponding parameters from the client who creates this object but we also dynamically assign the received values to the class instance variables and thus avoid hard-coding. We will conclude the class constructor discussion with a Windows Form constructor example:

Custom Constructor 3

```
Public Sub New()
    MyBase.New()
    'This call is required by the Windows Form Designer.
    InitializeComponent()
    'Add any initialization here.
```

```
End Sub
```

In one of your Windows application projects, expand the code region named "Windows Form Designer Generated Code" and find *Public Sub New* procedure. This is the form class custom constructor. It does not use parameters but it does initialize the form class by calling the *InitializeComponent* procedure. Pay attention that *MyBase.New* calls the base class constructor. In any derived class, the keyword *MyBase* is reserved to reference a base class.

Class Constructor Summary:

> ➢ Creating a class constructor is optional.
> ➢ A class may have multiple custom constructors (constructor overloading).
> ➢ A default constructor does not take parameters.
> ➢ A custom constructor may accept parameters.
> ➢ A constructor may be used to do class initialization work.
> ➢ In a derived class you may need to call a base class constructor.
> ➢ Base class constructors are not inherited by a derived class.
> ➢ Constructor parameters can be used to pass class configuration data.

Creating Class Methods

Now let's look at how class methods are created. Any function or subroutine defined in a class automatically becomes a class method. The visibility of a class method is determined by access modifiers used to declare it. Before creating a class method you should make a number of decisions. First, you need to decide what access modifier best suits a particular method's role in the class. For instance, if you plan to expose this method to the outside consumers of the class you should make it public. Apparently, if you plan to use this method as a helper procedure, it will make sense to declare it as private. Please note that a helper procedure is just a function or a subroutine that performs some auxiliary tasks.

Using Method Parameters

Subroutines, functions and property procedures can accept parameters. You may leave an argument list empty if you do not plan to receive input parameters or send back results. A decision of when to use parameters depends on many factors. In a most simplified explanation you may need a set of input and output parameters if your procedure needs some input data and generates results that should be returned to a caller. The above examples illustrated class methods without parameters. Now let's look at how to create methods that employ parameters. Here's a simple subroutine procedure that accepts one input parameter:

```
Public Sub ProcedureName(ByVal ParameterName As String)
        'Procedure implementation code
End Sub
```

In the following section, we will discuss the rules of method parameter declaration.

Declaring Method Parameters

When you create method parameters you should declare them almost the same way as variables. However, there are two differences. First, you need not use any access modifiers because all method parameters will automatically assume a local procedure scope, which means they are visible only inside that procedure. Second, you should begin your declaration with a parameter direction identifier: *ByVal* (by value) or *ByRef* (by reference). Use ByVal if you want to create an input parameter. To define an output parameter use ByRef. Please note that ByRef parameters can work both ways as output and input at the same time. How does the parameter direction identifier work? If ByVal is used the runtime creates a copy of the variable data and sends it to the called procedure. Thus, any changes made by a called procedure will not retain when execution returns to the calling procedure.

With ByRef parameters the data transfer mechanism is principally different. In fact, there is no data transfer because when you use ByRef a reference to the memory address of the variable is passed. Therefore, the called procedure will use that reference to directly access the variable and if it changes the value stored by it the change will hold.

Note:

Class methods are normally used to implement class functionality. They are typically given names that use verbs; for example, Connect, Open, Close, CleanUp, Dispose and so on. In most cases methods may need some parameters to pass data in and out. Values passed as method parameters must match declared procedure parameter data types. ByRef parameters can be used for both input and output.

Designing Class Properties

Class properties are used to describe an entity modeled by a class. They define class appearance. Using properties help to make each instance of a class unique by allowing it to have some individual characteristics. For instance, customer last name or address may be different in each instance of a Customer class. From a programming perspective, class properties may be divided into two main categories: declarative and procedural. A **declarative property** is created by simply declaring a class variable with an accessibility level that makes it visible outside the class.

In case of a **procedural property,** you need to create a property procedure that handles a class property. A great thing about a procedural property is that it allows executing any necessary code at the time when the property is read or written to. This is especially important for data validation or filtering.

Declarative Properties

By using a declarative method you cannot execute any property validation code so this method is more appropriate for simple properties that do not require any validation. A declarative method uses a public or friend class variable to hold the property value, which can be accessed directly whenever there is a need to read or write to the property.

```
Public Class Order
    Public strStoreID As String
    Friend dtOrderDate As DateTime
End Class
```

In the above code, a public class variable *strStoreID* and a friend variable dtOrderDate can be used to store property values that are accessible outside the declaration class.

Procedural Properties

A procedural property is defined as a procedure. Whenever such property is referenced the corresponding procedure will be executed. A procedural property has one advantage over a declarative one: you can execute any necessary code in it to validate or pre-process data before it is assigned to the property. This method requires more coding but it allows synchronizing data quality with the principals of class behavior that we spoke about in the encapsulation section. Creating a procedural property may be divided into two steps. First, declare a private class variable of a corresponding data type. This variable will be used to store the property value. Then write a property procedure that will implement the *Get* method that reads the property and the *Set* method that writes to the property. A simple class property procedure may look like the following:

```
Public Class OnlineStore
    Private strStoreRegion As String
    Public Property StoreRegion() As String
        Get
            Return strStoreRegion
        End Get
        Set(ByVal Value As String)
            strStoreRegion = Value
        End Set
    End Property
End Class
```

The first step is simple enough: you need to declare a private class variable to store a property data. Note that this variable should be private and be accessible within the class only. The second step potentially has more coding work. You need to write the Get procedure that will read the value stored in the private variable and return it to the caller and the Set method that will write to the variable. This is a place where you would, most probably, want to check the value passed through the *Value* variable and if it satisfies all verification criteria assign it to the property. Note that the Value variable should be declared as the Set method's input parameter.

Obviously, if you implement a property procedure in such a simple way as shown above, you are not taking advantage of running any validation or verification code. Let's enhance this example with a simple value length validation. After a small change your code should look like this:

```
Public Class OnlineStore
    Private strStoreRegion As String
    Public Property StoreRegion() As String
        Get
            Return strStoreRegion
        End Get
        Set(ByVal Value As String)
                    If Value.Length > 3 Then
                            strStoreRegion = Value
                    Else
                    Throw New Exception("Invalid region name")
                    End If
        End Set
    End Property
End Class
```

But what if you need to create a property that should not be changed by clients? In this case you need to declare a read-only property. But how would you initialize it? At runtime there is only one place from where a read-only property can be initialized: a class constructor. Here's an example of a read-only property initialized in the class constructor:

```
Public Class OnlineStore
    Public Sub New(ByVal strRegion as String)
        m_strStoreRegion = strRegion
    End Sub
    Private m_strStoreRegion As String = ""
    Public ReadOnly Property StoreRegion() As String
```

```
Get
    Return m_strStoreRegion
    End Get
  End Property
End Class
```

In the above class code, we declared a read-only property *StoreRegion* and initialized it with a value received through a class constructor parameter *strRegion*.

Programming Class Events

Programming class events can be divided into two main phases. First you need to define your custom event as an *Event* class instance using the keyword *Event*. If you do need to use any event parameters you should declare them in the event definition statement. For example, an event with one parameter may be look like the following:

```
Public Event AccountOpened(ByVal objAcctInfo As Object)
```

If you take a closer look at the above event definition statement, you will notice that it has the following elements: access modifier, the keyword *Event*, the event name and the event argument list. Once you are able to declare your class event it is ready to be used from anywhere in the class. There is only one way to use the event by simply raising it in any class procedure. You will need to use the *RaiseEvent* keyword, which takes one parameter—the event name. If your event takes parameters then you should pass parameter values as well.

```
Public Class BankAccount
Public Event AccountOpened(ByVal objAcctInfo As Object)
Private Function OpenAccount() As Boolean
```

```
      Dim objAcctInfo as Object
   'Procedure code
   RaiseEvent AccountOpened(objAcctInfo)
End Function
End Class
```

In the above code snippet, we defined *AccountOpened* event and then raised it in the *OpenAccount* procedure.

Note:

There is a principal difference between class methods and events. Class methods are normally invoked by a client application. Events can only be raised by a class itself. If a client is properly subscribed to receive object events, its event handler procedure will be executed.

Object Binding

In a simple explanation, object binding is a method of connecting an object variable with a corresponding class instance in memory. When we discussed variables in Chapter 5, we focused on one type of object binding—an early binding. Here we will tell you about another method of binding—a late binding. We will also compare both methods and give you more examples.

If you declare an object variable as a specific class and instantiate it with a corresponding class instance, you are using an early binding. In this case you are binding a class instance to an object variable in the most efficient way. All binding preparation work is done at the earliest possible time—design and compilation time. That's why it is called **early binding**. When you build such code, the compiler will check if a referenced DLL contains a definition for such type and will obtain all the necessary type information. Any reference or type mismatch errors are normally detected at this stage. Alternatively, you can declare an object variable as a generic object, which means any class instance can be assigned to it. Then later, typically, at runtime, you create a class instance and assign it an object variable. This method is called **late binding**.

Early Binding

When you declare an object variable as a specific class you can only instantiate it with that class instance. For example:

```
Dim objProduct As Product
objProduct =  New Product()
```

This type of object binding is called early binding because a significant part of the work to prepare the object variable to accept an instance of a corresponding class is done at design and compilation time. As a result, this type of binding is very fast, efficient and is less error prone because all references, dependencies and type checking are performed at an early stage.

Late Binding

In late binding, you declare an object variable as a generic object and assign a desired class instance to it later. The main disadvantage of this method is that it is significantly slower and error prone. However, it allows a lot of flexibility and freedom in assigning class instances at runtime. Here's an example of late binding:

```
Dim strClassType as String
Dim objGeneric As Object
```

```
If strClassType = "ClassA" Then
      objGeneric = New ClassA()
Else
      objGeneric = New ClassB()
End if
```

In the above code, we declare and instantiate a generic object variable *objGeneric*. Then based on a specified class name, we asign an instance of *ClassA* or *ClassB* to it. Note that this code will compile only if you set *Option Strict Off*.

However, the above example is only good enough to illustrate the idea of late binding. The truth is that it isn't a real late binding. Because in this case all type information is available to a compiler at compilation time and class instance assignments can be verified at compilation time. Thus, in this example only the object instance assignment occurs at runtime. And the only difference from a true early binding is in allowing a choice of class instance. We'll give an example of real late binding in the Advanced Late Binding section.

Note:

Object binding is all about how an object variable is declared and instantiated. Using early binding you assign a class instance to an object variable that exactly matches its type declaration statement. Early binding is fast and efficient. In late binding you declare a generic object variable that can accept any object type. Then at runtime you assign a certain class instance to it. Late binding is slow, error prone and violates the principles of strong typing.

Advanced Late Binding

Object variable creation can be divided into the following stages: object variable declaration, object creation and object assignment. When you declare an object variable for a specific class you make a request for a memory space built for that type. In the instantiation stage, an instance of that class is created and placed into that memory address. If a class instance type does not match the declared type a fatal error such as memory corruption may occur. The principle of strong typing is all about not allowing you to compile code that may attempt to do that.

As for late binding, it has many practical uses by providing flexibility in type manipulation. One example of true late binding, which is widely used, is when you declare a method parameter as an object and then in the method code convert it into a certain type and assign it to a generic object variable. This example was given in Chapter 8 when we discussed type casting. Here we will show you another type of late binding. In this case an object built from an assembly loaded at runtime is used. To test this example, first add the imports directive for *System.Reflection* namespace:

```
Imports System.Reflection
Dim objGeneric As Object
Dim objAssembly As Assembly = Assembly.LoadFrom _
                ("C:\Components\Products.dll")
objGeneric = objAssembly.CreateInstance("Product")
```

In the above code, a generic object variable is created. Then an *Assembly* object variable is instantiated using the static *LoadFrom* method of the Assembly class. Note that the LoadFrom method takes a path to the DLL assembly file that needs to be loaded. Then we use the Assembly object variable to create an instance of a specified class and assign it to a generic object variable.

Subscribing to Class Events

We discussed class events earlier in this chapter. But knowing how to program class events is only half of the work. The second half is about how to subscribe or capture events raised by a class and then handle them. To receive and process events raised by a class you need to subscribe to them. If you know that a certain class can generate events that you are interested to process, you should adjust your class variable declaration to subscribe to class events. This is done by adding the *WithEvents* keyword to your object variable declaration. For example:

```
Public Class ClassB
    Private WithEvents objClassA As ClassA
End Class
```

Once you have properly declared and instantiated your object variable, you are ready to create object event handlers. The easiest way to create an event handler procedure is by using the code editor method as we described in previous chapters. Open your consumer class in the code editor window. Click on the *Class Name* dropdown list box and select your object variable. Then in the *Method Name* dropdown double-click a desired event implemented by that class. When you do so the code editor will create an empty event handler subroutine for you. For example, the *AccountOpened* event handler that we mentioned earlier in this chapter should look like this:

```
Private Sub objClassA_AccountOpened(ByVal strAcctNumber _
                As String) Handles objClassA.AccountOpened
    'Event handler code
End Sub
```

If a class has multiple events, you may need to repeat the above procedure for each event. Of course, when you get more familiar with event handlers, you can write the wrapper lines of an event handler subroutine yourself. Remember, typically an event handler is a private sub. Its name is made of an object variable name plus the event name connected with an underscore character, followed by a parameters list, the keyword *Handles*, the object variable name and the event name.

Note:

Object variable declarations that contain the *WithEvents* keyword cannot be local procedure variables. They must be class member variables. If you try to place such a declaration in a procedure, you will get an error like the following: "WithEvents is not valid in a local variable declaration."

Using Object Browser

There will be many occasions when you need to lookup or learn the structure of a certain class in a certain assembly. It can be a standard .NET framework DLL, a third-party component or a custom assembly created by a fellow developer. Typically, what you may need to know is the assembly class structure, what methods and properties are implemented by a class and so on. The quickest and easiest way to picture the assembly's inner class structure is by using the Object Browser utility.

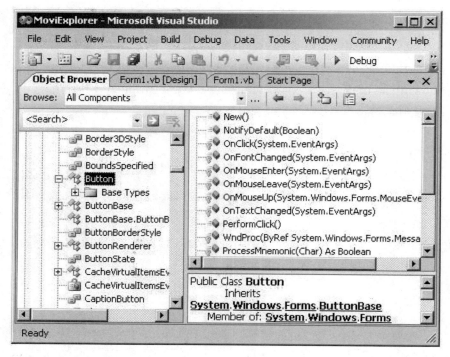

Figure 11.0 Object Browser.

A snapshot of the Object Browser is shown in Figure 11.0. The Object Browser provides a quick view of classes, methods, properties, constants and events implemented in a class. To open the Object Browser, click on its button on the toolbar or click on the View/Object Browser menu or press Ctrl + W, J. The Object Browser will normally show a list of namespaces or libraries referenced in your project including the project itself. Expand the library or namespace that you are interested in and you will see the classes that belong to it. To see the members of any class, highlight or expand the class and you will see all members of the class be it a method, an event or a property. If you want to get more details on any class member you need to select it in the left-hand pane and you will see the details in the right-hand pane.

Furthermore, if you select any method or property in the right-hand pane, you will see its definition in the bottom pane.

Summary

In this chapter, you have learned how to program class constructors, methods, properties and events. You were introduced to object-oriented programming concepts such as encapsulation, inheritance, polymorphism, object binding and learned how to use access modifiers to determine class member visibility.

Lab 11: Project MARS

MARS

In this Project:

You will practice programming a *TradeOrder* class and will create class methods, properties and events. Then you will use this class in a simple order management application to handle trade order data. This project will help you consolidate your knowledge of object-oriented programming principles acquired in Chapter 11.

Create a New Project

- ➢ Create the *Lab11* project folder.
- ➢ Open Visual Studio .NET
- ➢ Create a new Windows Application project.
- ➢ Set the project Location to C:\Labs\Lab11.
- ➢ Set the project Name to *MARS*.

Design User Interface

Add Controls

Add controls to the frmOrders form according to Table 1.

Table 1. The frmOrders form controls and properties.

Control Type	Property Name	Value
Form	Name	frmOrders
-/-	Text	Order Management System
-/-	AcceptButton	btnExecute
GroupBox	Text	Enter Order to Execute:
Label	Text	Symbol
Label	Text	BuySell
Label	Text	Quantity

Label	Text	Price
Label	Text	Execution Status:
Label	Text	Waiting...
-/-	Name	lblStatus
Button	Name	btnExecute
-/-	Text	&Execute
Button	Name	btnClear
-/-	Text	&Clear
Button	Name	btnClose
-/-	Text	Cl&ose
GroupBox	Text	Orders in System:
DataGridView	Name	dataGridView1

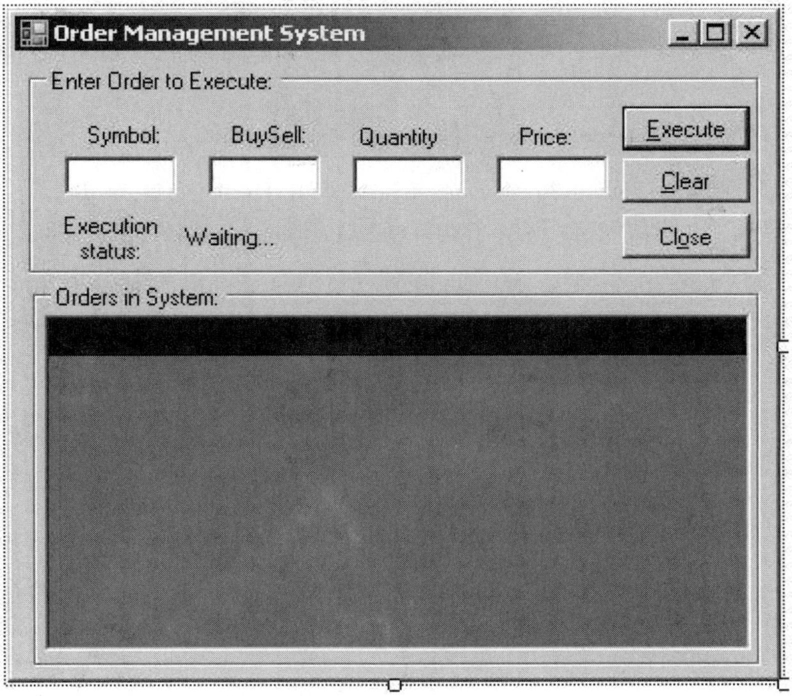

Figure 1. The frmOrders form.

When you finish the user interface design, your form should look like the one shown in Figure 1. There are a few things that you need to pay attention to when you design this form. The AcceptButton property of the form is used to set one button to accept the Enter key press. Set it to the btnExecute button. This button should be created prior to setting this property. The labels and the DataGridView control may keep their defaults.

Write Code

In this lab you will have two classes: the form class and the *TradeOrder* class. Begin coding with the TradeOrder class. Note that you will create code regions in this class that should help you to better structure your code. The entire class code is shown in Listing 1.

Create the TradeOrder Class

This class will model a trade order and processes related to it. Hence, it should implement such functionality as enter order, execute order, send order to the broker, show order status and so on. You will create the following class members: public and private methods, public events and properties and class variables. Please type code presented in Listing 1 into your project.

Listing 1. The TradeOrder class.

```
Imports System
Imports System.Threading.Thread

Public Class TradeOrder
#Region "Class Constructors"
Public Sub New()
End Sub
#End Region
#Region "Private Members"
Private m_strSymbol As String
Private m_intQuantity As Int32
Private m_strBuySell As String
Private m_sngPrice As Single
Private m_strStatus As String
Private m_objRandom As New System.Random(CInt(DateTime.Now.
Ticks Mod Int32.MaxValue))
```

```
#End Region
#Region "Class Events"
Public Event OrderExecuted(ByVal ExecutionTime As DateTime,
ByVal OrderStatus As String, ByVal OrderId As Integer)
#End Region

#Region "Public Properties"
Public Property Symbol() As String
Get
      Return m_strSymbol
End Get
Set(ByVal Value As String)
      m_strSymbol = Value
End Set
End Property
Public Property Quantity() As Int32
Get
      Return m_intQuantity
End Get
Set(ByVal Value As Int32)
      m_intQuantity = Value
End Set
End Property
Public Property Price() As Single
Get
      Return m_sngPrice
End Get
Set(ByVal Value As Single)
```

```vb
            m_sngPrice = Value
End Set
End Property
Public Property BuySell() As String
Get
        Return m_strBuySell
End Get
Set(ByVal Value As String)
        m_strBuySell = Value
End Set
End Property
Public Property Status() As String
Get
        Return m_strStatus
End Get
Set(ByVal Value As String)
        m_strStatus = Value
End Set
End Property
#End Region
#Region "Public Methods"
Public Function ExecuteOrder(ByRef tblOrders As DataTable) As
Boolean
    Dim strData As String
    Dim OrderID As Integer
    Dim strOrderStatus As String
    Dim strTmp As String
    Dim rowData As DataRow
```

```
Try
    OrderID = m_objRandom.Next
    rowData = tblOrders.NewRow()
    strOrderStatus = SendOrder(Quantity)
    rowData("OrderID") = OrderID
    rowData("Symbol") = m_strSymbol
    rowData("BuySell") = m_strBuySell
    rowData("Quantity") = m_intQuantity
    rowData("Price") = m_sngPrice
    rowData("Status") = strOrderStatus
    tblOrders.Rows.Add(rowData)
    RaiseEvent OrderExecuted _
    (DateTime.Now.ToShortDateString(), _
    strOrderStatus, OrderID)
    Return True
Catch ex As Exception
    Throw ex
End Try
End Function
#End Region
#Region "Private Methods"
Private Function SendOrder(ByVal OrderQuantity As _
                                    Integer) As String
Dim strOrderStatus As String
Try
    Sleep(2000)
    If OrderQuantity < 200 Then
        strOrderStatus = OrderQuantity & " Executed"
```

```
    ElseIf OrderQuantity Mod 200 = 0 Then
        strOrderStatus = OrderQuantity & " Executed"
    ElseIf OrderQuantity Mod 200 > 0 Then
        strOrderStatus = "200 Executed"
    ElseIf OrderQuantity > 1000 Then
        strOrderStatus = "Open"
    End If
    Return strOrderStatus
Catch ex As Exception
    Throw ex
End Try
End Function
#End Region
End Class
```

Add Code Regions

If you examine code in Listing 1, you should notice the #Region and #End Region directives. They are used to create labeled code blocks.

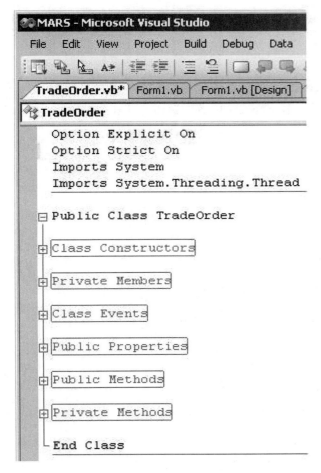

Figure 2. The TradeOrder class code regions.

This is a very helpful feature that we recommend you to use as it helps to better organize code and make it more readable. The region should begin with the *#Region* keyword followed by the region name in double quotes; for example: *#Region "Private Methods."* You should close the region with the *#End Region* line. In this class you created the following regions: Class Constructors, Public Properties, Private Members, Class Events, Public Methods and Private Methods. When you complete coding and collapse all regions your class code page should look like the one shown in Figure 2.

Declare Class Private Members

Create the "Private Members" code region that will contain declarations of class variables prefixed with (m_). Most of these variables will be used to store corresponding class public property values. Here's the code that you should write in this region:

```
#Region "Private Members"

    Private m_strSymbol As String
    Private m_intQuantity As Int32
    Private m_strBuySell As String
    Private m_sngPrice As Single
    Private m_strStatus As String
    Private m_objRandom As New Random _
            CInt(DateTime.Now.Ticks Mod Int32.MaxValue))

#End Region
```

Note that a *Random* object is used to generate random numbers that you will use as order IDs.

Create Class Events

The Class Events region will have one public class event called *OrderExecuted*. You will raise this event in the class whenever you successfully enter the order into the system and get the execution results. Your code should look like the following:

```
Public Event OrderExecuted(ByVal ExecutionTime As DateTime,
ByVal OrderStatus As String, ByVal OrderId As Integer)
```

Notice that the OrderExecuted event declares three parameters that will be used to pass order execution results to a client.

Save your Work

Add Class Public Properties

Write code to create public class properties that should be placed in the Public Properties region. These properties are used to describe the TradeOrder object features such as Symbol, BuySell, Price and so on. Each property procedure implements the Get and Set methods. The former reads the property value from the corresponding class private variable and returns the value to the caller. The latter writes a new value passed by the caller to the same private class variable. Here's an example of one property procedure code; you will find others in Listing 1:

```
Public Property Symbol() As String
    Get
        Return m_strSymbol
    End Get
    Set(ByVal Value As String)
        m_strSymbol = Value
    End Set
End Property
```

Write Class Public Methods

Write code in the Public Methods region. Note that the *ExecuteOrder* method does the main work of creating a DataTable row populated with trade order data passed by a client. Each time a user enters a new trade order, the client (the form class) will call this method to process the order. Trade orders are gradually accumulated in the DataTable object, which temporally replace a database. Please type the following code into your project:

```
Public Function ExecuteOrder(ByRef tblOrders As DataTable) As
Boolean
    Dim strData As String
    Dim OrderID As Integer
    Dim strOrderStatus As String
    Dim strTmp As String
    Dim rowData As DataRow
Try
    OrderID = m_objRandom.Next
    rowData = tblOrders.NewRow()
    strOrderStatus = SendOrder(Quantity)
    rowData("OrderID") = OrderID
    rowData("Symbol") = m_strSymbol
    rowData("BuySell") = m_strBuySell
    rowData("Quantity") = m_intQuantity
    rowData("Price") = m_sngPrice
    rowData("Status") = strOrderStatus
    tblOrders.Rows.Add(rowData)
    RaiseEvent OrderExecuted _
    (DateTime.Now.ToShortDateString(), strOrderStatus, OrderID)
    Return True
```

```
Catch ex As Exception
   MessageBox.Show( ex.Message)
End Try
End Function
```

The first line in the *ExecuteOrder* method gets a random number from the Random object and assigns it to the OrderID variable. Then a DataTable object *tblOrders* creates a new DataRow object and assigns it to the *rowData* variable. After that you call the *SendOrder* method and pass the order quantity value to it and write the order status return value to the *strOrderStatus* variable. Once you are done with the columns data you add a new DataRow to the DataTable object, raise the OrderExecuted event and pass a time stamp and order execution status to it.

Create Private Methods

Create the Private Methods region and type the *SendOrder* function in it. This method is designed to simulate the order execution process. First you call the *Sleep* function to cause a two-second delay in the execution. Then you create a few dummy execution conditions. Below is the code that does it:

```
Sleep(2000)
If OrderQuantity < 200 Then
     strOrderStatus = OrderQuantity & " Executed"
ElseIf OrderQuantity Mod 200 = 0 Then
     strOrderStatus = OrderQuantity & " Executed"
ElseIf OrderQuantity Mod 200 > 0 Then
     strOrderStatus = "200 Executed"
ElseIf OrderQuantity > 1000 Then
     strOrderStatus = "Open"
End If
```

```
Return strOrderStatus
```

Please locate this method's code in Listing 1 and type it into your class. Congratulations! You completed coding the TradeOrder class.

Code the Form Class

In this project, the form class will function as a client that will instantiate and use the functionality provided by the TradeOrder class. You will create a DataTable object and define its columns. In MarsPlus lab you will replace it with a real database table. Also note how you instantiate the TradeOrder class. It should be declared using the *WithEvents* keyword. This way you manage to declare an object variable and also subscribe to receive the class events. In this case you will receive the OrderExecuted event. Then you need to create the event handler procedure to process the event. The entire code of the frmOrders class is shown in Listing 2.

Listing 2. The frmOrders class code.

```
Private WithEvents objTradeOrder As New TradeOrder
Private tblOrders As New DataTable("Orders")

Private Sub btnExecute_Click(ByVal sender As Object, _
    ByVal e As EventArgs) Handles btnExecute.Click
    SubmitOrder()
End Sub

Private Sub SubmitOrder()
Try
    objTradeOrder.Symbol = txtSymbol.Text
```

```vb
        objTradeOrder.BuySell = txtBuySell.Text
        objTradeOrder.Price = txtPrice.Text
        objTradeOrder.Quantity = txtQuantity.Text
        objTradeOrder.ExecuteOrder(tblOrders)
        DataGrid1.DataSource = tblOrders
    Catch ex As Exception
        MessageBox.Show(ex.Message)
    End Try
End Sub
Private Sub InitiliazeDataTable()
    Dim clmOrderId As New DataColumn
    Dim clmSymbol As New DataColumn
    Dim clmQunty As New DataColumn
    Dim clmBuySell As New DataColumn
    Dim clmPrice As New DataColumn
    Dim clmStatus As New DataColumn
    Dim clmOrderType As New DataColumn
    Dim bln As Boolean = True
    Try
        clmOrderId.Caption = "OrderID"
        clmOrderId.ColumnName = "OrderID"
        clmOrderId.MaxLength = 12
        tblOrders.Columns.Add(clmOrderId)
        clmSymbol.Caption = "Symbol"
        clmSymbol.ColumnName = "Symbol"
        clmSymbol.MaxLength = 6
        tblOrders.Columns.Add(clmSymbol)
        clmQunty.Caption = "Quantity"
```

```
    clmQunty.ColumnName = "Quantity"
    clmQunty.MaxLength = 8
    tblOrders.Columns.Add(clmQunty)
    clmBuySell.Caption = "BuySell"
    clmBuySell.ColumnName = "BuySell"
    clmBuySell.MaxLength = 7
    tblOrders.Columns.Add(clmBuySell)
    clmPrice.Caption = "Price"
    clmPrice.ColumnName = "Price"
    clmPrice.MaxLength = 5
    tblOrders.Columns.Add(clmPrice)
    clmStatus.Caption = "Status"
    clmStatus.ColumnName = "Status"
    clmStatus.MaxLength = 18
    tblOrders.Columns.Add(clmStatus)
Catch ex As Exception
    MessageBox.Show(ex.Message)
End Try
End Sub


Private Sub ShowAllOrders()
Try
    DataGrid1.DataSource = tblOrders
Catch ex As Exception
    MessageBox.Show(ex.Message)
End Try
End Sub
```

```vb
Private Sub Form1_Load(ByVal sender As Object, _
      ByVal e As EventArgs) Handles MyBase.Load
      InitiliazeDataTable()
End Sub
Private Sub btnClose_Click(ByVal sender As Object, _
      ByVal e As EventArgs) Handles btnClose.Click
      Me.Close()
End Sub
Private Sub objTradeOrder_OrderExecuted(ByVal ExecutionTime As
Date, ByVal OrderStatus As String, ByVal OrderId As Integer)
Handles objTradeOrder.OrderExecuted
Try
   lblStatus.Text = OrderStatus
   ShowAllOrders()
Catch ex As Exception
   MessageBox.Show(ex.Message)
End Try
End Sub


Private Sub btnClear_Click(ByVal sender As Object, _
         ByVal e As EventArgs) Handles btnClear.Click
Try
   txtSymbol.Text = ""
   txtBuySell.Text = ""
   txtPrice.Text = ""
   txtQuantity.Text = ""
Catch ex As Exception
   MessageBox.Show(ex.Message)
```

```
End Try
End Sub
End Class
```

Write the InitializeDataTable Procedure

The *InitiliazeDataTable* procedure creates a DataTable object, which is passed by reference to a TradeOrder object that will populate it with data. Please find this procedure in Listing 2 and type it into your project.

Write the SubmitOder Procedure

The *SubmitOrder* method is designed to invoke the ExecuteOrder procedure and obtain order execution results. Please locate this method in Listing 2 and type it into your project. When you are done with this procedure, type one line of code in the *btnExecute_Click* event procedure, which will call this procedure.

Save your work

Create the ShowAllOrders Procedure

This is a helper method that will be called every time when you need to refresh the screen or show the most recent data stored in the DataTable object. There is only one line of code in this procedure, which assigns the DataTable object to the DataSource property of the DataGridView control.

Write the OrderExecuted Event Handler

Writing this event procedure should be a good practice in creating event handlers. In your code editor, select the *objTradeOrder* object in the Class Name dropdown and then open the Method Name dropdown and select OrderExecuted event. Please type the following two lines of code:

```
lblStatus.Text = OrderStatus
```

```
ShowAllOrders()
```

Save your work. Congratulations! You completed coding.

Test and Debug

Testing this application should be much easier than coding. However, there is one known bug in the code that can only be identified by testing. Thus, your first task is to test the application functionality. Then you will test a special case, debug the application and correct the problem.

Functionality Testing

Press F5 to run the application. Check if you can enter a new trade order and execute it. Enter any Symbol, BuySell, Quantity, Price and press Enter. Do the results of order execution appear in the data grid? If you get any errors investigate and fix them.

The second test case is related to the order execution logic. To simulate some fake execution conditions we made up the following conditions. If the order quantity is less than 200 then we execute a 100%. If the order quantity divided by 200 has no remainder then we execute a 100% otherwise we execute only the first 200. If the order quantity is greater than 1000 we leave it open meaning we may need to queue it for later execution.

Test each of the above-mentioned conditions. Enter an order with a quantity less than 200. Does it execute in full? Enter an order for 200 shares. Does it execute in full? Enter an order for 300 shares. Does it execute 200 only? Enter an order for 1100 shares? Does it execute 200?

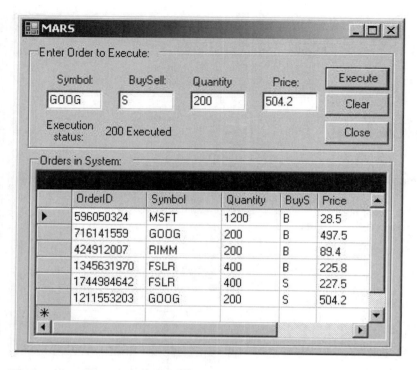

Figure 3. The MARS application at runtime.

Debug the Application

The last order execution result is not correct or at least it's not what you expect it to be. The execution status for orders over 1000 must be *Open*. This means you have a bug. This logic resides in the *SendOrder* procedure. Hence, place a breakpoint on the first line of code in that procedure. Press F5 to start debugging. Enter an order with a quantity over 1000 and press Enter. When execution breaks on its first line press F10 to execute code line by line. When you execute code, pay attention to when the If or Elseif condition is true and where code execution jumps into the Elseif block. You should see that on the second Elseif the test is True because 1100 divided by 200 will have a remainder greater than 0. Therefore, this logical test produces a wrong result. Can you figure out why? You may try to place the "OrderQuantity Mod 200 = 0" as the first ElseIf condition. However, if you do so you will fix one issue but create another. What if you enter 1200? It is greater than 1000 but divides by 200 without a remainder. How to fix this problem? Yes, you need to use "greater than 1000" as the first Elseif condition. Your modified code should look like the following:

```
Private Function SendOrder(ByVal OrderQuantity As Integer) As
String
    Dim strOrderStatus As String
Try
    Sleep(2000)
    If OrderQuantity < 200 Then
        strOrderStatus = OrderQuantity & " Executed"
    ElseIf OrderQuantity > 1000 Then
        strOrderStatus = "Open"
    ElseIf OrderQuantity Mod 200 = 0 Then
        strOrderStatus = OrderQuantity & " Executed"
    ElseIf OrderQuantity Mod 200 > 0 Then
        strOrderStatus = "200 Executed"
    End If
    Return strOrderStatus
Catch ex As Exception
    MessageBox.Show( ex.Message)
End Try
End Function
```

Test the application again by entering quantities 180, 200, 1000, 1100 and 1200. Did you get correct order execution results?

Congratulations! You completed Lab 11.

Chapter 12: Functions and Subroutines

Functions and Subroutines

In this Chapter:

You will consider functions and subroutines. Once you mastered the art of writing programming statements and using code libraries it is time to understand your code structurally. More importantly, you need to learn how to use procedure scope to control code visibility, how to branch your code into procedures to break a complex task into smaller pieces and to better control code execution flow. In this chapter, you will learn all these topics and much more.

Chapter 12 at a Glance

- ➤ Code Modularization
- ➤ Understanding Procedures
- ➤ Creating Subroutines
- ➤ Writing Functions
- ➤ Procedure Scope
- ➤ Advanced Procedure Scope
- ➤ Managing Procedure Calls
- ➤ Code Branching
- ➤ Repeated Code
- ➤ Execution Redirection

Code Modularization

When you examine any Visual Basic application code, you may notice that it consists of two major structural elements: modules and procedures. A program can have a number of modules and each module may contain a set of procedures. For example, an application can have one form class and a number of code classes. Why do we need multiple modules? Can't we put all code into one module? We can but it wouldn't be a good idea. By writing the application code in multiple modules we can divide the source code into separate specialized parts, which makes code easier to read and maintain. This approach is called code modularization. When you compile your project, your code modules will be compiled into one application assembly, which can be a DLL or an EXE.

In Visual Studio 2005, you can also do additional file-based modularization by using partial classes. In this case, one class can be coded in multiple partial classes, each located in its own file. Also, in .NET you can write code in separate modules, compile them into netmodule and when necessary use the assembly linker utility (AL) to link them into one assembly. This feature opens a lot of additional possibilities to divide application source code into parts that can be developed by different team members. In this chapter, we will focus on the main aspects of procedure programming and code branching.

Understanding Procedures

You will, probably, spend a lot of your development time writing various procedures. What is a code procedure? Functions, methods and subroutines all refer to approximately the same entity. They denote a relatively independent piece of code in a program that can perform a certain computation task and can be called from within that program. In other words, a procedure is the smallest callable piece of code in a program that can perform a certain task, can accept parameters and return results.

In most cases a procedure may contain the body, parameters and the return value. In a high-level programming language, procedure code boundaries are marked by the so-called wrapper lines that signal the beginning and the end of a procedure. The procedure name is embedded into the opening wrapper line. For example:

```
Public Sub GetAccountDetails()
```

The end of a procedure code is marked by the *End Sub* or *End Function* lines. All procedures must have an argument list enclosed in parentheses. The argument list, which can be empty, is used to declare procedure parameters. When a procedure is called, all executable code in it is executed. In Visual Basic .NET, there are two types of procedures: functions and subroutines. The only difference between them is that the former can return values while the latter cannot.

Are procedures created equal? No. Some procedures are *well-connected* (wired) while others are *stand-alone* (unwired). The source of this difference is pretty simple. All event handlers and property procedures are wired to corresponding events or properties. Wired procedures are automatically executed when the event fires or the property is referenced. All event handlers should be implemented as subroutines. Typically, they have a pre-defined arguments list. For example, all button click event procedures define two parameters: an *object* (sender) parameter, which represents a class that raised the event, and an event *arguments* parameter which carries the information about the event itself; for example, an *EventArgs* parameter. The sender parameter can be used to reconstruct the object that fired the event, which in our case is the button class. The *EventArgs* parameter can be used to get various characteristics of the event. For example, in case of a click event, it can tell which mouse button is clicked, the number of clicks and the cursor location. The unwired procedures are executed only if you call them from your code. They can be either subroutines or functions. You make this decision based on whether you plan to use the method's return value or not. In the rest of this chapter, we will talk about functions and subroutines in more detail.

Creating Subroutines

Creating a *Sub* should begin with writing the opening procedure wrapper line. If you manage to write it properly and press Enter, Visual Basic will insert the ending line for you. To write the opening line, you need to type the procedure access modifier keyword; for example, *Public,* the keyword *Sub* followed by the procedure name and the argument list. Making up procedure names should abide to the same naming conventions and rules as for variables, which we discussed in Chapter 5. Thus, a Sub's opening wrapper line should include the following elements:

- ➤ Access modifier.
- ➤ Keyword *Sub.*
- ➤ Procedure name.
- ➤ Argument list.

For example:

```
Private Sub ShowReport()
```

Writing Functions

Everything said about subroutines is relevant and will work for functions as well. However, there is one significant difference: A function can return a value while a sub cannot. Therefore, when you create a function procedure you should do the following: Replace the keyword *Sub* with the keyword *Function* and declare the function's return data type. The following is a simple function procedure that accepts no parameters and defines its return data type as *Single*:

```
Public Function GetAccountBalance() As Single
      Dim sngAmount as Single
```

```
    sngAmount = 9800.56
    Return sngAmount
End Function
```

Note that somewhere in the function body, typically at the end, you need to assign its return value. The return value data type must match the declared function return data type. If you do not assign a value, a default value will be used, which is normally equal to the Visual Basic .NET initialization value. For example, a string variable is initialized to an empty string (zero-length string), an integer – to 0 and so on.

There are two ways to set a function's return value. You can use the keyword *Return* followed by a literal value, an expression or a variable. Consider this a recommended way. Alternatively, you may use a VB 6 legacy method, in which case you should assign the return value to the function name. Here's how the above function would look in this case:

```
Public Function GetAccountBalance() As Single
    Dim sngAmount as Single
    sngAmount = 9800.56
    GetAccountBalance  = sngAmount
End Function
```

Note that in this case the function name is used as the return parameter and the return value is assigned to it.

Procedure Scope

In Chapter 11, we briefly introduced the access modifiers in the context of class declaration. Here we will consider this topic in relation to procedure scope. Procedure scope is determined by an access modifier used to declare it. In Visual Basic .NET, there are five access modifiers:

> ➤ Public – Has no access limitations.
> ➤ Private – Limits access to the declaration context only.
> ➤ Friend – Access limited to home assembly.
> ➤ Protected – Accessible in a derived class and in the containing class.
> ➤ Protected Friend – Combines accessibility of Friend and Protected.

These five code accessibility flags should be interpreted as follows. A *Public* flag is simple and imposes no access restrictions. The *Private*, on the contrary, is the most restrictive one. Its accessibility is limited to the class where it was declared, which constitutes its declaration context. A *Friend* access modifier provides access within a home assembly. Thus, if you have two assembly level classes in your home assembly then Friend methods in each class will be able to talk to each other. The *Protected* flag controls access to inherited code. If your class inherits from another class you will be able to access Public, Protected and Protected Friend methods of that class. By using access modifiers you can create the following procedure accessibility variations: global, inter-assembly, inter-class, derived class and declaration context.

Procedure Accessibility Categories:

> ➤ Global
> ➤ Inter-assembly
> ➤ Inter-class
> ➤ Derived class
> ➤ Declaration context

A global scope provides the capability of direct access from anywhere within the entire application. A global procedure can be created by declaring a public method in a public module. A *Module* is a specific Visual Basic .NET phenomenon. It is yet another VB 6 legacy item, where it was called a *Standard Module*. You should first add a module to your project and then create global methods, properties and variables.

The inter-assembly context can be established between a public method of a public class residing in one assembly, and a similar method and class in another assembly. All public procedures created in public classes are visible in the inter-assembly context. Procedures declared with Friend or Protected Friend access modifiers in classes visible inside an assembly can be visible in the inter-class context. Any procedure declared in an inheritable class using a Protected access modifier is accessible in the derived class context and in its declaration context. Finally, all private procedures are limited to their declaration context only. Now let's look at some examples.

Listing 1. Procedure scope.

```
Namespace AssemblyA
Public Class ConsumerA
      Public Sub TestMethod()
          Dim objServer As New ServerA()
          'Inter-class context calls
          objServer.FriendMethod()
          objServer.ProtectedFriendMethod()
      End Sub
End Class
Public Class ServerA
      Public Sub PublicMethod()
          'Declaration context method call
          PrivateMethod()
      End Sub
```

```
        Private Sub PrivateMethod()
        End Sub
        Friend Sub FriendMethod()
        End Sub
        Protected Sub ProtectedMethod()
        End Sub
        Protected Friend Sub ProtectedFriendMethod()
        End Sub
End Class
End Namespace
```

Listing 1 presents an assembly with two public classes and is used to illustrate the inter-class and declaration context levels of accessibility. From the *TestMethod* of a *ConsumerA* class you can call *ServerA* class methods: *PublicMethod, FriendMethod* and *ProtectedFriendMethod*. So these procedures exemplify the inter-class accessibility context. In a *ServerA* class there is a private method that is visible only within that class, which represents its declaration context.

Listing 2. Global and derived class contexts.

```
Namespace AssemblyB
Public Class ConsumerB
            Inherits ServerB
  Public Sub TestMethod()
        'Call a global method
        GlobalMethod()
        'Call the base class method
        ProtectedMethod()
```

```
    End Sub
    Public Overrides Sub MustOverrideMethod()
        'Overrides the base class method
    End Sub
    Public Overrides Sub OverridableMethod()
        'Overrides the base class method
    End Sub
End Class
Public MustInherit Class ServerB
    Protected Sub ProtectedMethod()
    End Sub
    Public Overridable Sub OverridableMethod()
    End Sub
    Public MustOverride Sub MustOverrideMethod()
    Public Sub PublicMethod()
    End Sub
End Class
End Namespace
Public Module Module1
    Public Sub GlobalMethod()
                    'Procedure code
    End Sub
End Module
```

Listing 2 presents examples of global and inherited code accessibility levels. It contains two classes and one module. A public method in Module1 module is an example of a global method. Note that you need not create an object variable or specify the module name to call a global method. *ConsumerB* and *ServerB* classes are used to illustrate the procedure scope in a derived class. The ConsumerB class inherits an abstract class ServerB, which contains Protected, MustOverride, Overridable and Public methods. A Protected method will flow into a derived class and will be visible anywhere in that class. A MustOverride method is not only visible in a derived class but must also be overridden in it.

Managing Procedure Calls

How do procedures get executed? As you may already know it depends on the procedure type. All event procedures are automatically executed when the corresponding event fires. The same is true about property procedures that are executed when you reference the property in code, i.e. when you read or write to a property. Unwired procedures are executed only if you call them from some other procedure. Thus, a procedure call can be made only from another procedure. In a procedure call chain one procedure acts as a calling procedure and the other as a called procedure. This distinction is important to understand our further discussion of procedure parameters and code execution flow. To call a procedure you need to specify the procedure name and pass required parameters. This creates an execution flow in which one procedure calls another procedure in a certain order or sequence. To optimize code execution flow you may need to branch your code.

Code Branching

You can significantly improve code execution efficiency by properly branching your application code. Code branching is all about understanding when and why you should break your code into separate procedures. Remember our question at the beginning of this chapter about a module? You can ask the same question about a procedure. Can you write all of your code in one procedure? Theoretically, you can. But it won't be a good idea. Then how do you know when to branch your code? Of course, many code branching decisions are up to a developer to make and some of these questions will be answered gradually in the process of acquiring programming experience. However, the knowledge of some basic principles will help to streamline this process from the very beginning. Let's consider a few cases where code branching is strongly recommended and may provide an optimized solution.

Code Branching Scenarios

➢ Handling repeated code.

➢ Redirection of code execution.

➢ Breaking a complex task into smaller logical units.

➢ Creating complex execution patterns.

Repeated Code

When you write code you should be aware of any repeated code sections. These pieces of code are good candidates for branching. Consider putting them into separate procedures within the execution context. It will not only improve performance but will also simplify future changes and maintenance. For example, if you have code that calculates taxes or discount amounts and is used in multiple procedures, you may consider putting it into a separate procedure.

Execution Redirection

Redirection of execution may be necessary when you want to execute certain pieces of code conditionally or based on certain calculation results. Here by redirection of execution we mean sending the execution pointer to a different section of code within the same procedure. Note that calling other procedures should not be treated as redirection. As a matter of fact, very often redirection may become necessary as a result of poor or no code branching. If you find yourself in a situation where within your procedure code you want to redirect the execution you should consider code branching. Your diligence in code branching should normally translate into creating procedures that need no redirection of execution.

However, if you think that redirection is inevitable then you can use the *goto* command to send the execution to a labeled block of code in your procedure. Goto is a legacy command inherited from VB 6. We do not recommend using it because of the following two reasons: First, any procedure that includes *goto* will not lend itself to procedure call in-lining optimization; second, code that includes *goto* is not easy to read and maintain. Also keep in mind that procedure call in-lining may not be applied if you use complex execution flow controls such as *Select Case*.

There is another execution control technique that you need to know. In some cases, you may want to stop code execution and exit before the end of the procedure is reached. Here you can use the *Return* command or one of the legacy commands such as *Exit Sub* or *Exit Function*. This may be useful when your data validation or calculation results make further code execution irrelevant or pointless. For example, if in your file open procedure you find out that the file path is not specified or is invalid, you may stop further code execution by calling the Return command.

In this context, it will also make sense to say a few words about the procedure return event. You may hear the phrase "when procedure call returns" very often. If you debug any code that contains procedure calls you will notice that when the called procedure completes, the execution control returns to the statement that made a procedure call. This creates a good checkpoint between the calling and the called procedure that allows you to check how the called procedure performed and then apply your decision-making logic. For example, if the called procedure completes successfully you may continue normal execution, and if it fails take other appropriate actions.

Creating Algorithms

One of the most exciting applications of code branching is probably designing
algorithms. Given that an algorithm is a schema of actions aimed at solving a complex
task then using code branching is a way to programmatically implement such a task.
In this case, dividing code into separate procedures allows you to break the main
task into smaller, logically related units and then execute them in a certain sequence.
Typically, algorithm efficiency greatly depends on optimal control of the code
execution sequence combined with the interpretation of return values and decision-
making.

Summary

In this chapter, you were introduced to topics related to programming functions and subroutines such as code modularization, procedure scope and code branching. Learning how to write procedures and branch your code are very essential programming skills. In Visual Basic .NET, there are subroutine and function procedures that differ only in whether they can return values or not. Procedures can accept parameters that are used to pass input data and return results. Procedure scope is a concept that explains how you can determine your procedure accessibility. The code branching concept describes the principles of when and why you should divide your code into separate procedures.

Lab 12: The File Utility Project

File Utility

In this Project:

You will practice creating subroutines, functions and code branching. You will practice coding a *TreeView* and a *ListView* controls, *OpenFileDialog* component and an *ImageList* class. In terms of functionality, a program that you will create in this project is relatively simple. It allows users to browse a file system and transfer files.

Create a New Project

- ➤ Create the *Lab12* project folder.
- ➤ Open Visual Studio .NET
- ➤ Create a new Windows Application project.
- ➤ Set the project Location to C:\Labs\Lab12.
- ➤ Set the project Name to *FileUtility*.

Design User Interface

Add Controls

In this project, you will use a TreeView, ListView, ImageList controls and an OpenFileDialog component. Add these and other controls to the project according to Table 1.

Table 1. The Form1 form controls.

Control Type	Property Name	Value
Form	Name	Form1
-/-	Text	File Transfer Program
GroupBox	Name	GroupBox1
TreeView	Name	TreeView1
ListView	Name	ListView1
Label	Name	Label1
Label	Text	Source:
Label	Name	Label2
Label	Text	Destination:
Label	Name	Label3
Label	Text	Status:
Label	Name	Label1
Label	Text	Source
Label	Name	lblStatus
Label	Text	Waiting...
TextBox	Name	txtDestination
TextBox	Name	txtSource
Button	Name	btnBrowse
-/-	Text	&Browse
Button	Name	btnTransfer
-/-	Text	&Transfer
Button	Name	btnClose
-/-	Text	&Close

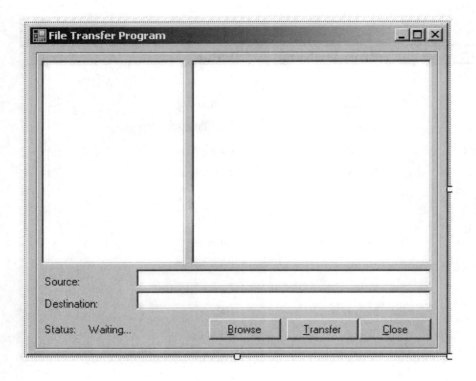

Figure 1. The File Transfer Program form.

When you complete the design work, your form should look like the one shown in Figure 1.

Write Code

Begin your application coding by typing the imports directive that will reference the *System.IO* namespace. This namespace contains various file manipulation classes that you will use in this project:

```
Imports System.IO
```

Add Form Variables

You will need at least two form level variables. The first one is named *m_ IconFilesFolder* and is used to store the icon images folder path. The second one is an *ImageList* object variable, which is used to store icon images. Place these declarations in the "Form Variables" region.

```
#Region "Form Variables"
    Private m_IconFilesFolder As String
    Private m_ImageList As New ImageList()
#End Region
```

Create Application Procedures

In this part of the project you will create application private procedures. These are standalone, unwired procedures that will be executed only if you call them from your code. Please type code presented in Listing 1 into your project.

Listing 1. Private methods.

```
#Region "Private Methods"
Private Sub InitializeFormObjects()
Try
    m_IconFilesFolder = "C:\Labs\Lab12\Icons"
    PopulateImageList(m_IconFilesFolder)
    ListView1.Columns.Add("File Name")
    ListView1.View = View.Details
Catch ex As Exception
    MessageBox.Show(ex.Message)
End Try
```

```
End Sub
Private Sub PopulateTreeView(ByVal strFolderPath As String)
    Dim objDirInfo As DirectoryInfo
    Dim arrDirInfos() As DirectoryInfo
    Dim objTopTreeNode As TreeNode
    Dim objNode As TreeNode
    Dim strTopDirName As String
    Dim strFolderNameOnly As String
    Dim strFullName As String
Try
    objDirInfo = New DirectoryInfo(strFolderPath)
    arrDirInfos = objDirInfo.GetDirectories("*", SearchOption.
    TopDirectoryOnly)
    strTopDirName = strFolderPath.Substring _
    (strFolderPath.LastIndexOf("\") + 1)
    objTopTreeNode = New TreeNode(strTopDirName, 1, 1)
    'Set a TreeView object to use the ImageList TreeView1.
    ImageList = m_ImageList
    'Set the default "folder" image index
    TreeView1.ImageIndex = 0
    For Each objDirInfo In arrDirInfos
        strFullName = objDirInfo.FullName
        strFolderNameOnly = strFullName.Substring _
        (strFullName.LastIndexOf("\") + 1)
        objNode = New TreeNode(strFolderNameOnly)
        objNode.Tag = strFullName
        objTopTreeNode.Nodes.Add(objNode)
    Next
```

```vb
        'We are done creating child nodes
        'Add nodes to the TreeView
        TreeView1.Nodes.Add(objTopTreeNode)
Catch ex As Exception
        MessageBox.Show(ex.Message)
End Try
End Sub
Private Sub ShowFolderFiles(ByVal strSelectedFolderPath As
String)
        Dim objDirInfo As DirectoryInfo
        Dim arrFileInfo() As FileInfo
        Dim objFileInfo As FileInfo
        Dim strFileName As String
        Dim strFullFileName As String
        Dim objListItem As ListViewItem
Try
        'Get selected folder path
        objDirInfo = New DirectoryInfo (strSelectedFolderPath)
        'Put files into FileInfo array
        arrFileInfo = objDirInfo.GetFiles()
        'Clean ListView previous state
        ListView1.Clear()
        ListView1.Columns.Add("File Name")
        ListView1.View = View.Details
        'Show files in the ListView
        For Each objFileInfo In arrFileInfo
                strFullFileName = objFileInfo.FullName
                strFileName = strFullFileName.Substring _
```

```vbnet
                (strFullFileName.LastIndexOf("\") + 1)
                objListItem = New ListViewItem(strFileName)
                objListItem.Tag = strFullFileName
                ListView1.Items.Add(objListItem)
        Next
    Catch ex As Exception
        MessageBox.Show(ex.Message)
    End Try
    End Sub
    Private Function TransferFiles(ByVal strSourceFilePath As
    String, ByVal strSorceFilename As String) As Boolean
        Dim strDestinationFolder As String

    Try
        lblStatus.Text = "Processing..."
        If strSourceFilePath.Length = 0 Or _
                strSorceFilename.Length = 0 Then
                Return False
        End If
        strDestinationFolder = txtDestination.Text
        If strDestinationFolder.Length = 0 Then
            MessageBox.Show("Please enter destination path")
            Return False
        End If
        File.Copy(strSourceFilePath, _
                strDestinationFolder + strSorceFilename)
        Return True
    Catch ex As Exception
```

```vbnet
        MessageBox.Show(ex.Message)
        Return False
    End Try
End Function
Private Sub PopulateImageList(ByVal strFolderPath As String)
    Dim objDirInfo As DirectoryInfo
    Dim objFileInfo As FileInfo
    Dim strFileName As String
Try
    'Create directory info
    objDirInfo = New DirectoryInfo(strFolderPath)
    'Get image file names and create image objects
    'Add them to the ImageList object
    For Each objFileInfo In objDirInfo.GetFiles
        strFileName = objFileInfo.FullName
        If Not strFileName.Contains("Thumbs") Then
            m_ImageList.Images.Add(Image.FromFile(strFileName))
        End If
    Next
Catch ex As Exception
    MessageBox.Show(ex.Message)
End Try
End Sub
#End Region
```

Note that in Listing 1 all application procedures are placed in the region called "Private Methods." After you are done with typing, we advise you to walk through the code and try to understand the logic of each statement.

Write Event Handlers

Type all event handlers shown in Listing 2 into your project. They are used to invoke worker procedures created earlier. Note that in the TreeView1_ NodeMouseClick event procedure you will extract the node object from the *TreeNodeMouseClickEventArgs* object and use it to read the node tag that should contain the path to a selected directory from where you will read the file names and show them in the ListView control.

Please remember a trick to get the wrapper lines of each event procedure typed for you. Right-click the control and select Properties. At the top of the Properties window, click on the lightning bolt icon, which represents the Events button. This should display all control events. Double-click the event for which you want to write an event procedure. This should open the code editor window and type the event procedure wrapper lines for you.

Listing 2. Event handlers.

```
#Region "Event Handlers"
Private Sub TreeView1_NodeMouseClick(ByVal sender _
    As System.Object, ByVal e As TreeNodeMouseClickEventArgs) _
    Handles TreeView1.NodeMouseClick
Try
    If e.Node.Tag Is Nothing Then
        Return
    End If
    ShowFolderFiles(e.Node.Tag.ToString())
Catch ex As Exception
    MessageBox.Show(ex.Message)
End Try
```

```vb
End Sub


Private Sub btnTransfer_Click(ByVal sender As System.Object,
ByVal e As System.EventArgs) Handles btnTransfer.Click
    Dim colListviewItems As ListView.
    SelectedListViewItemCollection
    Dim strFullFileName As String
    Dim strFileName As String
    Dim i As Integer
    Dim intCount As Integer
    Dim strErr As String
    Dim strStatus As String
Try
    strErr = ""
    intCount = 0
    colListviewItems = ListView1.SelectedItems
    For i = 0 To colListviewItems.Count - 1
        strFullFileName = colListviewItems.Item(i).Tag.ToString()
        strFileName = colListviewItems.Item(i).Text
        Try
            TransferFiles(strFullFileName, strFileName)
            intCount += 1
        Catch ex As Exception
            strErr += ex.Message
        End Try
    Next
    strStatus = intCount & " files transferred."
    If strErr.Length > 0 Then
```

```
        strStatus += " Errors: " & strErr
    End If
    lblStatus.Text = strStatus
Catch ex As Exception
    MessageBox.Show(ex.Message)
End Try
End Sub


Private Sub btnClose_Click(ByVal sender As System.Object, ByVal
e As System.EventArgs) Handles btnClose.Click
      Me.Close()
End Sub


Private Sub Form1_Load(ByVal sender As Object, _
                ByVal e As EventArgs) Handles MyBase.Load
    InitializeFormObjects()
End Sub
Private Sub btnBrowse_Click(ByVal sender As Object, _
                ByVal e As EventArgs) Handles btnBrowse.Click
    Dim strSourceFolder As String
    Dim i As Integer
Try
    'Get the source folder name and path
    'Show OpenFileDialog to select a file
    OpenFileDialog1.ShowDialog()
    strSourceFolder = OpenFileDialog1.FileName
    'Truncate the file name.
    'Use the last "\" as an offset
```

```
    i = strSourceFolder.LastIndexOf("\")
    strSourceFolder = strSourceFolder.Substring(0, i)
    PopulateTreeView(strSourceFolder)
    txtSource.Text = strSourceFolder
Catch ex As Exception
    MessageBox.Show(ex.Message)
End Try
End Sub


#End Region
```

When you complete coding, check your code for any possible typos and errors. A good method to quickly identify all errors is to try to build the project. Proceed to application testing only when you are able to successfully build the application.

Test and Debug

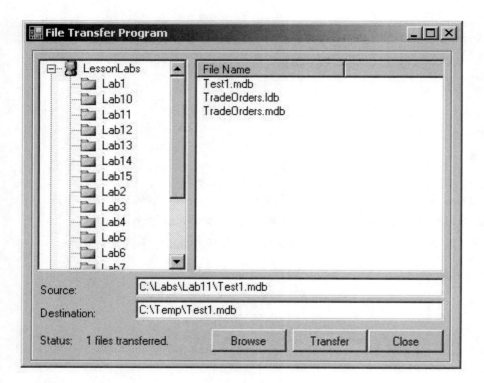

Figure 2. File Transfer program at runtime.

Pres Ctrl + F5 to run the application without debugging and test the following:

- Click on the Browse button. Does it display the Open File Dialog box?
- Select a file from any folder. The application should extract the path to that folder. Is the folder path correctly shown in the Source textbox?
- Check if all subfolders contained in the selected folder are displayed in the TreeView.

- Click on any node in the TreeView control. All files in that folder should be displayed in the ListView.
- In the Destination textbox type the file destination path and click on the Transfer button. Verify that the file is copied to the destination directory.

Congratulations! You successfully completed this project.

Extra Credit Task 1

The program has at least one known bug. If you find more you deserve a special credit. To activate the bug, perform the following test. Run the application and click on the Browse button. Navigate to any folder and without selecting any file click on the Cancel button. You should get an error message like the following.

Use all of your debugging skills learned so far and try to identify what line of code causes this error and why. Then figure out how to protect the program from this type of runtime error. Hint: Place a breakpoint at the beginning line of btnBrowse_Click event procedure and press F5 to start debugging. Step into each line of code until you get an error. Analyze why the error occurs and write code to prevent it. Good luck.

Extra Credit Task 2

A *MessageBox* dialog box can be configured to better represent the application that shows it. For example, the message box shown above does not display the application or procedure name. Can you program a *MessageBox* to show which procedure generated this error message and show the application name? Hint: You can do it by adding the second parameter to the *MessageBox.Show* method call.

Part YII   Application Data Access

Application Data Access

Chapter 13: Programming ADO .NET

Programming ADO .NET

In this Chapter:

You will learn how to program ADO .NET. Any program normally needs to connect to a database and manipulate data. Database connectivity is a very critical point of any application. That's why solid knowledge and understanding of application data access programming is so important. In this chapter, we will cover the main aspects of the ADO .NET functionality and will show you how to use them in your own projects.

Chapter 13 at a Glance

- ➤ ADO .NET Components
- ➤ How ADO. NET Works
- ➤ Connecting to Databases
- ➤ SQL Server Connections
- ➤ Oracle Connections
- ➤ MS Access Connections
- ➤ OleDB Connections
- ➤ SQL Server OleDb Connections
- ➤ Oracle OleDb Connections
- ➤ ODBC Connections
- ➤ DSN-Based Connections
- ➤ Non-DSN ODBC Connections
- ➤ Programming a DataAdapter
- ➤ Using a SqlDataAdapter
- ➤ Using a DataSet
- ➤ Programming a Command Object
- ➤ Using a DataReader

ADO .NET Components

The ADO .NET library contains four top-level components: SqlClient, OracleClient, OleDB and ODBC, which represent four data access providers. The first two are designed to provide access to the SQL Server and Oracle databases correspondingly while OleDB and ODBC can be used for almost any other database type.

When you use ADO .NET objects, your program acts as a client to a database server. This fact is reflected in the first two component names: SqlClient and OracleClient. These components belong to the so-called managed providers while OleDB and ODBC are unmanaged providers. From the binding perspective the SqlClient and OracleClient have one more common feature—both are early bound, which means that a corresponding database type is set at design time. For example, when you use the SqlClient connection class you do not have to specify the database provider because it is internally set to the SQL Server. The same is true about the OracleClient connection class. With the unmanaged providers such as OleDB and ODBC, the provider name is extracted from the connection string or from the DSN at runtime, which impacts performance.

Thus, when you prepare to code your database connection you have to make a decision as to which ADO .NET provider you will use. Your decision may be based on a number of factors, which may include the database type, application configuration, performance considerations, user machine setup, application deployment and some others. Each ADO .NET component contains a large number of classes. Here we will focus on a set of frequently used classes, which will include the following:

> Connection Class
> Command Class
> DataAdapter Class
> DataReader Class

Each ADO .NET database provider has an approximately similar class structure and all the above-mentioned classes are present in each of them. However, each component implements a database-specific version. For example, the SqlClient has a SqlConnection, SqlCommand, SqlDataAdapter and SqlDataReader classes. Similarly, the OracleClient contains the OracleConnection, OracleCommand, OracleDataAdapter and OracleDataReader. The functionality provided by these classes is very similar so if you learn how to program one of them you are ready to use others. First make sure that you know where these classes reside in the .NET FCL library of classes. The SqlClient, OleDB and ODBC components are located in *System. Data* namespace. The OracleClient component will also appear under *System.Data* but you need to add a reference to *OracleClient.dll* first. Note that in your Windows application projects the reference to *System.Data* is added by default. The following namespaces contain data access provider classes:

> *System.Data* – Contains all generic data access classes.
> *System.Data.SqlClient* – SQL Server provider classes.
> *System.Data.OracleClient* – Oracle provider classes.
> *System.Data.Odbc* – ODBC provider classes.
> *System.Data.OleDb* – OleDB provider classes.

How ADO .NET Works

Let's take a look at how ADO .NET classes work. What is associated with typical application data access functionality? For example, what is involved in a simple data retrieval task? First, you need to establish a connection to a database system. Second, you should execute a select query that returns a resultset. Then load data into a transportation device and move it to the client application site. Thus, retrieving data from a data source can be broken into three main stages: establishing a connection, data extract and data transportation to the client. Each of these three tasks is accomplished by a corresponding ADO .NET class: *Connection*, *Command* or *DataAdapter* and *DataSet* or *DataReader* classes.

The Connection class is obviously the first player in this game. It contacts a database manager and requests a connection session. The database manager always listens to such requests and if it has available recourses it will grant one to the caller. Once a connection is established, the work of a connection object is almost done. However, you will need to keep a connection open and a connection object alive until you finish retrieving data. The data extract part can be done by a *DataAdapter* or a *Command* object or both. These two objects act as data warehouse supervisors who are supposed to check if your SQL statement is correct and valid, send it to the database to execute and when necessary, load data into a transportation device.

There are two main programmatic data transportation devices: a *DataSet* and a *DataReader*. Typically, the DataAdapter is used to fill up a DataSet and the Command is used to load a DataReader. If you try to populate a DataSet manually as you did in the MovieExplorer lab, you will certainly appreciate the hard work accomplished by the DataAdapter. A DataSet is a heavyweight carrier that is more like a portable database. It takes all the data contained in the resultset and carries it to the client in one network trip. Additionally, it can have multiple DataTables and allows you to mimic the relationships between tables and much more. A database connection can be closed immediately after a DataSet is loaded.

A DataReader is a lightweight object that can carry only one record at a time. Hence, if your resultset contains a dozen records it has to make a dozen network trips to transport them to a client application. Of course, during this time the connection must be kept open. The Command and DataReader classes can also be used to do more specific and granular work. For example, extract a single value or a record or execute a stored procedure. Keep in mind that there are some limitations to the use of DataReaders. For example, only one active DataReader (active resultset) per application is allowed. In the rest of this chapter, we will show you how to program database connections, execute a Command object methods and use a DataSet and DataReader.

Connecting to Databases

Opening a connection to a database is a very critical and error-prone process. That's why it makes sense to have a dedicated procedure that will open and close a connection to a database and handle all potential errors. To properly configure your connection class object you need to know how to build a database specific connection string and instantiate a Connection object for each database type.

SQL Server Connections

To program a SQL Server database connection you should use a SqlConnection class contained in the SqlClient component. Make sure that you have referenced *System. Data* in your project and in your class code you may want to add the imports directive for *System.Data.SqlClient* namespace like this:

```
Imports System.Data.SqlClient
```

Then you should write a connection string and pass it your connection object. The connection string may contain a number of name value pair parameters separated by a semi-colon. In a typical connection string you may include the following parameters: a server name, user name, password and a database name. To connect using a SQL Server login you should provide a user name and password. The user name parameter is presented as *User ID* or *UID* and the password—as *Password* or *PWD*. Your connection string may look like this:

```
strCon ="Server= svr1;User ID=user;Password=password1;"
strCon += "Database=Products"
```

If the Windows authentication is used instead, you should replace the user name and password with the *Integrated Security* parameter. In this case your connection string may look like the following:

```
strCon = "Server=svr1;Integrated Security=true;"
strCon += "Database=Products"
```

Note that all parameter names are not case sensitive. In most cases it will make sense to build a connection string before you try to instantiate a connection object. Then you can pass the connection string at the object instantiation stage or assign it to the *ConnectionString* property after the object is instantiated. A *SqlConnection* class offers two constructors: the default constructor that does not take any parameters and a custom constructor that takes a connection string parameter.

Using a Parameterized Constructor:

```
Dim strCon As String
Dim objSqlCon As SqlConnection
strCon ="Server=svr1;Integrated Security=true;Database=DB1"
objSqlCon = New SqlConnection(strCon)
```

Alternatively, you may use a default constructor that does not take parameters and then later assign the connection information to a connection object's *ConnectionString* property:

Using a Default Constructor:

```
Dim strCon As String
Dim objSqlCon As SqlConnection
```

```
strCon   = "Server=svr1;Integrated Security=true;Database=DB1"
objSqlCon = New SqlConnection()
objSqlCon.ConnectionString = strCon
```

Once you have successfully built a connection string and instantiated a connection object, you may open a connection at any time by calling the connection object's *Open* method:

```
objSqlCon.Open()
```

Note that if you open a connection using the *Open* method you should make sure that you close it using the *Close* method.

Open Connection Procedure

If your application needs to open and close connections multiple times, it will make sense to create separate open and close connection procedures. In this case a connection object should be a class-level variable. This way you will make it accessible from anywhere in your class and also be able to ensure connection pooling. Here's a sample of an open connection procedure:

```
Private m_objSqlCon As SqlConnection
Private m_strCon As String
Private Function OpenSQLConnection() As Boolean
Try
    If m_objSqlCon Is Nothing Then
        m_objSqlCon = New SqlConnection(m_strCon)
    End If
    If m_objSqlCon.State = ConnectionState.Closed Then
        m_objSqlCon.Open()
```

```
    End If
    Return True
Catch sqlEx As SqlException
    Throw New Exception(sqlEx.Message)
Catch ex As Exception
    Throw ex
End Try
End Function
```

This procedure may be called from anywhere in your class. If a connection object is already instantiated or a connection is open, it will do nothing. Note that the way you handle errors in the Catch blocks should be in agreement with your application requirements.

SQL Server Connection String

Connection string parameters may differ from one database provider to another. The following parameters are used by the SQL Server and are common to most database types:

- Data Source (Server) – SQL Server database machine name.
- Initial Catalog (Database) – Database name.
- User ID (UID) – Database user name.
- Password (PWD) – Database user password.
- Integrated Security – Windows authentication parameter.

Note that most parameter names have aliases. For example, the *Data Source* parameter can be replaced with the *Server* and *Initial Catalog*—with *Database*. Remember that a connection string uses name-value parameters and their order is not important. Parameters must be separated by a semi-colon and no quotation marks are necessary.

Oracle Connections

To establish an Oracle connection, you need to do practically the same as for the SQL Server but using the *OracleClient* component and classes. However, there are some differences in the connection string. First, add a reference to *System.Data. OracleClient.dll* and the imports directive to your class:

```
Imports System.Data.OracleClient
```

Build an Oracle connection string and create an *OracleConnection* class object variable. Your code may look like the following:

```
Dim strCon As String
Dim objOraCon As OracleConnection
strCon = "Data Source=Database1;UID=user;PWD=password"
objOraCon = New OracleConnection(strCon)
objOraCon.Open()
```

In this chapter, we consider three database types: SQL Server, Oracle and MS Access. For the SQL Server and Oracle we recommend using corresponding managed providers discussed earlier. For MS Access there is no managed provider so your choice is limited to OleDB or ODBC. You can use OleDB and ODBC for the SQL Server and Oracle too but you should do so only if there is a strong reason for not using the managed providers. In the following sections, we will show you how to use OleDB and ODBC for all three database types.

MS Access Connections

The MS Access database is not supported by any managed provider so you should use OleDB or ODBC. We will discuss ODBC later in this chapter. In this section, we will show you how to connect to the MS Access database using the OleDB. First check if a reference to the *System.Data* is added to your project. Then add the imports directive for the OleDB namespace to your class. Now you are ready to code the OleDB connection. As usual, you need to build a connection string and create an OleDBConnection class object variable. Pay attention to the structure of the connection string. The first and most important difference is that you have to specify a database provider name. In our case it is a long name of the MS Access provider:

```
Microsoft.Jet.OleDb.4.0.
```

The second difference is the database name. Note that an Access database name will actually be a database file name and path. When you design an Access database you should create a database file. The User ID and Password are not required unless you decide to create a password-protected database. Thus, your OleDB open connection procedure may look like the following:

```
Private m_objOleDbCon As OleDbConnection
Private Function OpenOleDbConnection() As Boolean
   Dim strCon As String
   Try
      If m_objOleDbCon Is Nothing Then
          strCon = "Provider=Microsoft.Jet.OleDb.4.0;"
          strCon += "Data Source=C:\Labs\Lab11\Orders.mdb;"
          m_objOleDbCon = New OleDbConnection(strCon)
      End If
```

```
    If m_objOleDbCon.State <> ConnectionState.Open Then
        m_objOleDbCon.Open()
        Return True
    End If
    Catch oledbEx As OleDbException
        Throw New Exception(oledbEx.Message)
    Catch ex As Exception
        Throw ex
    End Try
End Function
```

In the above code, we have broken the connection string into several pieces so that it will fit the page line. You may type it as one uninterrupted statement.

OleDB Connection Strings

OleDB is a universal data access provider, which can be used to connect to various database types; for example, Paradox, FoxPro, Dbase and others. You may also use it to connect to the SQL Server and Oracle, although it is much more efficient to use the above-mentioned managed providers instead. The main difference of the OleDB connection string is that you have to include a provider parameter that tells OleDB which database type you want to connect to.

SQL Server OleDb Connections

An OleDb SQL Server connection string should contain the provider name, which in this case is *SqlOleDB*. The rest is similar to the managed provider connection string.

```
strCon = "Provider=SqlOleDb;"
```

Oracle OleDb Connections

An Oracle OleDb connection string is slightly different. The Oracle provider name is *MsdaOra* and the Data Source should be the database name not the server name:

```
"Provider=MsdaOra;Data Source=DBName;UID=user;PWD=pwd"
```

When you are done with the connection string you need to instantiate an OleDB Connection object and, if necessary, other data access objects. Find them in the *System.Data.OleDb* namespace. Your OleDb connection object instantiation code may look like this:

```
Dim strCon As String
Dim objOleDbCon As OleDbConnection
strCon = "Provider=MsdaOra;Data Source=DBName;
UID=user;PWD=pwd"
objOleDbCon = New OleDbConnection(strCon)
```

ODBC Connections

One of the main advantages of using the ODBC provider is the possibility of using DSN (Data Source Name). Using DSN-based connections has its advantages and disadvantages. As a disadvantage, we can mention the following: slower performance, availability issues, a DSN may be accidentally removed or re-configured and deployment issues.

The main advantages are: a DSN relieves your application from providing connection details such as a provider name, database name and so on. All the required connection information is entered when a corresponding DSN is created. You can create a DSN for any database type for which there is an appropriate driver installed on a user machine. A user may be allowed to select from a list of available DSNs and dynamically change the database connection.

DSNs are created using the ODBC Data Source Administrator utility, which can be opened from Administrative Tools\Data Sources (ODBC). A file DSN adds one more feature—portability and ease of deployment. As usual you should begin to code an ODBC connection byh adding the imports directive to the ODBC namespace as follows:

```
Imports System.Data.Odbc
```

If it is a DSN-based connection, you first need to create a DSN using the ODBC administrator utility.

DSN-Based Connections

A connection string for all DSN-based connections will have the same structure except for differences related to security protocols. For example:

```
strConnection="DSN=dsnName;UID=user;PWD=password"
```

For a file DSN, the main difference is that you need to replace the *DSN* parameter with the *FILE DSN* and specify a file path. Thus, your connection string may look like this:

```
strConnection="FILE DSN=FilePath;UID=user;PWD=password"
```

A code that opens a DSN-based ODBC connection may look like the following:

```
Dim strCon As String
Dim objOdbcCon As OdbcConnection
strCon = "DSN=dsnName;UID=user;PWD=password"
objOdbcCon = New OdbcConnection(strCon)
```

```
objOdbcCon.Open()
```

Non-DSN ODBC Connections

The ODBC provider is typically used to establish DSN-based connections. However, it can be used for non-DSN connections as well. In this case, the connection string should contain some additional parameters such as a provider name, server name, database name, user name and password. Here's how a connection string may appear:

SQL Server Connection String

```
"Driver={SQL Server};Server=;Database=;UID=;PWD=;"
```

Oracle Connection String

```
"Driver={Microsoft ODBC for Oracle};Server=;UID=;PWD=;"
```

MS Access Connection String

```
"Driver={Microsoft Access
                        Driver(*.mdb)};Dbg=FileName.
mdb;UID=;PWD=;"
```

Sybase Connection String

```
"Driver={SYBASE ASE ODBC Driver};
                              Srvr=ServerName;Uid=user;Pw
d=password"
```

Programming a DataAdapter

Once you have successfully passed the open connection stage and are able to establish a connection to a database, you are ready to retrieve data and use it in your application. As we mentioned earlier, you can transport data to your application by using a DataSet or a DataReader.

Using a SqlDataAdapter

A DataAdapter class is database-specific while a DataSet is generic. In this discussion, we will use a *SqlDataAdapter* class as an example. The other three DataAdapter classes *OracleDataAdapter*, *OleDbDataAdapter* and the *OdbcDataAdapter* are very similar and have a few minor differences. Hence, in most cases when coding for other database types you may just need to replace a SqlDataAdapter class with a corresponding database-specific class.

To start playing with a SqlDataAdapter you need to make sure that *System. Data* and *System.Data.SqlClient* imports directives are added to your class. Then create a select command and store it in a string variable. A select command in this case is a SQL select statement. After that, create a SqlConnection object and open a connection as we discussed earlier in this chapter. It is always helpful to check if the open connection procedure succeeds, i.e., if the connection is open before you proceed to the next step.

Create a SqlDataAdapter object variable. Note that a SqlDataAdapter class implements four constructors. If you use the default constructor, which means you will not pass any parameters, then you should pass the select command and the connection string to corresponding SqlDataAdapter object properties. The second constructor accepts a SqlCommand object that can contain your select statement and a connection object. The third constructor accepts a select command and a connection string. In this case, a SqlDataAdapter will internally create a connection object and open a connection for you. Thus, using this constructor relieves you from a necessity of creating any other objects (for example, a SqlCommand or a SqlConnection). The fourth constructor accepts a select command and a SqlConnection object. If you would like to use this constructor you need to build a select statement and then create a SqlConnection object and pass them to this constructor. Once you have successfully instantiated a SqlDataAdapter object, you may use its *Fill* method to load a DataSet:

```
objDataAdapter.Fill(objDataSet)
```

Note that the Fill method returns an integer value, which indicates how many records were retrieved and pumped into a DataSet object. Therefore, you may want to read this value and use it to check if the expected data is actually retrieved. If the value is 0 then it means that no records were returned by the query and the DataSet is empty. In this case, a DataSet object should not be used as a data source for the DataGridView or an error will occur. Below is a sample procedure that implements the above logic:

```
Private m_objCon As SqlConnection
Private Sub FillDataSet()
    Dim objDS As New DataSet
    Dim objDA As SqlDataAdapter
    Dim strSQL As String
    Dim intRecords As Integer
Try
        '1. Open a connection
        If Not OpenSQLConnection() Then
            MessageBox.Show("Failed to open connection.")
            Exit Sub
        End If
        '2. Build a select command
        strSQL = "Select * from Orders"
        '3. Create a SQLDataAdapter object
        objDA = New SqlDataAdapter(strSQL, m_objCon)
        '4. Call the Fill method and check its return value
        If objDA.Fill(objDS) = 0 Then
            MessageBox.Show("No records were found.")
```

```
        Exit Sub
    End If
    '5. Use the DataSet as a data source
    DataGridView1.DataSource = objDS.Tables(0)
Catch sqlEx As SqlException
    Throw New Exception(sqlEx.Message)
Catch ex As Exception
    Throw ex
End Try
End Sub
```

In the next section, we will consider various options of using a DataSet and a SqlDataAdapter *Fill* method.

Using a DataSet

First, let's walk through the *FillDataSet* procedure code. In the first step, we call the *OpenSQLConnection* procedure to open a connection. Note that for this to work a connection object should have a class scope and if the open connection procedure returns false we cannot continue. Then we build a SQL select statement. After that we create a SqlDataAdapter object and pass the select command and a connection object to its constructor. Then we call the data adapter's *Fill* method and pass a DataSet object to it. When the Fill method call returns, we check its return value. If it is 0 then we have no records retrieved from the database and it does not make sense to continue. You may want to write a return value to an integer variable and use it in code wherever necessary. Here's the code that does it:

```
'4. Call the Fill method
intRecords = objDA.Fill(objDataSet)
If intRecords = 0 Then
```

```
      MessageBox.Show("No records were found.")
      Exit Sub
End If
```

Programming a DataAdapter class for other database providers is similar to the SQL Server example discussed above. You just need to replace a SqlDataAdapter class as follows:

OracleDataAdapter

```
Dim objDA As OracleDataAdapter
objDA = New OracleDataAdapter(strSQL, objCon)
```

OleDbDataAdapter

```
Dim objDA As OleDbDataAdapter
objDA = New OleDbDataAdapter(strSQL, objCon)
```

ODBCDataAdapter

```
Dim objDA As OdbcDataAdapter
objDA = New OdbcDataAdapter(strSQL, objCon)
```

Using the *Fill* Method Parameters

The DataAdapter's Fill method is overloaded, which gives you a number of very useful options. The first version takes a DataSet object as a single parameter. Although in most cases this may be sufficient you should not totally ignore other options. Let's take a look at some of them.

Using Source Table Parameter

Did you know that you can name each data table created within your DataSet object? You can pass the table name as a second parameter of the Fill method. This option will allow you to build a collection of tables by passing the same DataSet object with different table name parameters:

```
objDataAdapter.Fill(objDataSet, "Products")
objDataAdapter.Fill(objDataSet, "Orders")
objDataAdapter.Fill(objDataSet, "Customers")
```

After you run this code your DataSet will contain three named data tables. Notice that if you provide the same source table name every time you call the Fill method, the corresponding table in a DataSet object will be refreshed. However, if you specify different table names, they will be added to the *Tables* collection. Then you can access these tables either by index or by name. Additionally, you can build relationships between these tables and further use a DataSet as a portable database and avoid any additional database trips.

Using StartRecord and MaxRecord Parameters

If there is a need to limit the total number of records returned or to skip a certain number of rows, you can use the overloaded version of the Fill method that takes the following four parameters: a DataSet, StartRecord, MaxRecords and a source table name. For example:

```
objDataAdapter.Fill(objDataSet, 10, 20, "Orders")
```

This Fill method call will return 20 records starting from the tenth and will create the "Orders" table in a *DataSet.Tables* collection.

Using a DataTable Array Parameter

If you want full control over your data tables or wish to create data tables outside a DataSet object, you can achieve this by creating an array of *DataTables* and passing it as a parameter to the Fill method. This version of the Fill method takes three parameters: StartRecord, MaxRecords and a data tables array. Your code may look like this:

```
Dim strSQL As String
Dim objDataAdapter As SqlDataAdapter
Dim strSQL As String
Dim arrDataTables() as DataTable
Dim tblProducts As DataTable
Dim tblOrders As DataTable
Dim tblCustomers As DataTable
ReDim arrDataTables(3)
arrDataTables(0) = tblProducts
arrDataTables(1) = tblOrders
arrDataTables(2) = tblCustomers
objDataAdapter = New SqlDataAdapter(strSQL, m_objCon)
objDataAdapter.Fill(0, 100, arrDataTables)
tblProducts = arrDataTables(0)
tblOrders = arrDataTables(1)
tblCustomers = arrDataTables(2)
```

There are a few things that you need to pay attention to when you use the above code. We assume that you will build a select query that returns three resultsets. Data tables will be assigned to your data tables array in accordance with your select statement. Table names will not correlate with the actual table names in the data source. After you run the Fill method, you can extract the individual tables from the array and use them. If you do not need to specify the start and the maximum records parameters, pass *Nothing* instead of a parameter value.

Using a DataTable Parameter

Finally, there may be situations when you want to save your resources and avoid using a heavy DataSet object or simply want to use a DataTable object directly. This can be done by passing a DataTable object but in this case you are limited to passing only one DataTable object at a time:

```
Dim tblProducts As DataTable
objDataAdapter.Fill(tblProducts)
```

Using a DataSet or a DataTable object after you run the Fill method may require additional precautions to avoid errors. We will talk about this in the next section.

Handling a DataSet Exceptions

Using a DataSet or a DataTable object without checking their status may cause exceptions. Depending on your application exception tolerance requirements you may want to reduce a potential risk of exceptions by validating these objects before you try to use them. For example, each of the following three lines of code may cause an exception if the underlying DataTable is not instantiated:

```
DataGridView1.DataSource = objDataSet.Tables(0)
DataGridView1.DataSource = tblProducts
tblProducts = objDataSet.Tables(0)
```

The following code may solve the problem and will allow you to check the status of each object without causing an exception.

Check if a DataSet object is instantiated:

```
If objDataSet Is Nothing Then
      'Handle the error
End If
```

Check if a DataSet contains a named DataTable:

```
If objDataSet.Contains("scrTableName") = False Then
      'Handle the error
End If
```

Check if a *Tables* collection count is zero:

```
If objDataSet.Tables.Count = 0 Then
      'Take appropriate action
End If
```

You can accomplish many data access tasks by using only a Connection and a DataAdapter objects. However, if you want a more granular access or wish to execute parameterized stored procedures, you may need to mobilize another ADO.NET team player—a Command class.

A Command Class

The ADO .NET Command class offers a wide range of functionality that can be used to perform various database transactions such as select, insert, delete and update. This class implements three major methods that allow leveraging performance, the style of data retrieval and methods of data transportation. In this section, we will show you how to code Command class methods.

As you may already know when coding any object, you have at least two choices: you may pass as many class instantiation parameters at the object creation stage or do it later when the object is created by using the object's public properties. In most cases, it is a matter of your personal preference. We recommend using the constructor parameters to pass instantiation parameters where it is possible. Note that the ADO .NET Command class constructor has four overloads: a default no parameters constructor, a constructor that accepts a command text parameter,

Microsoft Visual Basic .NET Programming Fundamentals

a constructor that takes a command text and a connection object and finally a
constructor that accepts a command text, a connection object and a transaction
object. For example, if you decided to pass a SQL statement and a connection object
your code should look like the following:

```
Dim objCom As OracleCommand
objCom = New OracleCommand(strSql, objCon)
```

For the above code to work you need to build a SQL statement and create a
corresponding connection object. And last but not least, you need to open a
connection. You may do it either before you instantiate the command object or after,
but always before you try to execute a command object's methods.

The ExecuteReader Method

The ExecuteReader method has a very straightforward task—to execute a SQL select
statement and return an instantiated DataReader object. Note that you cannot
instantiate a DataReader object; it can only be done by the Command object itself.
All you need to do is declare an appropriate type of a DataReader variable and assign
an object instance returned by the ExecuteReader method to it. Here is a sample
procedure that uses an OracleDataReader:

```
Private Sub ExecuteOracleDataReader(ByVal strSQL As String, _
            ByRef objDataReader As OracleDataReader)
    Dim objCom As OracleCommand
Try
    objCom = New OracleCommand(strSQL, objCon)
    objDataReader = objCom.ExecuteReader()
Catch sqlEx As OracleException
    Throw New Exception(sqlEx.Message)
Catch ex As Exception
```

```
      Throw ex
End Try
End Sub
```

The above procedure accepts a SQL select command and a reference to an OracleDataReader object variable. It calls an OracleCommand object's ExecuteReader method, which returns an instance of an OracleDataReader.

Using a DataReader

If you are able to successfully execute the ExecuteReader method, you can start using a DataReader object. Be aware of two potential errors. If the ExecuteReader method fails for any reason, it will not instantiate a DataReader and will return null. As a precaution you may always need to check if the returned DataReader object is null (*Nothing*). However, if the ExecuteReader method succeeds but your query returns an empty resultset, even though a DataReader object will be instantiated, it won't contain any data. Keep in mind that trying to read such a DataReader will cause an error. You can solve this problem by checking the DataReader's *HasRows* property. Below is the code that performs both checks:

```
If Not objDataReader Is Nothing Then
   If objDataReader.HasRows = True Then
      'Use a DataReader object
   End If
End If
```

Also, please remember that you cannot read a DataReader before you call its *Read* method. Calling the Read method tells the DataReader to make a round trip to the database and bring the first record. In fact, you need to call the Read method every time you want to extract the next record. The Read method returns a Boolean value that signals if it was able to get the next record. To automate this process you may want to create a loop in which you will check the Read method's return value in each iteration. When it returns False you should exit the loop. Your code may look like the following:

```
Private Sub ExecuteOracleDataReader(ByVal strSQL As String,
                ByRef objDataReader As OracleDataReader)
    Dim objCom As OracleCommand
    Dim objTmp As New Object()
Try
    objCom = New OracleCommand(strSQL, objCon)
    objDataReader = objCom.ExecuteReader()


    If Not objDataReader Is Nothing AndAlso

objDataReader.HasRows Then
        While objDataReader.Read() = True
            'Extract the first column value by index
            objTmp = objDataReader.Item(0)
            'Or by column name
            objTmp = objDataReader.Item("ColumnName")
        End While
    End If

Catch ex As Exception
    Throw ex
End Try
End Sub
```

As we already mentioned, a DataReader normally contains one record that may have multiple columns. There are two ways to extract the column value: by index or by column name. To access column values use the default *Item* property of a DataReader, which accepts either an integer column index or a string column name and returns an object that contains the column value. In the *ExecuteOracleDataReader* procedure we have shown both methods. Normally, you should convert the object into a data type that the column is expected to be. For example:

```
strTmp = objDataReader.Item(0).ToString
```

Using the ExecuteScalar Method

The *ExecuteScalar* method is designed for performance and situations when you want to retrieve a single value from a data source. This method returns an object so you may need to convert it to a corresponding data type. What happens if your SQL query returns multiple rows and columns? No matter how many rows or columns are selected this method will only return the value of the first column of the first record. Here is how your code may appear:

```
objCom = New SqlCommand(strSql, objCon)
obj = objCom.ExecuteScalar()
'Convert an object to a string
strData = Convert.ToString(obj)
```

The ExecuteNonQuery Method

The ExecuteNonQuery method is self-explanatory. It is designed to execute such commands as insert, delete and update. For example:

```
Dim objCom As SqlCommand
Dim intRecordsAffected As Integer
Dim strSQL As String
strSQL = "Delete from Products"
objCom = New SqlCommand()
objCom.Connection = objCon
objCom.CommandType = CommandType.Text
objCom.CommandText = strSQL
intRecordsAffected = objCom.ExecuteNonQuery()
```

The method returns an integer value that indicates how many records were affected by execution of the command. Apparently, if the number of records affected is 0 then the executed statement did not do anything and no records were inserted, deleted or updated.

Summary

In this chapter, you have learned how to use ADO .NET classes to implement various data access tasks. When you start programming database access functionality, the first decision to make is what database provider to use—managed or unmanaged. ADO .NET offers two managed providers: SqlClient and OracleClient and two unmanaged providers: OleDB and ODBC. Each of these data access components contains approximately the same library of classes and provides similar functionality. In Lab 13, we will give you more details on how to create a project that makes use of ADO .NET classes.

Lab 13: The MarsPlus Project

MarsPlus

In this Project:

You will redesign the MARS project created in Lab 11 to use a database instead of a DataTable. This will require considerable modification of the TradeOrder class as well as the form class. If you didn't create lab 11 we recommend you to create it first and then complete this lab. This project will give you a good chance to practice coding Connection, Command, DataAdapter, DataSet and DataReader objects to implement application data access functionality.

Create a New Project

> ➤ Create the *Lab13* project folder.
> ➤ Open Visual Studio .NET
> ➤ Create a new Windows Application project.
> ➤ Set the project Location to C:\Labs\Lab13.
> ➤ Set the project Name to *MarsPlus*.

Design User Interface

Add Controls

Add form controls and set their properties according to Table 1.

Table 1. The MarsPlus form controls.

Control Type	Property Name	Value
GroupBox	Text	Enter Order to Execute:
Label	Text	Symbol
Label	Text	BuySell
Label	Text	Quantity
Label	Text	Price
Label	Text	Execution Status:
Label	Text	Waiting...
-/-	Name	lblStatus
Button	Name	btnExecute
-/-	Text	&Execute
Button	Name	btnClear
-/-	Text	&Clear
Button	Name	btnClose
-/-	Text	Cl&ose
Form	Name	frmOrders
-/-	Text	Mars Plus
-/-	AcceptButton	btnExecute
GroupBox	Text	Existing Orders:
DataGridView	Name	dataGridView1

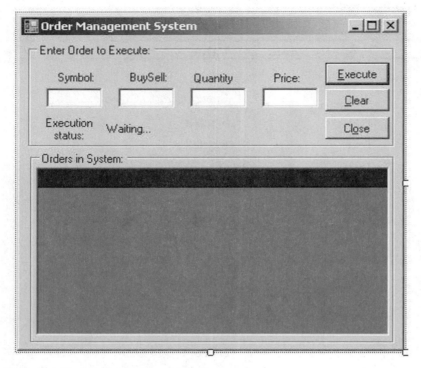

Figure 1. The MarsPlus form design view.

When you complete the user interface design, your form should look like the one shown in Figure 1. Note that in this project the AcceptButton property of the form should be set to the btnExecute button. Set this property only after the specified button is created. Most labels and the DataGridView control can keep their default names.

Write Code

In this lab you will write code in two classes: the TradeOrder class and the frmOrders form class. You will use ADO.NET objects in the TradeOrder class.

Write the TradeOrder Class

This project is a modification of the MARS project. You will have to modify the code in the *TradeOrder* class to use ADO .NET. The entire code of this class is presented in Listing 1.

Listing 1. The TradeOrder class code.

```
Imports System
Imports System.Threading.Thread
Imports System.Data.OleDb
Public Class TradeOrder
#Region "Class Constructors"
Public Sub New()
End Sub
Public Sub New(ByVal mdfFile As String)
    m_MdbFileName = mdfFile
End Sub
#End Region
#Region "Private Members"
   Private m_MdbFileName As String
   Private m_strSymbol As String
   Private m_intQuantity As Int32
   Private m_strBuySell As String
   Private m_sngPrice As Single
   Private m_strStatus As String
   Private m_objRandom As New
   System.Random(CInt(DateTime.Now.Ticks
   Mod Int32.MaxValue))
```

```vb
    Private m_objCon As OleDbConnection
#End Region

#Region "Class Events"
Public Event OrderExecuted(ByVal ExecutionTime As DateTime, _
     ByVal OrderStatus As String, ByVal OrderId As Integer)
#End Region

#Region "Public Properties"
Public Property MdfFileName() As String
Get
     Return m_MdbFileName
End Get
Set(ByVal Value As String)
     m_MdbFileName = Value
End Set
End Property
Public Property Symbol() As String
Get
     Return m_strSymbol
End Get
Set(ByVal Value As String)
     m_strSymbol = Value
End Set
End Property
Public Property Quantity() As Int32
Get
     Return m_intQuantity
```

```vb
End Get
Set(ByVal Value As Int32)
      m_intQuantity = Value
End Set
End Property
Public Property Price() As Single
Get
      Return m_sngPrice
End Get
Set(ByVal Value As Single)
      m_sngPrice = Value
End Set
End Property
Public Property BuySell() As String
Get
      Return m_strBuySell
End Get
Set(ByVal Value As String)
      m_strBuySell = Value
End Set
End Property
Public Property Status() As String
Get
      Return m_strStatus
End Get
Set(ByVal Value As String)
      m_strStatus = Value
End Set
```

```
End Property
#End Region
#Region "Public Methods"
Public Function ExecuteOrder() As Boolean
    Dim strInsertStm As String
    Dim OrderID As Integer
    Dim strOrderStatus As String
    Dim objCom As OleDbCommand
Try
    OrderID = m_objRandom.Next
    strOrderStatus = SendOrder(Quantity)
    strInsertStm = "INSERT INTO Orders Values('"
    strInsertStm += OrderID & "','" & m_strSymbol & "','"
    strInsertStm += m_strBuySell & "," & m_intQuantity & ","
    strInsertStm += m_sngPrice & "','" & strOrderStatus & "')"
    If Not OpenConnection() Then
        Throw New Exception("Failed to open connection")
    End If
    objCom = New OleDbCommand
    objCom.Connection = m_objCon
    objCom.CommandText = strInsertStm
    objCom.CommandType = CommandType.Text
    If objCom.ExecuteNonQuery() <> 1 Then
        Throw New Exception("Insert order Failed")
    End If
    objCom = Nothing
    RaiseEvent OrderExecuted(DateTime.Now.ToShortDateString(),
    strOrderStatus, OrderID)
```

```
      Return True
Catch ex As Exception
      Throw ex
Finally
      CloseConnection()
End Try
End Function
Public Function GetExistingOrders(ByVal strSQL As String, _
                ByRef dsOrders As DataSet) As Boolean
   Dim objDA As OleDbDataAdapter
Try
      If Not OpenConnection() The
         Throw New Exception("Failed to open connection")
      End If
      objDA = New OleDbDataAdapter(strSQL, m_objCon)
      If objDA.Fill(dsOrders) = 0 Then
         Throw New Exception("No orders found")
      End If
      objDA = Nothing
Catch ex As Exception
      Throw (ex)
Finally
      CloseConnection()
End Try
End Function
#End Region

#Region "Private Methods"
```

```
Private Function OpenConnection() As Boolean
Try
    If m_objCon Is Nothing Then
        m_strCon = "Provider=Microsoft.Jet.OLEDB.4.0;"
        m_strCon += "Data Source = " & m_MdbFileName
        m_objCon = New OleDb.OleDbConnection(m_strCon)
    End If

    If m_objCon.State = ConnectionState.Closed Then
        m_objCon.Open()
    End If
    Return True
Catch ex As Exception
    Throw ex
End Try
End Function


Private Function CloseConnection()
If Not m_objCon Is Nothing Then
    If m_objCon.State <> ConnectionState.Closed Then
        m_objCon.Close()
    End If
End If
End Function
Private Function SendOrder(ByVal OrderQuantity As Integer) As
String
    Dim strOrderStatus As String
Try
```

```
    Sleep(2000)
    If OrderQuantity < 200 Then
        strOrderStatus = OrderQuantity & " Executed"
    ElseIf OrderQuantity > 1000 Then
        strOrderStatus = "Open"
    ElseIf OrderQuantity Mod 200 = 0 Then
        strOrderStatus = OrderQuantity & " Executed"
    ElseIf OrderQuantity Mod 200 > 0 Then
        strOrderStatus = "200 Executed"
    End If
    Return strOrderStatus
Catch ex As Exception
    Throw ex
End Try
End Function


#End Region


End Class
```

Add the Imports Directives

Begin by adding the imports directives. Note that in this version of the TradeOrder class you will use the *System.Data.OleDb* namespace. The beginning of your class code should look like this:

```
Imports System
Imports System.Threading.Thread
Imports System.Data.OleDb
```

Add Code Regions

If you examine code in Listing 1, you should notice that we are using regions to divide and label sections of class code. This is a very helpful code editor feature that we recommend you to use. In this project, you will create the following regions: Class Constructors, Public Properties, Private Members, Public Methods, Private Methods and Class Events.

Write Class Constructors

In the previous version you had a default class constructor only. Add the following custom constructor to your code:

```
Public Sub New(ByVal mdfFile As String)
          m_MdbFileName = mdfFile
End Sub
```

The above constructor accepts one string parameter that is used to pass the database file name and path. In this procedure, you assign its value to the class variable *m_MdbFileName*. If a client chooses not to use the custom constructor and use the default one instead, then it should pass this value through the *MdfFileName* public property.

Add Private Class Members

The next section of class code should be enclosed in the region called "Private Members." It will contain declaration statements of class variables prefixed with (m_). Most of these variables are used to store corresponding class public property values. Here's the code that you should write in this region:

```
#Region "Private Members"
     Private m_strCon As String
```

```
Private m_MdbFileName As String
Private m_strSymbol As String
Private m_intQuantity As Int32
Private m_strBuySell As String
Private m_sngPrice As Single
Private m_strStatus As String
Private      m_objRandom As New System.
Random(CInt(DateTime.Now.Ticks Mod Int32.MaxValue))
#End Region
```

Create Class Events

The "Class Events" region will have one public class event called *OrderExecuted*. You will raise this event whenever an order is successfully entered into the system. Your code that declares this event should look like the following:

```
Public Event OrderExecuted(ByVal ExecutionTime As DateTime,
ByVal OrderStatus As String, ByVal OrderId As Integer)
```

The *OrderExecuted* event declares three parameters that are used to pass order execution results from a class object to the client, which includes order execution time, order status and order ID.

Save your Work

Create Class Properties

Write code to create public class properties in the "Public Properties" region. All these properties are used to describe *TradeOrder* object features such as Symbol, BuySell, Price and so on. Notice that each property procedure implements the Get and Set methods. The former reads the property value from the corresponding class module private variable and returns the value to the caller. The latter writes a new value passed by the caller to the same private class variable. In this lab, you will add one more public property, called *MdfFileName,* which will be used to set or get the value of the database file name. Please locate public properties code in Listing 1 and type them into your project.

Create Class Methods

Write code in the "Public Methods" region. Compared to the original MARS project you will have a considerably modified *ExecuteOrder* procedure and will add the *GetExistingOrders* method.

Write the ExecuteOrder Method

Listing 2. The ExecuteOrder function code.

```
Public Function ExecuteOrder() As Boolean
    Dim strInsertStm As String
    Dim OrderID As Integer
    Dim strOrderStatus As String
    Dim objCom As OleDbCommand
Try
    OrderID = m_objRandom.Next
    strOrderStatus = SendOrder(Quantity)
    strInsertStm = "INSERT INTO Orders Values('"
    strInsertStm += OrderID & "','" & m_strSymbol & "','"
    strInsertStm += m_strBuySell & "'," & m_intQuantity & ","
    strInsertStm += m_sngPrice & ",'" & strOrderStatus & "')"
    If Not OpenConnection() Then
```

```
        Throw New Exception("Failed to open database connection")
    End If
    objCom = New OleDbCommand
    objCom.Connection = m_objCon
    objCom.CommandText = strInsertStm
    objCom.CommandType = CommandType.Text
    If objCom.ExecuteNonQuery() <> 1 Then
        Throw New Exception("Failed to insert a new order")
    End If
    objCom = Nothing
    CloseConnection()
    RaiseEvent OrderExecuted(DateTime.Now.ToShortDateString(),
    strOrderStatus, OrderID)
    Return True
Catch ex As Exception
    Throw ex
Finally
    CloseConnection()
End Try
End Function
```

Let's walk through the *ExecuteOrder* function code. First you declare local variables such as the *strInsertStm, OrderID, strOrderStatus* and *objCom*. Then you get a number from a Random object and assign it to the order ID variable. Then call the *OpenConnection* procedure to open a connection to the database; instantiate the OleDB command object, set its Connection property to the connection object; set the Command Type property to Text. Then set the Command Text property to the insert string variable.

Proceed to call the command object's *ExecuteNonQuery* method. If the method completes successfully, it returns a number of rows affected. You will use this value for additional verification of how the procedure completed. If the returned value is not equal to 1, throw a new exception signaling to the caller that you failed to insert a new record into the database. If everything goes well and the method returns 1, continue processing and raise the *OrderExecuted* event and pass all required parameters to it. Add some cleanup to this method, in which you set the command object variable to *Nothing* to signal that you don't need it anymore and it can be garbage collected. Although this is a local variable, it is still a good practice to perform. Then call the *CloseConnection* procedure to close a database connection if it is open. Also add a *Finally* block to your Try block in which you will call the CloseConnection procedure. This will guarantee the execution of this method. **Save your Work.**

Write the GetExistingOrders Method
Listing 3. The GetExistingOrders method code.

```
Public Function GetExistingOrders(ByVal strSQL As String, _
                ByRef dsOrders As DataSet) As Boolean
   Dim objDA As OleDbDataAdapter
Try
   If Not OpenConnection() Then
      Throw New Exception("Failed to open database connection")
   End If
   objDA = New OleDbDataAdapter(strSQL, m_objCon)
   If objDA.Fill(dsOrders) = 0 Then
      Throw New Exception("No orders found")
   End If
```

```
    objDA = Nothing
Catch ex As Exception
    Throw (ex)
Finally
    CloseConnection()
End Try
End Function
```

The *GetExistingOrders* is a new method in this class. You will design it to retrieve data from the Orders table and populate a DataSet object. In this method, you will declare two parameters—the *strSQL* as a string and the *dsOrders* as a DataSet. The string parameter is used to pass the SQL query. A DataSet parameter is declared with the *ByRef* parameter direction keyword to make it work as an output parameter. To populate a DataSet with data you need to create a DataAdapter object. Then open a connection to the database by calling the *OpenConnection* procedure. When you instantiate an *OldDbDataAdapter* object you pass two parameters to its constructor: a SQL query and a connection object. Then you call its Fill method and pass a DataSet object as a parameter. Note that a DataAdapter's Fill method returns a numeric value that signals how many records were placed into a DataSet.

Write Private Class Methods

The last portion of this class code is placed in the "Private Methods" region. You will have only one method here: the *SendOrder* function. Functionality wise, this method is designed to simulate the order execution process. First, you call the *Sleep* function to simulate a two-second delay in the execution process. Then create a few dummy execution conditions coded in the *if* block. Please locate this method in Listing 1 and type it into your class.

Congratulations! You successfully finished coding the TradeOrder class.

Changes in the Form Class

Code in the form class will have noticeable modifications as compared with the MARS project. First, you will get rid of a DataTable initialization procedure. You don't need it anymore since you are going to use a database table instead. With the new version of the TradeOrder class you have almost all details of implementation hidden in the class. Pay attention to how the TradeOrder class is instantiated. You will declare a TradeOrder object variable using the *WithEvents* keyword and pass one parameter to the class constructor. Here is how the statement should appear:

```
Private WithEvents objTradeOrder As New
                                    TradeOrder(m_strMDBFile)
```

By doing so not only are you declaring and instantiating the object, but also subscribing to receive the object's events. Then you create the corresponding event handler procedure so that you can take necessary actions when the event fires. The entire form class code is presented in Listing 4.

Listing 4. The frmOrder form class code.

```
Public Class Form1
Private m_strMDBFile = "C:\Labs\Lab13\TradeOrders.mdb"
Private WithEvents objTradeOrder As New

TradeOrder(m_strMDBFile)
Private Sub btnExecute_Click(ByVal sender As System.Object, _
        ByVal e As System.EventArgs) Handles btnExecute.Click
        SubmitOrder()
End Sub
Private Sub SubmitOrder()
```

```
Try

    objTradeOrder.Symbol = txtSymbol.Text

    objTradeOrder.BuySell = txtBuySell.Text

    objTradeOrder.Price = txtPrice.Text

    objTradeOrder.Quantity = txtQuantity.Text

    If objTradeOrder.ExecuteOrder() = False Then

        MessageBox.Show("Failed to execute order")

    End If

Catch ex As Exception

    MessageBox.Show(ex.Message)

End Try

End Sub

Private Sub ShowAllOrders()

    Dim dsOrders As New DataSet

    Dim strSQL As String

Try

    strSQL = "Select * from Orders"

    objTradeOrder.GetExistingOrders(strSQL, dsOrders)

    DataGrid1.DataSource = dsOrders.Tables(0)

Catch ex As Exception

    If ex.Message = "No orders found" Then

        lblStatus.Text = "There are no orders in system"

    Else

        MessageBox.Show(ex.Message)

    End If

End Try

End Sub

Private Sub Form1_Load(ByVal sender As Object, ByVal _
```

```vb
                            e As EventArgs) Handles MyBase.Load
        ShowAllOrders()
End Sub


Private Sub btnClose_Click(ByVal sender As Object, _
        ByVal e As EventArgs) Handles btnClose.Click
        Me.Close()
End Sub


Private Sub objTradeOrder_OrderExecuted(ByVal ExecutionTime _
          As Date, ByVal OrderStatus As String, ByVal OrderId _
          As Integer) Handles objTradeOrder.OrderExecuted
Try
    lblStatus.Text = OrderStatus
    ShowAllOrders()
Catch ex As Exception
    MessageBox.Show(ex.Message)
End Try
End Sub
Private Sub btnClear_Click(ByVal sender As System.Object, _
        ByVal e As System.EventArgs) Handles btnClear.Click
Try
    txtSymbol.Text = ""
    txtBuySell.Text = ""
    txtPrice.Text = ""
    txtQuantity.Text = ""
Catch ex As Exception
    MessageBox.Show(ex.Message)
```

```
End Try
End Sub
End Class
```

Write the SubmitOder Procedure

The main mission of the SubmitOrder procedure is to invoke the ExecuteOrder method of the TradeOrder class. Note that you submit the order data by setting corresponding TradeOrder object public properties. Then you call the ExecuteOrder method and if it returns false, display a failure message. Please locate this method in Listing 4 and type it into your project. When you are done, type one line of code in the btnExecute_Click event procedure, which calls the SubmitOrder procedure.

Save your work

Create the ShowAllOrders Procedure

This procedure is modified considerably compared to the previous version of MARS. Now it is set to call the *GetAllExistingOrders* method of the TradeOrder class and passes a SQL query and a DataSet object variable. It will be called from the Form Load event procedure or when you need to refresh the screen to display recent data stored in the database.

Create the OrderExecuted Event Procedure

Writing this event procedure should be a good practice in creating custom event procedure handlers. In your code editor window, locate the Class Name dropdown box and select a *TraderOrder* object. Then in the Method Name dropdown, select the OrderExecuted event. When you do so, your code editor will create the wrapper lines of the new event procedure for you. Now all you need to do is type code in this procedure. Write two lines of code. One will update the lblStatus label Text property and the other will call the ShowAllOrders method to refresh the screen. Please type this code into your project. Then write code in the Clear and Close button click event procedures. Save your work. Congratulations! You are done with coding. Now it's time to test the application.

Test and Debug

To test this project you need to create a Microsoft Access database file according to the instructions below. Note that you won't be able to test the program without this database file.

Create a Database File

To create a database file, do the following: Open Microsoft Office Access. On the File menu choose New. Then in the right-hand pane click on the Blank Database link. Navigate to C:\Labs\Lab13 folder. In the FileName textbox type "TradeOrders" and click Create. This should open a TradeOrders Database objects dialog box like the one shown in Figure 2.

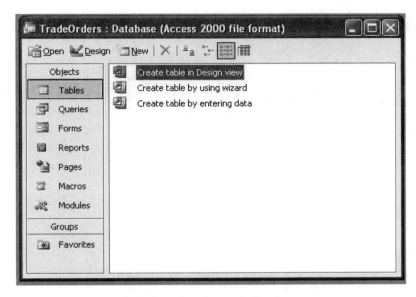

Figure 2. A TradeOrders Database dialog box.

Double-click *Create Table in Design View*, which should open a Table Design Form. All you need to do is type a column name and select a data type from the dropdown menu. When you complete the table design, your design window should look like the one in Figure 3.

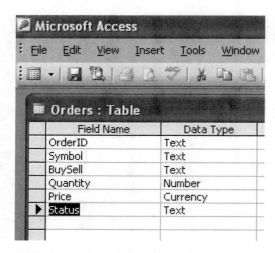

Figure 3. A database table design form.

When you are done, click on the Save button. You should see a small dialog box asking you to enter the name of the table. Type *Orders* and click OK. You will see a message box asking if you would like to create a primary key. Click No. Now you have your database file ready for testing. Please make sure that you saved the database file in the project directory.

Test the Application

Press F5 to run the application. Note that the ShowAllOrders procedure is called from the form load event. This means that whenever you start the application, this procedure will be automatically executed. It is very likely that you will get database connection errors. Check the hard-coded value of the *m_strMDBFile* variable at the top of the frmOders form class. Make sure that the database file name and path are valid and are exactly the same as the file you saved in C:\Labs\Lab13 directory when you created a database. Once you pass a database connection related errors you may start testing the application functionality.

First you need to test general program functionality. Check if you can enter a new trade order and execute it. Enter any Symbol, BuySell, Quantity and Price and press Enter. Does the order data appear in the DataGridView? If yes, then the application passed the first test. Enter a few more orders and check if they appear in the data grid.

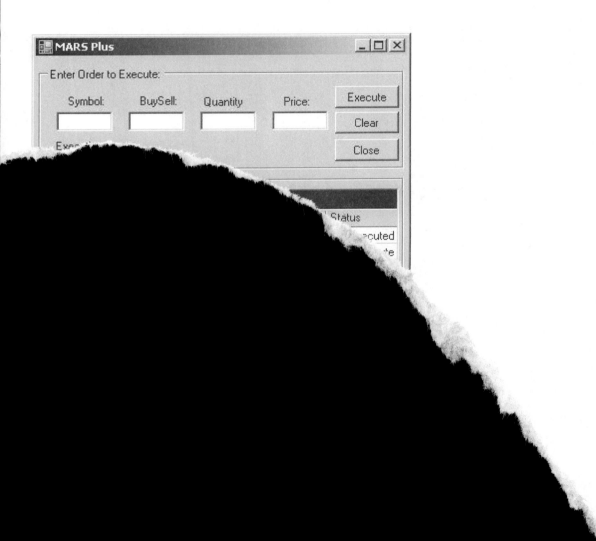

Part YIII   Application Installation

Application I

Chapter 14: Application Build Process

Application Build Process

In this Chapter:

You will learn how to configure project compilation, optimization and debugging options and use the project Property Pages tool. You will find out how to build the application from Visual Studio .NET and from the command prompt. You will be introduced to the methods of running an application executable file.

Chapter 14 at a Glance

- ➢ Application   Build Process
- ➢ Building in VS .NET IDE
- ➢ Project Property Pages
- ➢ Project Debugging Options
- ➢ Application Optimizations
- ➢ Project Compile Options
- ➢ Errors vs. Warnings
- ➢ Preparing to Build
- ➢ Command Line Compilation
- ➢ Running Application Executable
- ➢ Application Execution Tools

Building an Application

A final goal of any application development process is to make it available to end users. When design and testing are in the past and the application behavior is considered satisfactory, it is time to think about how the application will be built, shipped to customers and installed on the end-user machines. This phase of project development may include two tasks: generating an application executable and creating an installation package. We will discuss application installation in Chapter 15. Here we will consider topics related to the application build process.

Visual Studio .NET allows you to create various build flavors of one and the same project by using multiple build configurations. If you do not create your own build configurations you can always use the Debug or Release build that are already created for you. Note that when you create a new project, the Debug build is active by default. The main difference between them is that the Release build has the default optimizations enabled and it does not contain the debugging symbols, so it is smaller in size and faster. In the Debug build, optimizations are turned off and the debugging symbols are added, which makes a larger and slower executable.

Build configuration settings is a new useful feature in Visual Studio .NET, which allows having multiple build configurations for the same project. In the previous (non .NET) versions of Visual Basic, in order to achieve this you would have to reset project properties manually for each build configuration.

Each time you build a project you need to let the compiler know which build configuration to use. Use the Solution Configurations dropdown located to the right of the Run button to choose the active solution configuration. Your choices are:

- Debug
- Release
- Configuration Manager...

What happens when you build a project? A Visual Basic .NET compiler converts your human readable programming statements into executable binary code. This code is created in the Intermediate Language (IL) and then saved in your program's executable file. When you run the application this code is converted into a native machine code and then executed. Thus, with the application executable file in hand, you can run your newly created program on any machine that has a compatible version of Windows and the Microsoft .NET framework installed.

Essentially, there are two main ways to build an application. You can build it in Visual Studio .NET or from the DOS command prompt. We recommend learning both methods. Building from the Visual Studio IDE is simpler and offers a convenient way to set many compilation options. Building from the command prompt has its own advantages but requires learning the command line syntax and the use of switches. Let's begin with the first method.

Building from Visual Studio

As previously mentioned, building a project is synonymous with compiling it. Its main goal is to generate the application executable file. If you build a project from Visual Studio, you can set multiple project properties that affect the way the application is compiled by using convenient tools. If you choose not to set any of these properties, your project will use the defaults set by Visual Studio. To take a full advantage of building from the Visual Studio integrated development environment, it is essential to understand how various project properties may effect the application compilation. The first place to look at is the project Property Pages.

Project Property Pages

Project Property Pages is a Visual Studio .NET utility designed to help you set various project build properties, options and much more.

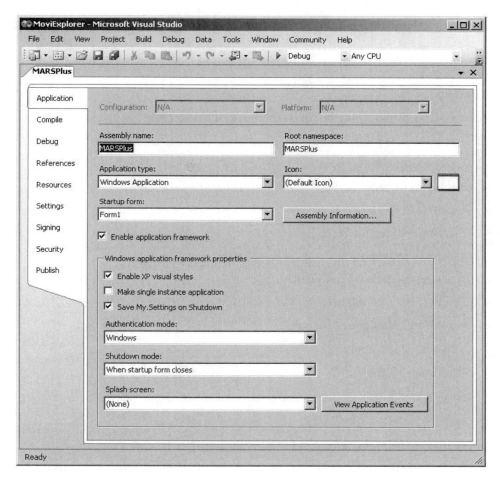

Figure 14.0   Project Property Pages.

To open project Property Pages, highlight your project name in the Solution Explorer and choose Properties. You should see a tabbed document interface like the one shown in Figure 14.0. As many other Visual Studio .NET tools, project Property Pages is designed as a tabbed document interface. It has multiple configuration sections that can be accessed via a corresponding link. The tool exposes a total of nine sections: Application, Compile, Debug, References, Resources, Settings, Signing, Security and Publish. Let's first briefly describe each section's role and then consider some of them in more detail.

Application

This section exposes a number of application-specific properties, which include:

- ➤ Compiled Assembly Name
- ➤ Project Root Namespace
- ➤ Project Application Type
- ➤ Executable File Icon
- ➤ The Project Startup Form
- ➤ Assembly Information
- ➤ Enable Application Framework
- ➤ Enable XP Visual Styles
- ➤ Make Single Instance Application
- ➤ Authentication Mode
- ➤ Shutdown Mode
- ➤ Splash Screen
- ➤ View Application Events

The application name is set to a project name by default. This is going to be your executable file name, which you can change at any time. The *Root* namespace is equal to a project namespace and also defaults to the project name. You should determine the application type when you create a project, so normally you would not change it here. The *Icon* property allows you to set the image that will be associated with the project executable file. The default is the form icon. The *Startup Form* can be either one of the project forms or a *Sub Main* procedure. By default, it is set to the first form in the project.

The *Assembly Information* comprises a set of project characteristics such as application title, product name, and file version and so on. If you click on the button it will open the project *AssemblyInfo* file where you can enter this information. The *Enable Application Framework* checkbox will toggle the second half of the settings, which include more or less self-explanatory features such as *Enable XP visual styles, Make single instance application, Save My Settings on Shutdown, Authentication mode, Shutdown mode, Splash screen* and *View Application Events*. If you added a splash screen to the project, you can select it here. This will relieve you from writing code to show it.

Project Compile Options

In this section, you can select a build configuration and platform and set a build output path, which is where the project executable file will be created. The default location is *bin\Debug* or *bin\Release* depending on the active solution configuration. You can specify the executable file location through the *Output Path* property, which will tell the compiler exactly where to put the executable file. Keep in mind that you can specify a full (absolute) path or a relative file path. For example, if you type a full path like *C:\Labs\Lab14\Executables,* the executable file will be created there. However, if you specify a relative path—for example, *exe\Dev*—the compiler assumes that the path entered is relative to the project folder and will look for it there. If the destination folder is not found, the compiler will create one for you. Note that: *bin\Debug* and *bin\Release* are both relative paths. The *Advanced Compile Options* button opens a small dialog box to set a number of advanced compile options. Here you can enable optimizations or remove integer overflow checks. Initially, you may not need to do anything here. If you examine the default settings for the Debug and Release builds, you will notice that in the Debug build Optimizations are turned off while in the Release build they are on. Of course, you can change these settings at any time but bear in mind that enabling optimizations is important for Release builds as it improves application performance. The debug build needs debug symbols information to do its job properly. Also note that removing integer overflow checks may increase overall application responsiveness but will also heighten the possibility of application crashes and runtime errors. Setting the Option Explicit and Option Strict options are essential for any project build. As previously mentioned, for both Debug and Release builds, Option Explicit is on and Option Strict is off. Turning the Option Strict on is a good idea but it will throw tons of conversion work on you. You can use the *Condition and Notification* table to tighten error handling on many different items. For example, depending on your project fault tolerance requirements you may want to enable *Treating of Warnings as Errors*, which again will make you sweat but will protect your application from many potential errors.

Errors vs. Warnings

When you build your application, the compiler may generate errors and warnings and show them in the build output window. The difference between errors and warnings, as you may guess, is not cut in stone. For example, declaring a variable and not using it is a candidate for a warning. It is not an error but it can be a signal for investigation that may lead to a potential error. That's why we do not recommend *Disabling all Warnings*. Although setting Treat all Warnings as Errors may be a good idea, you should use it only if you code your project so well that you do not leave dozens of candidates for warnings around.

Debug Options

In the *Debug* section as in the *Compile* section, you can select build configuration and platform and can set *Start Action, Start Options* and *Enable Debuggers*. Initially, you will most probably use the defaults. If your project should be started by another application, you can use the *Start Action* section to specify which project will start a debugging session. You have three options: *This Project, External Project* and *Start from URL.* The first option is probably most often used and is the default. Thus, normally if you do not change anything, the current application is used as a startup project. The second and the third options may be relevant when, for example, you test your application within a group of projects and want it to be invoked from within that group or for any other reason want another project to initiate the process and start your application. The Start from URL may be particularly useful when your project is a part of a web application. By using the *Start Options* properties you can set the command line arguments if your application is designed to accept and process command line parameters and set the working directory. If you would like to start the application on a remote computer, you may want to check *Use Remote Machine* and enter the remote machine name. If you want to include unmanaged code into the debugging process or add execution of SQL Server scripts, you need to check these options as well.

References

This section will provide a view of all your project references. The *Unused References* button may be useful to quickly identify those that are not used in the project. You can also add or remove references from here.

Resources

When you start building complex applications to support multiple cultures, languages and regions you will need resource files. This section helps you to manage project resources. For example, you can add or remove resource files.

Settings

This part of the Property Pages is initially empty. Here you can create application settings variables. Keep in mind that you can create two types of variables:

application and user. All application-type settings are read-only at runtime and can be set at design time only. User settings can be set and reset both at design and runtime. This means you can use user variables to save user preferences and keep the application level variables for common application settings. Remember that creating application settings will automatically generate an application configuration XML file. This file will be created by Visual Studio for you and after compilation it will appear in the project directory under *ApplicationName.exe.config* file name.

Assembly Signing

This section is designed to ease your task of creating a strongly named assembly. If you need to make your executable file strongly named, you have a number of ways to do it. This is the simplest one. First, using the *sn.exe* utility create a key file. Then check the *Sign the Assembly* checkbox. This action will enable the *Choose a Strong Name Key File* dropdown list box. Click on the <Browse> line in the dropdown box and navigate to your key file. Save project changes. There is one complication here, which you should keep in mind. When you sign the project assembly, you may start getting strange error messages when running in the debug mode. We recommend turning off signing when you need to debug. Simply uncheck the *Sign the Assembly* checkbox. You can enable signing whenever you need it. Visual Studio will remember your strong name key location, so you will not need to set it again.

Publish

This is one the most exciting additions in Visual Studio .NET 2005. It allows you to set the properties of the *ClickOnce* installation package if you decide to create one. Here you can set the *Publish Location, Install Mode, Publish Version* and much more. We will talk about ClickOnce in Chapter 15.

Preparing to Build

Now we have reached the point where you collected enough information on how to set the application build properties. Open a project in Visual Studio .NET. To build a project, click on the *Build* menu and select *Build Solution* or *Rebuild Solution*. Remember that if you have multiple projects in your solution, you will have two choices: build the entire solution by using the *Build Solution* menu or build a single project. If it is a single project, you should first highlight the project in the Solution Explorer and then choose *Build ProjectName* menu.

If you do not have any errors in your project, Visual Studio will compile your project and create your program's executable file. Errors are shown in the Output window at the bottom of the screen. This window is normally docked to the bottom of the main window. Correct errors and compile again until all errors are fixed and the executable is created.

Command Line Compilation

Compiling from the .NET command prompt is obviously more challenging and requires knowledge of command line syntax and the use of switches. This method allows you to compile your project source files into binary executable code and gives you a number of options that are not available in Visual Studio IDE. It also gives you direct control over how you compile your source code and does not require opening the project in Visual Studio. To master this method you need to learn the command line syntax of Visual Basic .NET compiler *vbc.exe*.

➤ Open Visual Studio .NET Command Prompt.

➤ On the Start menu, choose Programs\Microsoft Visual Studio .NET\Visual Studio .NET Tools\Visual Studio .NET Command Prompt.

➤ You should see a typical DOS screen.

First, let's consider a few most basic compiler command line switches and then create some examples.

/target:	This parameter is used to specify the output type. Shorthand is /t:
/target:exe	Creates a console application.
/target:winexe	Creates a Windows application.
/target:library	Creates a DLL assembly.
/target:module	Creates a module that can be added to an assembly.
/out:	This switch accepts the name and path of the output executable file.
/reference:	This parameter takes the name and path of referenced components. Shorthand /r:

Let's say you have a Visual Basic .NET class file named *TestClass.vb*. You may compile it into a DLL or an EXE, depending on application type, using one of the following commands:

```
vbc /target:exe /out:TestApp.exe C:\Temp\TestClass.vb
vbc /target:library /out:TestDll.dll C:\Temp\TestClass.vb
```

In the above examples, we did not provide the file path in the /out: switch. Obviously, in real-world projects you should provide it otherwise you may have to look for your executable file in the following default directory:

C:\windows\Microsoft.NET\Framework\v2.0.50727

If your project references other custom libraries, you won't be able to compile unless you include a proper *Reference* switch and specify the referenced library file name and path. Note that this does not apply to standard .NET framework classes. The use of the reference switch is simple:

```
/r:C:\Projects\Dependencies\TradeOrder.dll
```

Note that if you have multiple dependency files, you can type them separated by a space:

```
/r:TestAssembly1.dll TestAssembly2.dll TestAssembly3.dll
```

You can also use a wild card to indicate that you want to reference all libraries in a certain directory with a certain filename extension. For example:

```
/r:C:\Projects\Dependencies\*.dll
```

Once you successfully pass the build process stage, it will always make sense to test the executable file. There are a number of ways of how to run an executable, which we will discuss in the next section.

Running Executables

When you successfully build the application executable, your work is not yet complete. It is essential to give the newly created executable at least two tests: one outside the Visual Studio environment and one on a non-developer machine. Let's begin with the first one.

To run the application outside Visual Studio, you need to copy the application executable file to a designated directory and make sure that all dependencies are copied as well. Then you can use the Windows Explorer or the Run dialog box or the command prompt to run the application. To run an application executable on a non-developer machine, you need to add to the previous test a check of the presence of the following pre-requisites:

Compatible Windows operating system.

➤   Required .NET Framework.
➤   Application executable file.
➤   Application dependencies

To successfully accomplish the above tasks, you may also need to know how to use application execution techniques.

Application Execution Tools

If you are familiar with DOS, Run dialog box and the Windows Explorer, skip this section. There are three main tools that you can use to run an application executable:

➤   The Windows Explorer
➤   The Run Dialog Box
➤   The DOS Command Prompt

Using the Windows Explorer

To use the Windows Explorer to run an application, do the following:

➤   Open the Windows Explorer.
➤   Navigate to the folder where your application executable file is located.
➤   Double-click the file or right-click and select *Open*.

Using the Run Dialog Box

Using the Run dialog box to execute a program is simple. The only difficult thing type the exact path to the folder where the program executable file is located.

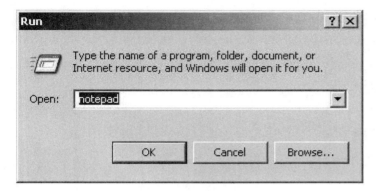

Figure 14.1 The Run dialog box.

Here is what you need to do to run a program from the Run dialog box.

- ➤ On the Start menu, choose Run.
- ➤ In Vista: Start/All Programs/Accessories/Run
- ➤ Type a full path to the executable file and press Enter or click OK.

<u>Cool Trick:</u>

Here's a cool trick that can free you from typing the executable file path. Open the Windows Explorer and resize it so that it will not take a part of the screen. Then open the Run dialog box. Try to make sure that both are at least partially visible on the screen. Then select the executable file in the Windows Explorer and drag and drop it onto the Run dialog box. The file path will be copied into the Run dialog box. You are ready to go.

Using the DOS Command Prompt

Using the DOS command prompt, especially for novice users, may be challenging but we advise you to master it as soon as possible and keep your skills alive thereafter. To open the DOS command prompt, do the following.

> ➢ Click Start and select Run.
> ➢ Type *cmd* and press Enter.

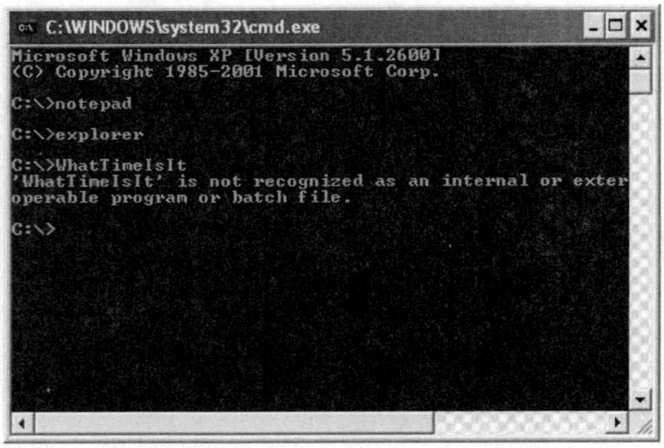

Figure 14.2 The DOS command prompt.

You should see a typical black DOS window like the one shown in Figure 14.2. To run a program all you need is to type the *start* command followed by a full file path. The *start* command is optional so you may just type the file name and path and press Enter. We recommend you to try to open some well-known programs. For example, practice running the *Notepad* and the *Windows Explorer* programs. Type *notepad* or *explorer* and press Enter. Note that you don't need to provide the path to well-known programs—Windows knows where to find them. Since your executable may not be well known to Windows, you have to enter the exact path to the folder where your program file is located. If you fail to do so you will get an error like this: *ShowTime.exe is not recognized as internal or external operable batch file.* You will practice running and testing application executables in Lab 15.

Summary

In this chapter, you have learned how to build an application executable. A project build process is one of the last stages in the project development cycle. It should be preceded by a proper project build configuration work. Visual Studio .NET offers a powerful tool to accomplish this task—the project Property Pages. A project build configuration will determine how a program exactable is generated. Building from the Visual Studio environment is the most convenient method but it is not the only option. You can also build your application from the DOS command prompt. It requires knowledge of compiler command line syntax and switches. When the build process is complete it is strongly recommended to test the application executable in a non-development environment.

Lab 14: The File Manager Project

File Manager

In this Project:

You will practice coding a number of widely used Windows Forms controls such as *MenuStrip, ToolBarStrip, StatusBarStrip* and *DataGridView*. This project will help to consolidate your skills in the following areas: creating event handlers for menus and toolbar buttons, using *For... Next* loops, populating ComboBoxes and DataGridView controls.

Create a New Project

> ➢ Create the *Lab14* project folder.
>
> ➢ Open Visual Studio .NET
>
> ➢ Create a new Windows Application project.
>
> ➢ Set the project Location to *C:\Labs\Lab14*.
>
> ➢ Set the project Name to *FileManager*.

Design User Interface

Add Controls

From a functionality perspective, this program allows you to view and edit text files. The application will have three forms. The main form called the *FileManager* form and two auxiliary forms: the *frmLogin* and *frmEdit*. Add these forms to the project, place control and set their properties according to corresponding control properties tables. Begin with the FileManager form.

Table 1. The FileManager form controls.

Control Type	Property Name	Value
Form	Name	FileManager
MenuStrip	Name	Default
MenuItem	Name	FileMenuItem
MenuItem	Name	OpenMenuItem
MenuItem	Name	ExitMenuItem
MenuItem	Name	ToolsMenuItem
MenuItem	Name	AddMenuItem
MenuItem	Name	EditMenuItem
MenuItem	Name	HelpMenuItem
MenuItem	Name	AbotMenuItem
ToolStrip	Name	Default
GroupBox	Name	Default
Label	Name	Default
-/-	Text	Selected File:
TextBox	Name	txtSelectedFile
DataGridView	Name	Default
StatusStrip	Name	Default

Add Container Controls

In this form, you will use three container controls: *MenuStrip, ToolStrip* and *StatusStrip*. These controls can host other controls. There are two ways to add controls to them: You can do it through the form designer window or programmatically. In this project, you will do both.

Add menus to the *MenuStrip* through the form designer. Type a menu Text in the white rectangle and then reset its Name property according to Table 1. Remember, you need to reset the default names before you start adding menu click event handlers. The main problem with the default names is that they are not meaningful and they are different from what we use in code. Note that you will add buttons to the *ToolStrip* control programmatically so you just need to place it on the form under the menu bar. When you complete the design work your form should like the one presented in Figure 1.

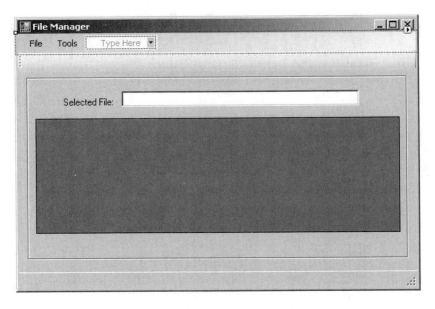

Figure 1. The FileManager form.

Create the frmEdit Form

The frmEdit form will be used to display current field values of a selected file record and to accept values for an edited or a new record. Therefore, it will contain four labels, four textboxes and two buttons as shown in Table 2.

Table 2. The frmEdit form controls.

Control Type	Property Name	Value
Form	Name	frmEdit
-/-	Text	Edit Form
Label	Text	ProductID:
Label	Text	Quantity:
Label	Text	User:
Label	Text	Date Changed:
TextBox	Name	txtUser
TextBox	Name	txtProductID
TextBox	Name	txtQuantity
TextBox	Name	txtDateChanged
Button	Name	btnSave
-/-	Text	&OK
-/-	DialogResult	OK
Button	Name	btnCancel
-/-	Text	&Cancel
-/-	DialogResult	Cancel

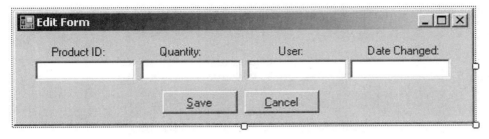

Figure 2. The frmEdit form.

The frmEdit form is shown in Figure 2.

Design the frmLogin Form

This is the smallest form in this project. The login form will contain two labels, two textboxes and two buttons. Please remember to set the *PasswordChar* property of the *txtPassword* textbox and the DialogResult property of both buttons according to Table 3.

Table 3. The frmLogin form controls.

Control Type	Property Name	Value
Form	Name	frmLogin
-/-	Text	Login
GroupBox	Name	Default
Label	Name	lblDisplayMsg
TextBox	Name	txtUser
TextBox	Name	txtPassword
-/-	PasswordChar	*

Button	Name	btnOK
-/-	Text	&OK
-/-	DialogResult	OK
Button	Name	btnCancel
-/-	Text	&Cancel
-/-	DialogResult	Cancel

Figure 3. The frmLogin form.

The frmLogin form is the last element in this project's GUI. Its snapshot is shown in Figure 3.

Write Code

This project's code is divided into three main parts: form initialization code, private procedures and control event handlers. To keep things better organized and make code more readable and maintainable, we recommend you to write it in three code regions. Although the sequence of regions is not principally important, we advise you to complete your coding work in the following order. First, type code for all form initialization procedures in the region called "Initialization Procedures." Then create private procedures in the "Private Methods" region. Finally, create all control event handlers including the form load event handler in the region called "Event Handlers." This applies only to coding the FileManager form. In other forms there will be much less code so you won't create code regions there.

Code the FileManager Form

Type the imports directives at the top of the form class code:

```
Imports System
Imports System.IO
Imports System.Text
Imports System.Data
```

Type the following class variable declarations:

```
Private m_strIconsFolder As String = "c:\Labs\Lab14\Icons"
Private m_objImgList As New ImageList
Private m_strSelectedFile As String = ""
Private m_strUser As String = ""
Private m_strLineToAdd As String = ""
Private m_strEditedLine As String = ""
Private m_intSelectedRowIndex As Integer = -1
Private m_strCellValues As String = ""
Private m_dicAuthorizedUsers As New Dictionary(Of String,
String)
```

Write Form Initialization Procedures

Listing 1 presents all initialization procedures, which includes: *LoadImages, LoadUsers, InitToolBar* and *InitStatusBar*. Please type this code in the "Initialization Procedures" region.

Listing 1. Initialization procedures.

```
#Region "Initialization Procedures"
Private Sub LoadUsers()
    m_dicAuthorizedUsers.Add("nWhite", "12551212")
    m_dicAuthorizedUsers.Add("vHoff", "34999233")
    m_dicAuthorizedUsers.Add("mNeil", "99123488")
End Sub
Private Sub LoadImages()
    Dim objDirInfo As DirectoryInfo
    Dim objFileInfo As FileInfo
    Dim objFileInfoArr() As FileInfo
Try
    objDirInfo = New DirectoryInfo(m_strIconsFolder)
    objFileInfoArr = objDirInfo.GetFiles()
    For Each objFileInfo In objFileInfoArr
        m_objImgList.Images.Add(Image.FromFile _
        (objFileInfo.FullName))
    Next
Catch ex As Exception
    ShowErrorMessage(ex.TargetSite.ToString, ex.Message)
End Try
End Sub
```

```vb
Private Sub InitToolBar()
    Dim OpenFileBtnEvnHandler As EventHandler
    Dim EditBtnEvntHandler As EventHandler
    Dim AddBtnEvntHandler As EventHandler
    Dim CloseBtnEvntHandler As EventHandler
Try
    OpenFileBtnEvnHandler = New EventHandler _
    (AddressOf OpenToolBtnClick)
    EditBtnEvntHandler = New EventHandler _
    (AddressOf EditToolBtnClick)
    AddBtnEvntHandler = New EventHandler _
    (AddressOf AddToolBtnClick)
    CloseBtnEvntHandler = New EventHandler _
    (AddressOf CloseToolBtnClick)
    ToolStrip1.ImageList = m_objImgList
    ToolStrip1.Items.Add("Open", m_objImgList.Images(0), _
    OpenFileBtnEvnHandler)
    ToolStrip1.Items.Add("Add", m_objImgList.Images(1), _
    AddBtnEvntHandler)
    ToolStrip1.Items.Add("Edit", m_objImgList.Images(2), _
    EditBtnEvntHandler)
    ToolStrip1.Items.Add("Close", m_objImgList.Images(3), _
    CloseBtnEvntHandler)
Catch ex As Exception
        ShowErrorMessage("InitToolBar", ex.Message)
End Try
End Sub
Private Sub InitStatusBar()
```

```
Try
    m_strUser = Environment.UserName
    StatusStrip1.Items.Add("Current User: " + m_strUser)
    StatusStrip1.Items.Add("          ")
    StatusStrip1.Items.Add("Current date: " & DateTime.Now.
    ToShortDateString)
Catch ex As Exception
    ShowErrorMessage(ex.TargetSite.ToString, ex.Message)
End Try
End Sub
#End Region
```

Please note that the *LoadImages* subroutine reads all image files stored in the images folder and loads them into an *ImageList* object, which is used to provide icon images for *ToolStrip* buttons. The *InitToolBar* procedure programmatically creates all toolbar buttons. The *LoadUsers* subroutine populates a *users* dictionary, which is used to authenticate users. Finally, the *InitStatusBar* method displays the current user's name and date time on the status bar. These subroutines are invoked from the form load event procedure.

Write Private Methods

The second large code region is called "Private Methods." Write this section of code before connecting these procedures to the event handlers. Please type code shown in Listing 2.

Listing 2. Private methods.

```
#Region "Private Methods"
```

```vb
Private Function AuthenticateUser(ByVal strUserID As _
String, ByVal strPassword As String) As Boolean
Try
    If m_dicAuthorizedUsers(strUserID) = strPassword Then
        Return True
    Else
        Return False
    End If
Catch ex As Exception
    ShowErrorMessage("AuthenticateUser", ex.Message)
End Try
End Function
Private Function Browse() As Boolean
    Dim OpenFileDlg As OpenFileDialog
Try
    OpenFileDlg = New OpenFileDialog()
    OpenFileDlg.ShowDialog()
    m_strSelectedFile = OpenFileDlg.FileName
    txtSelectedFile.Text = m_strSelectedFile
    If m_strSelectedFile.Length <> 0 Then
        Return True
    Else
        Return False
    End If
Catch ex As Exception
    ShowErrorMessage("Browse", ex.Message)
End Try
End Function
```

```
Private Function CheckIsFileSelected() As Boolean
Try

    If m_strSelectedFile.Length = 0 Then

        MessageBox.Show("Please select a file.")

        Return False

    Else

        Return True

    End If

Catch ex As Exception

    ShowErrorMessage("CheckIsFileSelected", ex.Message)

End Try

End Function

Private Function DisplayFileRecords() As Boolean

    Dim objFileOpenDlg As New OpenFileDialog()

    Dim strLine As String

    Dim i As Integer

    Dim j As Integer

    Dim strArr() As String

    Dim objDataTable As New DataTable()

    Dim objRow As DataRow

    Dim arrAllLines As String()

Try

    'Check if a file is selected

    If Not CheckIsFileSelected() Then

        Return False

    End If

    'Initialize DataTable columns:

    objDataTable.Columns.Add("Product ID")
```

```vb
            objDataTable.Columns.Add("Quantity")
            objDataTable.Columns.Add("User")
            objDataTable.Columns.Add("Date Changed")
            arrAllLines = File.ReadAllLines(m_strSelectedFile)
            For j = 0 To arrAllLines.Length - 1
                strLine = arrAllLines(j)
                strArr = strLine.Split("|")
                'For each record in file create a new row
                objRow = objDataTable.NewRow()
                'Add each field value to columns
                'We access row columns by index
                    For i = 0 To strArr.Length - 1
                        objRow(i) = strArr(i).ToString()
                    Next
                'Add this row to the table
                objDataTable.Rows.Add(objRow)
            Next
            'Now a DataTable is loaded with data
            'Use it as a datasource for DataGridView
            DataGridView1.DataSource = objDataTable
        Catch ex As Exception
            ShowErrorMessage("DisplayFileRecords", ex.Message)
        End Try
    End Function
    Private Function EditFileData() As Boolean
        Dim i As Integer
        Dim strTmp As String = ""
        Dim objRow As DataGridViewRow
```

```vb
    Dim arrOldLines As String()
    Dim arrNewLines As String()
    Dim strOldLine As String = ""
    Dim strNewLine As String = ""
    Dim strTmpLine As String = ""
    Dim strText As String = ""
    Dim strNewFileContent As String = ""
    Dim frmEditForm As New frmEdit()
    Dim arrFields As String()
    Dim isSave As Boolean
Try
    If m_intSelectedRowIndex = -1 Then
        MessageBox.Show("Select a row to edit")
        Exit Function
    End If
    ReDim arrFields(3)
    objRow = DataGridView1.Rows(m_intSelectedRowIndex)
    For i = 0 To objRow.Cells.Count - 1
    If (strOldLine.Length = 0) Then
        strOldLine = objRow.Cells(i).Value.ToString()
        arrFields(i) = objRow.Cells(i).Value.ToString()
    Else
        strOldLine += "|" & objRow.Cells(i).Value.ToString()
        arrFields(i) = objRow.Cells(i).Value.ToString()
    End If
    Next
    frmEditForm.StartEditForm(arrFields, isSave)
    frmEditForm.Close()
```

```vb
    frmEditForm = Nothing
    For i = 0 To arrFields.Length - 1
        If strNewLine.Length = 0 Then
            strNewLine = arrFields(i)
        Else
            strNewLine += "|" & arrFields(i)
        End If
    Next
    arrOldLines = File.ReadAllLines(m_strSelectedFile)
    'Redim statement resets the size of array
    'to a number of lines in the file.
    ReDim arrNewLines(arrOldLines.Length)
    For i = 0 To arrOldLines.Length - 1
        strTmpLine = arrOldLines(i)
        If strTmpLine.Equals(strOldLine) Then
            arrNewLines(i) = strNewLine
        Else
            arrNewLines(i) = strTmpLine
        End If
    Next
    For i = 0 To arrNewLines.Length - 1
        If Not arrNewLines(i) Is Nothing Then
            strNewFileContent += arrNewLines(i) & vbCrLf
        End If
    Next
    File.WriteAllText(m_strSelectedFile, strNewFileContent)
    Return True
Catch ex As Exception
```

```
        ShowErrorMessage("EditFileData", ex.Message)
        Return False
    End Try
End Function
Private Function AddLine() As Boolean
    Dim frmEditForm As New frmEdit()
    Dim arrFields As String()
    Dim isSave As Boolean
    Dim strNewLine As String = ""
    Dim i As Integer
    Dim objStreamWr As StreamWriter
Try
    If Not CheckIsFileSelected() Then
        Return False
    End If
    ReDim arrFields(3)
    frmEditForm.StartEditForm(arrFields, isSave)
    If isSave = False Then
        Return False
    End If
    For i = 0 To arrFields.Length - 1
        If strNewLine.Length = 0 Then
            strNewLine = arrFields(i)
        Else
            strNewLine += "|" & arrFields(i)
        End If
    Next
    objStreamWr = New StreamWriter(m_strSelectedFile, True)
```

```vb
    objStreamWr.WriteLine(strNewLine)
    objStreamWr.Close()
    objStreamWr.Dispose()
    Return True
Catch ex As Exception
    ShowErrorMessage("AddLine", ex.Message)
End Try
End Function
Private Sub ShowErrorMessage(ByVal strProcedure As _
                        String, ByVal errMsg As String)
Try
    MessageBox.Show("Error in " & strProcedure & _
                            " Details " & errMsg)
Catch ex As Exception
    Throw ex
End Try
End Sub
#End Region
```

All procedures shown in Listing 2 can be called helper routines since they implement tasks that are required to accomplish certain parts of the main action invoked from a corresponding public method. In most cases, breaking code into smaller helper procedures makes code much more efficient and allows better reusability. For example, the *DisplayFileRecords* procedure is called from the folowing procedures in this project: *OpenToolBtnClick, AddToolBtnClick, EditToolBtnClick, OpenMenuItem_Click, EditMenuItem_Click and AddMenuItem_Click*. By placing this piece of code into a seprate helper procedure, you make it reusable. You may also notice that the demand for this and many other procedures in this project is doubled because the same methods can be called from both the menu bar and the toolbar.

Write Event Handlers

In the last section of the FileManager form class you will write the event handler procedures. Please type code shown in Listing 3 into your project.

Listing 3. Event handlers.

```
#Region "Event Handlers"

Private Sub FileManager_Load(ByVal sender As Object,
             ByVal e As EventArgs) Handles MyBase.Load

    Dim frmLoginForm As New frmLogin()
    Dim strUserId As String = ""
    Dim strPassword As String = ""
    Dim blnLoginOK As Boolean = False
    Dim i As Int32
    Dim strDisplayMsg As String = ""
Try
    LoadUsers()
    For i = 0 To 2
    If (frmLoginForm.VerifyLogin(strUserId, strPassword,
                              strDisplayMsg)) Then
    'Authenticate a user
    'Check if UserID and Password are in the dictionary
    If AuthenticateUser(strUserId, strPassword) Then
       blnLoginOK = True
       Exit For
    Else
```

```
            strDisplayMsg = "Invalid UserID or Password"
            Continue For
        End If
        Else
            blnLoginOK = False
        Exit For
        End If
        Next
        frmLoginForm = Nothing
        If Not blnLoginOK Then
            Me.Close()
        End If
        LoadImages()
        InitToolBar()
        InitStatusBar()
Catch ex As Exception
    ShowErrorMessage(ex.TargetSite.ToString(), ex.Message)
End Try
End Sub


Private Sub OpenToolBtnClick(ByVal sender As Object,
                                        ByVal e As EventArgs)
    If Browse() = True Then
        DisplayFileRecords()
    End If
End Sub
Private Sub AddToolBtnClick(ByVal sender As Object,
                                        ByVal e As EventArgs)
```

```
    If AddLine() = True Then
        DisplayFileRecords()
    End If
End Sub


Private Sub EditToolBtnClick(ByVal sender As Object,
                                      ByVal e As EventArgs)
    If EditFileData() = True Then
        DisplayFileRecords()
    End If
End Sub


Private Sub CloseToolBtnClick(ByVal sender As Object,
                                      ByVal e As EventArgs)
    Me.Close()
End Sub


Private Sub AddMenuItem_Click(ByVal sender As System.Object,
        ByVal e As System.EventArgs) Handles AddMenuItem.Click
    If AddLine() = True Then
        DisplayFileRecords()
    End If
End Sub


Private Sub EditMenuItem_Click(ByVal sender As System.Object,
        ByVal e As System.EventArgs) Handles EditMenuItem.Click
    If EditFileData() = True Then
```

```
        DisplayFileRecords()
    End If
End Sub
Private Sub OpenMenuItem_Click(ByVal sender As System.Object, _
        ByVal e As System.EventArgs) Handles OpenMenuItem.Click
    If Browse() = True Then
        DisplayFileRecords()
    End If
End Sub


Private Sub ExitMenuItem_Click(ByVal sender As System.Object, _
        ByVal e As System.EventArgs) Handles ExitMenuItem.Click
        Me.Close()
End Sub


Private Sub DataGridView1_CellClick(ByVal sender As Object, _
            ByVal e As DataGridViewCellEventArgs) Handles _
                                DataGridView1.CellClick
        m_intSelectedRowIndex = e.RowIndex
End Sub


Private Sub DataGridView1_CellContentClick(ByVal sender As _
        Object, ByVal e As DataGridViewCellEvent) Handles _
                        DataGridView1.CellContentClick
        m_intSelectedRowIndex = e.RowIndex
End Sub


#End Region
```

Note to generate a click event handler you just need to double-click a selected button. For other events open the Properties window and click on the lightning bolt icon. This will display all events associated with the control. Double-click a desired event. The wrapper lines for the event handler will be inserted for you. When you return back to the Properties window you should see the event handler procedure name in the right-hand column.

Code the frmLogin Form

In this form, you will write one public function procedure that will be called from the main form when you need to authenticate a user. Notice that you do not need to capture any button click events because you are using the button *DialogResult* values that are handled by the form. For this to work you need to set the *DialogResult* properties of both buttons.

Please type code shown in Listing 4.

Listing 4. The frmLogin form code.

```
Public Class frmLogin

Public Function VerifyLogin(ByRef strUserID As String, ByRef _
    strPassword As String, ByVal strMsg As String) As Boolean
Try
    If strMsg.Length > 0 Then
        lblDisplayMsg.Text = strMsg
    End If
    If Me.ShowDialog() = Windows.Forms.DialogResult.OK Then
        strUserID = txtUser.Text
        strPassword = txtPassword.Text
```

```
        Me.Hide()
        Return True
    Else
        Me.Hide()
        Return False
    End If


Catch ex As Exception
    Throw ex
End Try
End Function
End Class
```

Code the frmEdit Form

Listing 5. The frmEdit form code.

```
Imports System.Windows.Forms


Public Class frmEdit
Public Sub StartEditForm(ByRef arrFields As String(), _
                                    ByRef isSave As Boolean)
    Dim dlgResult As DialogResult
Try

    txtUser.Text = arrFields(0)
    txtOldPwd.Text = arrFields(1)
    txtNewPwd.Text = arrFields(2)
```

```
    txtDateChanged.Text = arrFields(3)
    dlgResult = Me.ShowDialog()
    If dlgResult = Windows.Forms.DialogResult.OK Then
        arrFields(0) = txtUser.Text
        arrFields(1) = txtOldPwd.Text
        arrFields(2) = txtNewPwd.Text
        arrFields(3) = txtDateChanged.Text
        isSave = True
    Else
        isSave = False
        Me.Hide()
    End If

Catch ex As Exception
    Throw ex
End Try
End Sub


End Class
```

The main mission of the frmEdit form is to display user-selected record fields and if the user modifies them and clicks on the Save button transport the data back to the main form.

Test and Debug

Test the Login Function

Before you begin testing, pay attention to the following. User authentication is initiated from the *FileManager_Load* event handler. Here you display the login form to authenticate a user. The *VerifyLogin* function implemented in the frmLogin form is a simple solution to communicate data between the two forms. Also note that the *For ... Next* loop is coded to allow a user at least three attempts to login after which you shut down the application by closing the *FileManager* form.

Test a valid login

Run the application and try to login using a valid user name and password. Does the application successfully process the login and display the FileManager form?

Test an invalid login

Try to login with invalid credentials. Does the application display a login failure message? If yes, continue testing and check if you can make three attempts to login with an invalid password or user name. Does the application shut down after the third attempt?

Test the Toolbar Buttons

To prepare for this test you need to create the *Icons* folder that may contain the following files: *FolderOpen.ico, GenericPicDoc.ico, InFile.ico* and *NewFolder.ico*. You may use icons of your own choice but make sure you have at least four files in the following location: *C:\Labs\Lab14\Icons*. Run the application and check if all toolbar buttons are displayed correctly. Then test the functionality of the *Open, Add, Edit* and

Close buttons. Note the *Add* function should allow you to add a new record to the file and the *Edit* should save the changes made to a selected record.

Test the File Manager

Login with a valid user name and password and check if all menu items are displayed correctly. Create a simple text file with the following format:

SONY CMR220|200|nWhite|2/23/2008

The file should contain four fields separate by a pipe character (|) in the following order: *Product ID, Quantity, UserID* and *Date Changed.* A test file may have any name and filename extension. After you created a file, check if you can navigate to that file using the Open menu or button. Try to open the file. Does the application display the file data correctly? Test the following menus: *File/Exit, Tools/Add* and *Tools/Edit.*

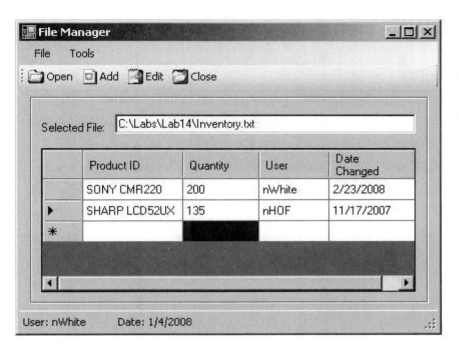

Figure 4. The File Manager program.

If the *Open* file function works properly and you were able to create a valid test file, your application should display data as shown in Figure 4.

Congratulations! You completed Lab 14.

Extra Credit Tasks

We tried to keep this project as simple as possible. Of course, it is far from being perfect. But that leaves a lot of room for enhancements and improvements where you can practice your new skills and earn a lot of extra credits. Try to test break the application from various perspectives and find vulnerabilities and weak points or bugs. Weak points are the best candidates for improvements. Then compare your findings with our extra credit task suggestions.

1. When the login form opens, it would be nice to have the cursor moved to the *User* textbox so that a user can start immediately.

 2. Notice that when a user clicks on the *Edit* toolbar button, while no file is open yet the message box says "Please select a row first." This is a bug. It should say that the file is not open yet. In this case you should write code to check if the file is selected and open before you try to read a selected row. Add this logic to the *EditFileData* method.

3. When there are multiple textboxes in a form it is more user-friendly if the textboxes have a consecutive Tab index. This will allow users to tab from one textbox to another. Hint: in the frmEdit you should reset each textbox tab index in the order that you expect the user to tab through the textboxes.

4. It would be nice to give a user the ability to delete a record. Try to add a delete record functionality. Hint: to delete a record from a file, you should use the same or similar approach as for the edit procedure. First store the record selected for delete then loop through the file content and write each record into a new file content variable. Compare each line with the record marked for deletion. When you identify

the record, skip it, do not include it into new file content, then write the new file content to the file.

5. You can make this program more generic and universal if you can automatically detect what data seperator is used and what columns a file contains. This can be easily done by adding a header record to the source file. The header line should have a seperator character and a list of column names seprerated by a pipe or a comma. In the application you should first read the header and use it to identify what seperator is used and what columns are needed and then initialize a *DataTable* object accordingly. Good luck.

Chapter 15: Application Installation

Application Installation

In this Chapter:

You will learn how to prepare the application for installation. In .NET, installation has become an easy procedure that can be as simple as file copy. However, this is only true for very simple applications. When you deal with real-world projects, things get complicated. For instance, you may need to create an application file system, check if dependencies are installed and if not install them, copy and install multiple resource files, add an application shortcut to the Start/Programs menu and so on. A long list of installation chores may urge you to start looking for how to automate this process by using a setup project or something as nice as ClickOnce installation. In this chapter, we will show you how to accomplish these tasks.

Chapter 15 at a Glance

- ➢ Application Installation
- ➢ Building Setup Project
- ➢ Adding Setup Project
- ➢ Creating Project Output
- ➢ Target Machine File System
- ➢ Setup Primary Output
- ➢ Setup Project Properties
- ➢ Setup Installation Files
- ➢ ClickOnce Technology
- ➢ ClickOnce Publish Properties
- ➢ ClickOnce Publish Wizard
- ➢ ClickOnce Installation Files
- ➢ ClickOnce Install URL

Application Installation

In .NET, application installation and deployment is significantly simplified. First of all there is no component (DLL) registration. That should certainly save you of the scary "DLL hell" issues. Of course, you may have some additional work around strongly named assemblies but that's nothing compared to the DLL registration.

It is true that in .NET application installation can be as simple as *xcopy*. As you may know *xcopy* is a DOS command, which is used to copy the entire directory file structure. However, this deployment method may be used when an application is really simple and there is no need to build the application infrastructure and do all installation and deployment chores that we mentioned earlier. Also *xcopy* deployment cannot replace a setup project, which does a lot of work to make the installation complete. This becomes especially important when the application is complex and has multiple dependencies. Thus, for a relatively complex application you need to create an installation project that will not only automate the process but will also allow customization of installation.

Visual Studio .NET offers a number of installation automation solutions. Among them is the old and a very well-known setup and deployment project that is based on the *Setup Project* template. And in Visual Studio .NET 2005, there is a new and very simple installation method called *ClickOnce*. This method is fully integrated with a Visual Studio project so you do not have to build a separate installation project. In this chapter, we will consider both.

Building Setup Project

A setup program created in Visual Studio can do much more than just copy application files to a user machine. It can also install a required .NET framework if it is not installed, check if previous or newer versions of the application already exist on the target machine and much more. Based on the complexity of the underlying project for which you want to create a setup project, the amount of work may differ considerably. To briefly describe this process we created a list of major tasks that may be required to implement a relatively simple setup project.

Building Setup Project Tasks

- ➤ Create a Setup Project
- ➤ Add Application Output
- ➤ Create a Target Machine File System
- ➤ Set Project Output Properties
- ➤ Set Setup Project Properties
- ➤ Build Setup Project

Adding a Setup Project

You should begin working on a setup project only after you are done with the application design, testing and build. The sequence of actions in creating a setup project may vary and is largely a matter of your personal preference. We recommend the following order:

- ➤ Open a target project in Visual Studio .NET.
- ➤ Add a Setup Project to it.
- ➤ On the *File* menu choose *Add Project/New Project*.
- ➤ In the *Add New Project* dialog box, expand *Other Project Types* node.
- ➤ Select *Setup and Deployment*.
- ➤ In the *Templates*, select *Setup Project* and click OK.

If you take a closer look at the Templates pane, you may see the following templates: Setup Project, Web Setup Project, Merge Module Project, Cab Project and Setup

Wizard. Each of these project templates has its own use. Let's consider the Setup Project template.

Select the Setup Project template and then enter the project name and location as usual. We do not recommend keeping the default Setup1 project name. Change it to something meaningful that may, for example, contain the target project name plus "Setup" or "Install." For example, for this demo we chose the *MoviExplorer* project and named the setup project *MoviExplorerSetup*.

Creating Project Output

Examine your new setup project in the Solution Explorer. You may notice that it has only one item: an empty folder called "Detected Dependencies." It is clear from the name that this folder is meant to store application dependency files that will be copied and installed on a user machine during the installation process. Now you need to tell the setup project what its output will be. In the Solution Explorer, right-click the setup project name, in our case it is the *MoviExplorerSetup*, and on the context menu, choose *Add\Project Output* as shown in Figure 15.0.

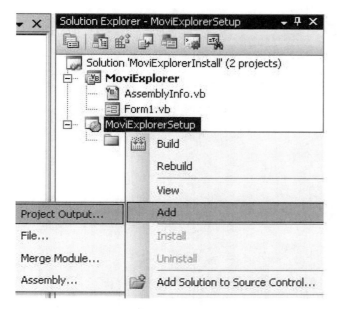

Figure 15.0   The Add / Project Output menu.

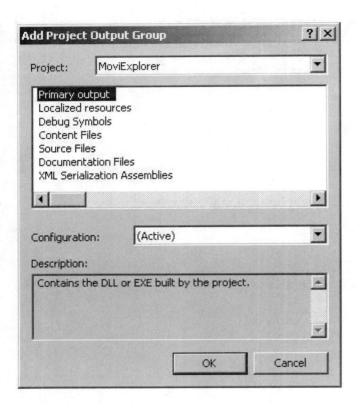

Figure 15.1 Add Project Output Group window.

This action should bring up the *Add Project Output Group* window show in
Figure 15.1. Essentially, this dialog box is designed to help you specify which EXE
or DLL file should be used as the main application output. Keep in mind that the
main goal of the setup project is to copy your application executable file and its
dependencies to an appropriate directory on the target machine. The *Add Project
Output Group* should list the following output types: Primary Output, Localized
Resources, Debug Symbols, Content Files, Source Files, Documentation Files and
XML Serialization Assemblies. If you highlight any of these options, its explanation
will be displayed in the *Description* section below. For example, if the *Primary*

Output is selected the description should say "Contains the DLL or EXE built by the project." Note that this option should be selected by default. To continue just select the *Primary Output* and click OK.

If you have multiple projects in your solution, they will be listed in the *Projects* dropdown. You should select a primary project or the one that is used as a startup project. In our case there is only one project named "MoviExplorer." Note that when you click OK Visual Studio will add two items to your setup project. In Visual Studio 2005, it will be the Microsoft .NET Framework and your application executable called *Primary Output ApplicationName*. In Visual Studio 2003, it will add the .NET redistributable runtime file named "dotnetfxredist_x86.msm" and the application executable file.

You have completed the first part of your setup project. The rest of your work may be focused on adding other application dependencies and setting or changing the properties of each item. To keep things simple, accept the default settings and proceed to building the project. Building the setup project will allow you to test the setup project and check the installation files created by it. After verifying the installation files, we recommend that you continue with the setup project and build the target machine file system.

Target Machine File System

In most typical installations, you may want to create an application folder that will store all application-specific files and, possibly, a shortcut on the *Start/Programs* menu. These tasks can be easily completed by the setup, if you instruct it what file system should be created on the target machine and how the files should be copied to it. This can be done by modeling the application file system in the setup project item called the *Target Machine File System*. Here you can create all the application folders and add files to them.

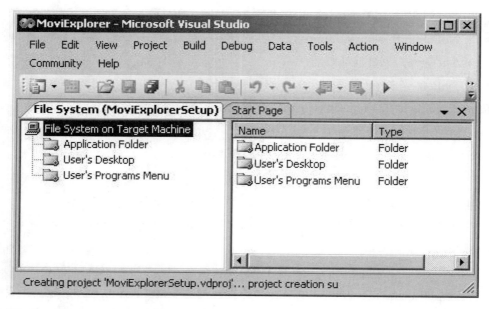

Figure 15.2 Target Machine File System tab.

File System Properties

To begin playing with the File System and to better visualize what we are talking about, make sure that the File System tab is displayed. If it's not, in the Solution Explorer, right-click the setup project and choose *View/File System*. This should display a default File System created by Visual Studio for you. You can accept it as is and modify it later or create your own. If you examine the File System tab snapshot shown in Figure 15.2, you will see two panes. The left-hand pane displays a File System with three suggested folders:

- ➢ Application Folder
- ➢ User's Desktop
- ➢ User's Programs Menu

The right-hand pane should display files contained by each folder. Highlight any folder and check if there are any files. You should see that the *Application Folder* contains the primary output file, if you did add the primary output prior to this test. Other folders should be empty. You can change, delete or add any items as needed. You may need to create a custom file system according to the project file system specifications. Once you are done with the file structure, you may want to assign appropriate files to each folder. When you complete this part of the setup project work, you need to set each folder's properties.

Setting the file system folder properties is essential for a number of reasons. The main reason is that the default Visual Studio settings may not always be what you want. You should always check and if necessary modify the following properties: *AlwaysCreate* and *DefaultLocation*. By default, *AlwaysCreate* is set to False, which means the folder will not be created on the target machine during the installation process. The *DefaultLocation* property is set to "Program Files\Manufacturer\ ProductName." You can change this at design time to add the real project characteristics.

Furthermore, a user may change it at installation time. Once you are satisfied with the future target machine file structure, you should make sure that all required files are added to their directories and only then continue setting the setup project. Keep in mind that invalid property settings may cause setup build errors. For example, if you create a shortcut to the application executable in the *User's Programs Menu* folder and *AlwaysCreate* is set to False you may get a long error message like the following: "ERROR: The target of shortcut 'Shortcut to User's Programs Menu' is invalid. The *AlwaysCreate* property of folder User's Programs Menu must be set to True."

Note:

When working with a Target Machine File System, remember that any folder created by Visual Studio will have the *AlwaysCreate* property set to False by default. These folders will not be created on a target machine unless you reset this property.

Setup Primary Output

The *Primary Output* file properties represent the main application executable file properties, which you would normally create in the application build process as discussed in Chapter 14. This file, as any other file included in a target machine file system, has a number of properties. The way you set these properties will determine how the file is installed on a target machine. They help you to control the following:

- What application dependencies should be included in the installation package.
- What dependency files should be excluded.
- Should the files be compressed.
- Should the files be hidden.

Setup Primary Output Properties:

- ➢ Dependencies
- ➢ Exclude
- ➢ Exclude Filter
- ➢ Hidden

> ➤ Key Output
> ➤ Outputs
> ➤ Package As

Dependencies

The *Dependencies* is a read-only property, which lists application dependency files included in the setup package. Click on this property and then click on the *Ellipsis* button. This should bring up a small dialog box with all dependency files. Here you may see the Microsoft .NET Framework and other libraries referenced by your application. If you have any application data or configuration files they will be listed here as well.

Exclude

Setting the *Exclude* to True will exclude the application executable from the setup package. Normally, you would not want to do this because otherwise you would have to deploy this file manually. But you can use this property to exclude other files from the installation package.

Exclude Filter

The *Exclude Filter* property can be used to set filters for certain file types. It can be individual files or file groups. Click on this property and then on the *Ellipsis* button. In the *Filter* dialog box enter your filter statement.

Hidden

The *Hidden* property can be used to create hidden files. By default, this property is set to False.

Outputs

The *Outputs* is a read-only property that lists all EXE or DLL files listed in your application project folder. Only one file can be set as the primary application output. For example, if your project contains multiple EXE files, one of them will act as a startup program and others may be used whenever necessary.

Package As

The *Package As* property is used to determine how the setup package should be built. There are two options: *vsdpaDefault* and *vsdpaLoose*. The former will compress files included into the setup package while the latter will leave them as is (loose).

.NET Redistributable File Properties

This property is valid for Visual Studio .NET 2003 only. As we mentioned earlier, the merge module contains the .NET redistributable runtime file. If included in the setup, it can be used to install the .NET Common Language Runtime on the target machine.

Note:

If after you started creating a setup project you decided to make some changes to your application that may alter the file structure, you can synchronize the setup project by simply refreshing dependencies. Right-click the *Detected Dependencies* folder and select *Refresh Dependencies*.

Setup Project Properties

The setup project properties represent the overall setup features. They contain a number of essential properties that may affect many aspects of the installation procedure. Here are some of these properties:

- ➢ AddRemoveProgramIcon
- ➢ Author
- ➢ DetectNewerInstalledVersion
- ➢ Localization
- ➢ ProductName
- ➢ RemovePreviousVersion
- ➢ SupportPhone
- ➢ SupportURL
- ➢ Title
- ➢ Version

AddRemoveProgramIcon

The *AddRemoveProgramIcon* property can be used to assign an icon to a program executable file, which will serve to distinguish it from other executable files. To assign an icon you need to select it from your application file system. If the icon file is not included, you need to add it to your application file system. Select an appropriate application file system folder and click on *Add File* button, navigate to an icon file and click OK.

Author

The *Author* property could be a manufacturer company name or an individual developer name that created the program.

DetectNewerInstalledVersion

The *DetectNewerInstalledVersion* feature could be very useful to include in your setup. If you set this property to True, it will produce the following effect. At runtime the setup will try to detect if a newer version of this application is already installed on a target machine. If yes, the setup will inform the user about the fact and will offer to replace it with the older version. The user will have an option to abort the installation or continue and overwrite the existing version.

Localization

The *Localization* property will come into play only when you need to create various international versions of the application to address region and culture differences. Therefore, by specifying the localization, you may create a setup package for a particular language and culture combination.

RemovePreviousVersion

The *RemovePreviousVersion* property can be used to handle previous installations of the same application. If set to True, it will instruct the setup to automatically remove any older versions of the application on a target machine.

SupportPhone and SupportURL

The *SupportPhone* and *SupportURL* properties are self-explanatory. If you add this information to your setup project, it will be displayed in the *Add/Remove Programs* screen so that a program user can get technical help or support.

Note:

Keep in mind, if you do not reset some default properties you may have inconsistent titles and headers in the installation process. For example, if you keep the default setup project name Setup1, your setup screen title will look like this "Welcome to Setup1 Setup Wizard." Also if you keep the defaults for *Author* and *ProductName* properties, your application installation path will look like this: "C:\ Program Files\Default Company Name\Setup1\." Where *Default Company Name* stands for the *Author* and Setup1 – for *ProductName*. Obviously, changing these defaults to something meaningful will make a lot of sense.

Setup Installation Files

Once you are done with the files and properties you may build the setup project. Building the setup project is different from the application build mostly in terms of the output. An application project build produces an executable file, while a setup project generates an installation package, which includes multiple files. To build the setup project, on the Build menu, choose *Build SetupProjectName*. Visual Studio .NET 2005 will create two files: *SetupProjectName.msi* and *Setup.exe*. Visual Studio 2003 will create three files: *SetupProjectName.msi, Setup.exe, Setup.ini*. If you did not change the Visual Studio defaults these files should appear in the *SetupProjectFolder\Release* directory.

Now you can give your setup package a good test. To start the installation of the application on a target machine, double-click the *Setup.exe* file. In Visual Studio 2003, the installation process reads the *Setup.ini* file to get the MSI loader name, the supported version of .NET runtime and then invokes the Microsoft Windows Installer that will actually accomplish the installation work. In Visual Studio 2005, the MSI loader name is embedded into the Setup.exe, so there's no need for the Setup.ini.

The main role of the *SetupProjectName.msi* file is to provide the Microsoft Windows Installer with the necessary configuration information, application-specific files and dependencies.

ClickOnce Technology

The *ClickOnce* technology is a new and very exciting feature of Visual Studio .NET 2005. Compared to a setup project it is a walk in the park and fun. The entire process of creating the application installation package is streamlined by Visual Studio for you. You do not have to create a setup and deployment project. All you need to do is *Publish* the installation files created by Visual Studio to a virtual or physical directory from where the users will install the application.

ClickOnce is an exciting new application deployment and installation methodology. Not only does it fully automate both code deployment and application installation but it is also tightly integrated with your Visual Studio project. From your Visual Studio project you need to publish the application installation files to either a virtual directory hosted by a website or to a shared physical directory. Then you provide all potential users with a URL or UNC that should point to the *Publish.htm* page, which is used to start the installation process. We will talk about the specifics of building the URL and UNC later in this chapter.

ClickOnce, besides many other things, allows centralizing the application installation code base, which simplifies installation, deployment and maintenance. The underlying installation is MSI based. The IIS (Internet Information Server) may be used not only to store code base but also to control access and enforce security. Now let's consider the details.

ClickOnce Publish Properties

Creating a ClickOnce installation package should begin with setting the *Publish* method's properties. This can be done using the project *Property Pages* that we introduced in Chapter 14.

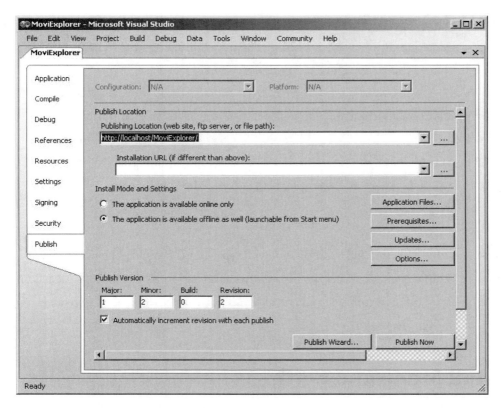

Figure 15.3 Project Property Pages Publish section.

As you can see in Figure 15.3, the Property Pages interface has a Publish section that brings together all the necessary tools to prepare a project for publishing and even invoke the *Publish* method or the *Publish Wizard*. You can skip setting the publish properties and invoke the *Publish* method directly from the *Build* menu. However, if you do so you will still have to set the main Publish method properties by answering the Publish Wizard's questions. We strongly recommend setting all properties in the Property Pages and only then publish the application installation files. Now we will briefly explain the meaning of each publish property.

Publish Location

First, you need to set the *Publish Location* property. This could be a website, an FTP server or a shared directory. Thus, the location can be:

A physical folder on a local disc, for example: C:\Projects\Install\ApplicationName.
A file share on a network drive, for example: \\Server1\Share1\ApplicationName.
An FTP Server, for example: ftp://ftp.MyFTP.com/ApplicationName.
A website virtual directory, for example: http://www.MyWebsite.com/ApplicationName.

When you know your publish location, you can type it or if possible browse to it. Keep in mind that each location type has its strengths and weaknesses. Your decision should be based on the availability of corresponding resources such as a website or FTP server and project requirements.

Install Mode and Settings

When you set the *Install Mode and Settings* you can make the application run directly from the publish location by selecting *This Application is Only Available Online*. Alternatively, you can select *This Application is Available Online or Offline*, which will allow running it locally and it can be uninstalled via *Add/ Remove Programs*. As for the application version, you can manually set it each time you publish the installation files or allow Visual Studio to increment it at each publication by checking the *Automatically Increment Revision with Each Publish* checkbox. When ready, click on the *Publish Now* button. Visual Studio will create the installation files and when done will show you the *Publish.htm* page.

ClickOnce Publish Wizard

You can also publish the application from the *Build* menu by choosing the *Publish* menu. In this case you will invoke the *Publish Wizard* that will assist you in accomplishing the task. To start the process click on *Build/Publish* menu.

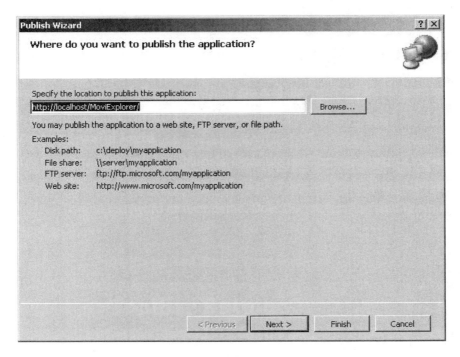

Figure 15.4 ClickOnce Publish Wizard.

You will see a *Publish Wizard* dialog box shown in Figure 15.4, which will ask you where you want to publish the application. If you did setup the publish properties, the publish location will be set accordingly. However, if you did not, Visual Studio will set it to a default:

http://localhost/ApplicationName/

When you click *Next*, the wizard will ask you how the users will install the application. The choices are: From a website, from a UNC path or file share, from a CD-ROM or DVD-ROM. Make a selection according to your publish location setting and click *Next*. The wizard will ask you if you want the application to check for updates and if yes, specify a location. You can select *The Application will Check for Updates from the Following Location* or *The Application will not Check for Updates* according to your project specifications.

ClickOnce Installation Files

Which publish method you will use is not principally important. What is more important is where you publish the installation files. Keep in mind that for each publish location option the list of files created may be slightly different. Let's consider a website publish location option, which we consider more flexible. For example, if you publish the *MoviExplorer* application to *http://localhost/MoviExplorer*, Visual Studio will create the following installation items in the publish location:

- ➤ MoviExplorer _1_0_0_0 folder
- ➤ MoviExplorer _1_0_0_0.application
- ➤ Setup.exe
- ➤ Publish.htm

The *MoviExplorer_1_0_0_0* folder should contain the following files for each published application version:

- ➤ MoviExplorer.exe.deploy

➢ MoviExplorer.exe.manifest

Note that Visual Studio will also create these files in your application project folder in: *bin\MoviExporer.publish* folder. In real-world projects, you may need to move installation files from the development environment to other environments such as QA, UAT or production. In this case, publishing to a local website will allow you to propagate the same files to other environments easily. To deploy the installation package on other web servers you need to do the following:

- On the target web server create a physical directory.
- Copy your ClickOnce installation files to it.
- Create a virtual directory on the default website.
- Point virtual directory to the physical directory.

ClickOnce URL

This is your final task; you are almost there. You need to create a URL that will be provided to all eligible application users. Your ClickOnce URL should consist of the following elements:

http://ServerName/VirtualDirectoryName/Publish.htm.

Now you are ready to test the ClickOnce installation. When the user invokes the URL, the *Publish.htm* page, like the one shown in Figure 15.5, should be displayed.

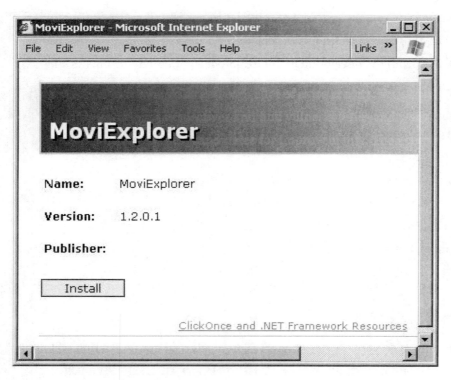

Figure 15.5 ClickOnce Publish.htm page.

The users are expected to do one thing: click once on the *Install* button and the installation process will start.

Summary

In this chapter, you have learned how to design a setup project and publish an application using the ClickOnce technology. Installation and deployment are the final stages of application development where you make the application available to the users. In real-world situations, both deployment and installation if not properly automated may require a lot of manual work. The setup project method represents an older but very straightforward and highly customizable installation solution. ClickOnce is a relatively new but very efficient installation technology. It works from inside of your project and has a lot of advantages. It can easily provide remote installation and centralizing code deployment, installation and updates.

Lab 15: The Setup Project

Setup Project

In this Project:

You will build a setup project for the *MarsPlus* application that you developed in Lab 13. We recommend that you review Chapter 15 before you start this lab. Note that MarsPlus will be used as a target application from which you will create a setup project. In this lab you will practice creating a setup and deployment project.

Open the MarsPlus Project

In this lab you will create a new solution that will include both the target project and the setup project. This will simplify the connection between them when you create this solution. Open *MarsPlus* project in Visual Studio .NET.

Build MarsPlus

To build MarsPlus executable, in the Solution Configurations dropdown, choose Release build. Then on the Build menu, choose *Build MarsPlus*. This should recompile the application and create *MarsPlus.exe*. When the build is complete, verify if the executable file was created. Look for the executable in: Labs\Lab13\ MarsPlus\Bin\Release folder. Check the build output window for errors and warnings. Note that the build procedure report shows how many projects succeeded, failed or skipped. This is important when your solution includes multiple projects. Pay attention to warnings. They may not stop compilation but should always be checked to identify potential errors.

Add Setup Project

Add a setup project to your solution. On the File menu select *Add/New Project*. This will bring up the *Add New Project* window. Select *Setup and Deployment* for the project type and for the template choose *Setup Project*. Change the project name from the default *Setup1* to *MarsPlusInstall*. Set the Location to *C:\Labs\Lab15* and click OK. When a setup project is created, Visual Studio will automatically display the Solution Explorer and the File System tab. Spend some time examining the default folders: *Application Folder, User's Desktop* and *User's Programs Menu*. If you click on any folder you will see files contained by it in the middle pane. There should be no files in these directories at this time.

Add Project Output

Add the project output to the setup project. The essence of this action is to show the setup project where your application executable is located. The rest is done for you behind the scenes. The setup will examine the executable to find out what version of .NET it was compiled with and will also check the application dependencies.

Check Dependencies

Application dependencies include two major categories: platform prerequisites and application-specific files. Since this application is based on the Microsoft .NET platform, there are two prerequisites: the .NET Common Language Runtime and the .NET Framework. They will appear as one item: .NET Framework. Application-specific dependencies may include: custom libraries, third-party libraries, application configuration and resource files. Application dependencies are detected when you add the project primary output to your setup project. When you add the project output, the *Detected Dependencies* folder is updated.

Add Project Primary Output

Add the primary output to the setup project.   In the Solution Explorer, right-click the *MarsPlusInstall* project and select *Add\Project Output*. This should bring up the *Add Project Output Group* dialog box that will by default show *MarsPlus* and will highlight *Primary Output* as the output type and select the active project solution. At this point, you should keep all defaults and click OK. Verify what dependencies are added. Setup should add the following to the *Detected Dependencies* folder:
In Visual Studio 2005 Microsoft .NET Framework is added.
In Visual Studio 2003 Dotnetfxredist_x86.msm is added.

Set Target Machine File System

This part of your setup project work is necessary if you want to make sure that the setup creates the application folder and possible sub-folders on the target machine. Remember if you leave the default settings, the application folder will not be created. In the Solution Explorer, right-click the setup project and select *View/Files System*. In the *File System on Target Machine* pane, right-click the *Application Folder* and select Properties. Set *AlwaysCreate* property to True. This will ensure that the application folder will be created on the target machine. Notice that by this time the *Application Folder* should contain one item: primary output from MarsPlus. This is your application executable file.

Set User's Programs Menu

Right-click the *User's Programs Menu* folder and select *Add/Project Output*. You should see that the project output item is created in this folder. Now right-click the *User's Programs Menu* folder again and select Properties. Set *AlwaysCreate* property to *True*.

Setup Project Properties

This should be the last item of the setup project configuration work before you are ready to compile the project. Highlight the setup project in the Solution Explorer. On the toolbar, click on the Properties button. Review all setup project properties. Change the Author property to something meaningful; for example, company name or product group name. Set the ProductName property to "MarsPlus." Set the Title property to "MarsPlus Program."

Build the Setup Package

Now you are ready to build the setup package. On the *Build* menu select *Build MarsPlusInstall*. Visual Studio will show the output window where you can monitor the build progress. If you take a closer look at your Solution Explorer, you should see that the MarsPlus solution hosts two projects: MarsPlus and MarsPlusInstall. When you build the MarsPlusInstall setup project Visual Studio will recompile both projects. Check the installation files. The setup package files must be in *Labs\Lab15\ MarsPlusInstall\Release* folder. It should include the following files:

MarsPlusInstall.msi

Setup.exe

Test the Installation Package

The last task in this lab is to test the installation package. You need to test if the setup can install the application. You may first run this on your machine and then repeat the test on another machine. Hence, if you perform this test on the build machine, all you need to do is double-click the *Setup.exe* file and follow the instructions of the Windows Installer wizard. If the installation is going to be on another machine, you need to copy all setup package files into a directory on the target machine and then run the Setup.exe. After the installation is complete, check the following:

> ➢ If the application folder is created.
> ➢ If the shortcut to the application is displayed on the Programs menu.
> ➢ Try to start the application.

Congratulations! You completed Lab 15.

Order Now

Give the Gift of Microsoft Visual Basic .NET Programming Fundamentals to Friends or Colleagues.

□ Yes, I want _____ copies of Microsoft Visual Basic .NET Programming Fundamentals for $49.95 each.

□ Yes, I included $3.99 shipping and handling for one book and $1.99 for each additional book. New York residents must include applicable sales tax. Payment must accompany orders. Allow 3–4 weeks for delivery.

My check or money order for $ _____ is enclosed.

Send the book to this address:

Name_____

Organization_____

Address_____

City/State/Zip_____

Phone_____

E-Mail_____

Signature_____

Make your check or money order payable to *Frontenac* and return to

Frontenac

P.O. Box 322

Huntington, NY 11743-0322

INDEX

A

B

D

Your Opinion Matters

Frontenac writes books for you.
Please send us your remarks and
suggestions about this book.
Your comments are always valued at
Frontenac.

Send comments to:
FrontenacBooks@gmail.com
To download lab project source code
visit: www.begenius.net